Eastern
Orthodox Christianity

Stephen J. Shoemaker

Eastern
Orthodox Christianity

A Western Perspective

Second Edition

Daniel B. Clendenin

Baker Academic

A Division of Baker Book House Co
Grand Rapids, Michigan 49516

© 1994, 2003 by Daniel B. Clendenin

Published by Baker Academic
a division of Baker Book House Company
P.O. Box 6287, Grand Rapids, Michigan 49516-6287
www.bakeracademic.com

Printed in the United States of America

             Library of Congress Cataloging-in-Publication Data
Clendenin, Daniel B.
     Eastern Orthodox Christianity : a western perspective / Daniel B. Clendenin.—2nd
   ed.
        p.   cm.
     Includes bibliographical references and index.
     ISBN 0-8010-2652-0 (pbk.)
     1. Orthodox Eastern Churches—Doctrines. I. Title.
   BX320.3.C58 2003
   230'.19—dc21   2003052312

Contents

Preface to the Second Edition

For far too long Christians generally have thought of our extended family as limited to either Catholic or Protestant communities. We can no longer afford the luxury of remaining ignorant of our siblings who belong to what is generally described as Eastern Orthodox Christianity. When we come to know this part of our Christian family, as I hope that this book and its companion anthology will help to facilitate, I am confident that we will be grateful for the many ways that Orthodoxy can enrich our own Christian experience. My own hope is that this newly revised edition will contribute to the "peace of the whole world, the stability of the holy churches of God, and the union of all" (*Liturgy of Saint John Chrysostom*).

In this revised edition, I have added an epilogue in which I have updated some of the demographic and statistical information about global Orthodoxy. In addition, I examine at some length one particular aspect of Orthodoxy's intersection with Protestantism, that of its growing exchange with evangelicalism. This is not only one of the most interesting but also one of the most important ecumenical developments of the last two decades. Protestants of all stripes, but especially evangelicals, continue to convert to the Orthodox church. In the new epilogue, I have incorporated a good portion of some of the emerging literature of this dialogue. I also have offered my own critique of the Orthodox-evangelical exchange in a more substantial way than I did in the first edition.

Readers should note that I have also revised the companion anthology, *Eastern Orthodox Theology: A Contemporary Reader*, that accompanies this present volume. In the revised anthology, I have kept all of the original selections and added two selections on the Orthodox-evangelical dialogue.

I would like to thank Cam Anderson, national director for the graduate and faculty ministry of InterVarsity Christian Fellowship, for his encouragement to take time out from my campus ministry responsibilities at Stanford University in order to undertake these revisions. Chris Sugden and Hillary Guest of the Oxford Center for Mission Study provided me with gracious and expert help in Oxford. Brian Bolger of Baker Academic encouraged me along the way. Bradley Nassif also provided timely help by sharing with me his work, which at the time had not been published.

Preface to the First Edition

The present volume is designed to be used together with its companion, *Eastern Orthodox Theology: A Contemporary Reader* (Grand Rapids: Baker, 1994), which contains thirteen readings by eight contemporary Orthodox theologians on major motifs in Orthodox Christianity. Together these two volumes attempt to introduce some of the major aspects of Orthodox history and theology to Protestant Christians who might otherwise have had no occasion to study Eastern Christianity, although I am quick to add that I make no pretense of having attempted anything near an exhaustive treatment.

In the present volume, after introducing the subject (chaps. 1–2), I focus descriptively on four theological themes in Orthodoxy: apophaticism, icons, Scripture and tradition, and theosis (chaps. 3–6). Although I differentiate them from similar themes in Protestant Christianity, there is no reason why the worlds of Orthodoxy and Protestantism cannot be seen as complementing rather than contrasting with one another. By and large there is nothing to prevent us from enjoying the best of both worlds. The final chapter draws some critical conclusions about Orthodox theology.

As has already been indicated, my primary focus is to compare and contrast Orthodoxy with Protestantism, and occasionally with Catholicism. Of course, these three traditions agree and disagree with one another at different points. Orthodoxy tends to see Protestants and Catholics as opposite sides of the same coin, similar, for example, in their juridical frameworks and appeals to external theological authorities (Scripture alone for Protestants and the papacy for Catholics). Protestant and Orthodox believers join together in their rejection of the Roman papacy. Catholics and Orthodox are similar in their sacramental and liturgical frameworks, Mariology, veneration of saints and images, and the like. Perhaps these three traditions are best viewed as three siblings of the same family, each similar and dissimilar to the other two in various ways. But the present text focuses primarily on the Orthodox and Protestant traditions.

In the former Soviet Union and Eastern Europe, home to about 85 percent of worldwide Orthodoxy, the relationship between Orthodoxy and other Christian confessions has been notably strained. There is no doubt, for example, that the Russian patriarchate aggressively supported the law proposed in the summer of 1993 to the Russian Parliament that would have banned or greatly restricted the operations of foreign religious groups in Russia. As will be apparent in the final chapter, my own stance toward Orthodoxy is not uncritical, but in the main it is nonpolemical. In other words, the strained confessional relationships call for greater efforts at mutual understanding.

I hope that this book, and its companion anthology, will contribute to a spirit of mutual respect, toleration, and even support. Relevant here are the words of Maximus the Confessor (580–662), one of Orthodoxy's greatest theologians, which spoke forcefully to me as I researched this volume. In the foreword to his *Four Hundred Texts on Love*, Maximus advised its addressee, one Father Elpidios, that this tome

> may not fulfil your expectations, but it was the best that I could do. . . . If anything in these chapters should prove useful to the soul, it will be revealed to the reader by the grace of God, provided that he reads, not out of curiosity, but in the fear and love of God. If a man reads this or any other work not to gain spiritual benefit, but to track down matter with which to abuse the author, so that in his conceit he can show himself to be the more learned, nothing profitable will ever be revealed to him in anything.

This is the spirit with which, as a Protestant believer, I have tried to engage Orthodoxy, and it is the spirit I ask of the reader.

A number of people and organizations offered assistance of various sorts toward the completion of this project, and it is my pleasure to thank them here: Donald Bloesch, Father John Breck, W. David and Nancy Buschart, Mark Elliott, the Grace Evangelical Presbyterian Church of Farmington Hills (Mich.), Father Evgeny Grushetsky and Vladimir Dunaev of the Humanitarian University of Minsk, Kent Hill, Daniel Hubiak, Constantine Ivanov and his colleagues at the Society for Open Christianity (Saint Petersburg), Dennis Kinlaw, Ludvik and Trudy Koci, Alexander Krasnikov, Natasha Krikounova, Sharon Linzey, Bradley Nassif, Cyril Nikonov, Thomas Oden, Gary and Jeannie Parsons, Phil and Nancy Payne, John and Madelle Payne, Anton Petrenko, Alexander Popov, Phil and Rachel Rohrer, Roger and Mary Simpson, James Stamoolis, Mel and Donna Stewart, Donald and Cindy Thorsen, James and Dorothy Wood, Ken and Laurel Wrye, Priscilla Young, and my seminar students at Moscow State University.

I would like to acknowledge in a special way the International Institute for Christian Studies (P.O. Box 12147, Overland Park, Kansas 66212), for their aggressive efforts in supporting Christian scholarship and teaching in public universities around the world. Special thanks go to Executive Director Daryl McCarthy, Dana Preusch, Debbie Warner, Marsha Wilson, and the board of directors. Special thanks are also due to Ray Wiersma, senior editor at Baker Book House.

My wife Patty read and critiqued the entire manuscript and offered valuable corrections. For her and my three children, Matthew, Andrew, and Megan, I am especially grateful.

On Smells and Bells

An Apologia for Orthodoxy

We do not wish to embark on a "comparative theology": still less to renew confessional disputes. We confine ourselves here to stating the fact of a dogmatic dissimilarity between the Christian East and the Christian West. ... If while remaining loyal to our respective dogmatic standpoints we could succeed in getting to know each other, above all in those points in which we differ, this would undoubtedly be a surer way towards unity than that which would leave differences on one side. For, in the words of Karl Barth, "the union of the Churches is not made, but we discover it."

—Vladimir Lossky

They come from radically different backgrounds. Franky Schaeffer, son of the late evangelical theologian Francis Schaeffer, grew up as a Presbyterian. Anthony Scott and Tom Walker were Southern Baptists. Paul O'Callaghan came from a devoted ethnic, Roman Catholic family. John Morris, a Fulbright scholar and a professor of history, was raised in the United Methodist Church. Maria King, an associate professor of nursing at the Medical College of Georgia, was an Episcopalian nun who had served as a missionary in Liberia for two years. David Giffey had spent several months in a Hindu monastery. Tom Avramis was a campus leader and course instructor for Campus Crusade for Christ. Gordon Walker and Peter Gillquist likewise hailed from Campus Crusade. Others have come from organizations like Youth for Christ, Young Life, the Evangelical Free Church, and the Christian and Missionary Alliance.

They attended radically different schools: Oral Roberts University, Fuller Seminary, Dallas Theological Seminary, Wheaton College, Columbia Bible College, Westminster Theological Seminary, Western Conservative Baptist Seminary, Biola University, Asbury Seminary, Southwestern Baptist Theological Seminary, Luther Rice Seminary, Trinity Evangelical Divinity School, General Theological Seminary, Louisville Presbyterian Seminary, Nyack College, and Zion Bible College.[1]

Despite these varied backgrounds, all of these people have a common story to tell: they are all Christians who have converted to Orthodox Christianity. Many if not most of these converts have traveled deeply personal and private journeys to the Eastern church.[2] Others converted en masse, as did the group led by Peter Gillquist.[3] It was in 1987 that Gillquist and several close friends culminated a fifteen-year theological pilgrimage by leading a group of two thousand believers from seventeen congregations to join the Antiochian Orthodox Christian Archdiocese of North America. Since then, another fifteen congregations have followed suit; and today, according to Gillquist, who is an archpriest and chairman of the archdiocese's Department of Missions and Evangelism, "there are so many inquiries, I don't have time to scratch up new contacts. Evangelicals have a growing awareness of reductionism—what's been left out—and a true hunger for worship. They need something more."[4]

Within Orthodoxy itself there are signs of growing vigor and renewal. At St. Vladimir's Orthodox Seminary in New York 50 percent of the students are from non-Orthodox backgrounds. In the Orthodox Church in America about half of the bishops are from non-Orthodox backgrounds. Strongly evangelical movements within Orthodoxy include the "Zoe" movement in Greece, the "Lord's Army" in Romania, the "Orthodox Brotherhood of Saint Simeon the New Theologian" in America (led by Archimandrite Eusebius Stephanou, an evangelical charismatic priest of the Greek Orthodox diocese), and the denominational merger of the Evangelical Orthodox Church with the Antiochian Orthodox Church of North America in 1987.[5] One publisher today even advertises a specifically Orthodox study Bible.

1. "'New' Orthodox Attract Evangelicals," *Christianity Today* 36.6 (May 18, 1992): 50, 53.

2. Thomas Doulis, ed., *Journeys to Orthodoxy: A Collection of Essays by Converts to Orthodox Christianity* (Minneapolis: Light and Life, 1986); Frank Schaeffer, *Dancing Alone: The Quest for Orthodox Faith in the Age of False Religions* (Brookline, Mass.: Holy Cross Orthodox, 1993).

3. Peter E. Gillquist, *Becoming Orthodox: A Journey to the Ancient Christian Faith* (Brentwood, Tenn.: Wolgemuth and Hyatt, 1989); idem, *Making America Orthodox: Ten Questions Most Asked of Orthodox Christians* (Brookline, Mass.: Holy Cross Orthodox, 1984); idem, ed., *Coming Home: Why Protestant Clergy Are Becoming Orthodox*.

4. Quoted in "'New' Orthodox," 50.

5. Bradley Nassif drew my attention to these renewal movements.

Despite numerous difficulties faced by converts to Orthodoxy, they often convey a sense of having found a pearl of great price or a long lost treasure.[6] Just what is it that has attracted such a diversity of Christians to the common denominator of Orthodoxy? How can we explain what draws a *xenos* (outsider) to a largely immigrant church which by its own admission is often plagued by intense ethnocentrism? Why would Christians leave familiar communities of worship, and often their families, for the strange world of smells and bells, of incense, icons, priestly vestments, and a liturgy that is often still chanted in a foreign language? Exactly what deficiency in their previous Christian experience has Orthodoxy filled for these converts? More starkly put, to recall Peter Gillquist's words in reference to the experience of his parishioners, "Whatever would so possess two thousand Bible-believing, blood-bought, Gospel-preaching, Christ-centered, lifelong evangelical Protestants to come to embrace this Orthodox faith so enthusiastically?"[7]

These questions are as complex as they are fascinating, and one purpose of this book is to explore possible answers.[8] The beauty and power of Orthodoxy's liturgical ornament, liberation from arid and reductionistic rationalism, the celebration of "sacred materialism" free from legalism, the wholehearted embrace of majesty and mystery, and stability that outlasts the latest theological or ecclesiastical innovations and that is born of an unwavering devotion to the theology and life of the patristic fathers—all these are common themes cited by converts to Orthodoxy. They are also strange-sounding themes to some Western believers, and they set us on notice that in large part and for most people in the West Orthodoxy is either completely unknown or a religious enigma.

The World of Orthodoxy: Anonymity and Mystery

For the most part Orthodoxy in America has had to endure a certain degree of anonymity or cultural invisibility.[9] Devotees, and in particular

---

6. For the difficulties see Doulis, *Journeys*, 39, 91. It would likewise be interesting to study people who have *left* Orthodoxy and the reasons they give.

7. Gillquist, *Becoming Orthodox*, 6.

8. I will focus only on Orthodox theology; the political fortunes of Orthodoxy, its complex church-state history, its links with the KGB, etc., are outside the scope of this study. For insightful critiques of Orthodoxy on these points see Kent R. Hill, "The Orthodox Church and a Pluralistic Society," in *Russian Pluralism* (New York: St. Martin's, 1993); Anthony Ugolnik's unpublished paper, "The Orthodox Church and Contemporary Politics in the USSR" (1991); and regular newspaper stories such as "In Hard Times, No Time to Hunt Down KGB Agents," *International Herald Tribune*, 2 February 1992, on exposed KGB agent Metropolitan Pitirim of the Russian Orthodox Church.

9. Constance Tarasar, ed., *Orthodox America, 1794–1976: Development of the Orthodox Church in America* (Syosset, N.Y.: Orthodox Church in America, 1975).

highly committed converts like those listed at the beginning of this chapter, like to think of Orthodoxy as America's best-kept secret, but more realistic is the judgment of Thomas Doulis that "Orthodox Christianity is the great unknown among American religious denominations."[10] James Stamoolis notes that until Orthodoxy was recognized as America's fourth major religion, the identification tags of Orthodox believers who served in the American military bore the inscription *Protestant*.[11] Several factors converge to explain this anonymity of Orthodoxy.

First, most Americans have been conditioned to think about religion in America in terms of the Big Three. Thus Will Herberg's significant sociological study of religion in America was entitled *Protestant, Catholic, Jew* (1955). Many textbooks and seminary courses in church history barely cast a fleeting glance at the unique contributions and ethos of Eastern Christianity. Others omit it altogether; the Pelican History of the Church series, for example, contains no volume on Eastern Christianity.[12]

Second, for the most part the Orthodox Church in America, like some other denominations here (German Baptists, the Scandinavian Free Church, and Latvian Evangelical Lutherans), has been primarily an immigrant church, a "tribal domain" to use Doulis's description, whose strength and weakness have both resided in its pervasive ethnicity. Consequently, its presence in any given larger community is likely to be small and in some ways socially marginal. Assimilation into the larger arena of American religious life and society has not been a hallmark of Orthodoxy. Despite the specific cases mentioned earlier, the efforts and success of this tribal domain at attracting new converts, as Doulis notes, have been typically restricted to the spouses of ethnic believers.

Third, specifically *Russian* Orthodox Christians in America have faced the political prejudice of growing up in a country where as recently as the late 1980s the popular media, culture, and even the church stigmatized and stereotyped their homeland and forebears as "the evil empire." America, on the other hand, in this scenario, was the object of God's special favor and delight. Recall the movie *Rocky IV* where Sylvester Stallone defeats a bionic-looking Russian, or the gush of patri-

---

10. Doulis, *Journeys*, 7. Cf. the similar lament in the preface of Carnegie S. Calian, *Theology without Boundaries: Encounters of Eastern Orthodoxy and Western Tradition* (Louisville: Westminster/John Knox, 1992).

11. James J. Stamoolis, *Eastern Orthodox Mission Theology Today* (Maryknoll, N.Y.: Orbis, 1986), 1–2. Stamoolis attributes this example to John E. Paraskevas and Frederick Reinstein, *The Eastern Orthodox Church: A Brief History* (Washington, D.C.: El Greco, 1969), 3, 88.

12. See Anthony Ugolnik, *The Illuminating Icon* (Grand Rapids: Eerdmans, 1989), xv.

otism over the American Olympic hockey team's victory at Lake Placid, and then imagine the reaction of a Russian-American believer. And how many of us have heard passionate sermons based on Ezekiel or some other prophet that pretentiously offer up an intricate interpretation of future history in which Russia is the great beast swooping down upon Israel?[13] It rarely occurs to Americans that Holy Russia was home to Christianity eight hundred years before the United States became a nation. In short, the Cold War legacy has prevented many of us from knowing, or even wanting to know, Russian Christians.

Finally, Orthodoxy has operated with a degree of anonymity because of its confusion with Catholicism (and that despite being lumped together with Protestantism!). The German Protestant theologian Ernst Benz notes our "natural tendency to confound the ideas and customs of the Orthodox Church with familiar parallels in Roman Catholicism."[14] For the casual observer, some outward similarities make this confusion understandable, especially from the vantage point of Protestantism. But it is also a gross error, for the religious and political history, theology, worship, and entire frame of reference of Orthodoxy are all very different from Catholicism. Indeed, from the Orthodox perspective, Protestantism and Catholicism are simply opposite sides of the same coin, and much more similar to each other than either is to Orthodoxy. Eastern Christianity is a different world altogether. The nineteenth-century Russian lay theologian Alexei Khomiakov (1804–60) put it this way: "All Protestants are Crypto-Papists. . . . To use the concise language of algebra, all the West knows but one datum a; whether it be preceded by the positive sign +, as with the Romanists, or with the negative sign –, as with the Protestants, the a remains the same. Now a passage to Orthodoxy seems indeed like an apostasy from the past, from its science, creed and life. It is rushing into a new and unknown world."[15] Orthodoxy is not Catholicism, and if we are to understand it we must leave behind this common misconception.

Even among those who should know, Orthodoxy is often an unknown entity. I well remember my shock and dismay as a doctoral student when on one of my comprehensive examinations I encountered a question that

13. Ugolnik, *Illuminating Icon*, 174–81, draws attention to the problems with this "central theme of American apocalyptic preaching." The other examples cited are mentioned in his first chapter.

14. Ernst Benz, *The Eastern Orthodox Church: Its Thought and Life*, trans. Richard and Clara Winston (Garden City, N.Y.: Anchor Books, 1963), 1.

15. Quoted in Timothy Ware, *The Orthodox Church* (Baltimore: Penguin, 1964), 9. Thomas Hopko makes the same point in Jordan Bajis, *Common Ground: An Introduction to Eastern Christianity for the American Christian* (Minneapolis: Light and Life, 1991), ix n. 2.

required me to interact with some theologians I had never heard of; I am sure I had never seen their names before. They were complete unknowns to me. To my embarrassment, I was ignorant of some great Orthodox theologians. Patrick Henry's words applied to me, and no doubt to many Western Christians today, that "ignorance of Eastern Orthodoxy is the scandal of Western Christianity."[16]

Most of those Western people who have in some way encountered Orthodoxy experience its religious life as strange and peculiar, even awesome and exotic, something totally foreign to and different from almost all other expressions of Christianity they have known in the West. Not unlike the emissaries of Russia's Prince Vladimir who were awestruck at the liturgy they encountered at the Church of Holy Wisdom in Constantinople,[17] it is not uncommon for converts to Orthodoxy to recall with vivid clarity the first Orthodox liturgy they ever experienced.[18] I will always remember my first Orthodox liturgy, which I experienced in Nizhni Novgorod (formerly Gorki), Russia. Even before entering the church one is taken aback by the unusual architecture—the glittering onion domes that sparkle like diamonds on a sunny day. Once inside, the Western Christian is likely to experience a virtual sensory overload: the absence of any chairs or pews; the dim lighting; the scarves worn by all the women as a sign of reverence; the multitude of icons and frescoes that cover almost every inch of space on the walls and ceilings; the massive iconostasis separating the priest and worshipers; the smoky smell of incense and the crackling of hundreds of candles that burn in memory of the dead; the priest resplendent in his ornate vestments, massive beard, and resonant voice; the worshipers who repeatedly prostrate themselves, kiss the icons, and make the sign of the cross; and, in Russia, the chanting of the liturgy in ninth-century Church Slavonic along with the professional choirs whose voices echo from the balconies throughout the high ceilings of the church. All of this is accompanied by a sense of extreme awe and reverence, as I soon discovered. In Saint Petersburg I made the mistake of standing with my hands in my pockets, only to have an old babushka order me to remove them. In Moscow I made the mistake of standing on a small piece of carpet that ran beneath a lectern, and was ordered to get off by a babushka—I was standing on holy ground! The sum total of the Orthodox liturgical experience creates an

16. Quoted in Ugolnik, *Illuminating Icon*, 30.

17. James H. Billington, *The Icon and the Axe: An Interpretive History of Russian Culture* (New York: Random House, 1966), 6–7.

18. See, e.g., the recollections by Anthony Scott, Paul O'Callaghan, and Victoria Smith in Doulis, *Journeys*, 26, 37, and 100–101.

atmosphere that is worlds away from the typical Protestant church found in most American communities.

It is no wonder, then, that even those who have some familiarity with Orthodoxy find it a very strange and mysterious environment, certainly far removed from most expressions of Christianity in America. Khomiakov was right when he advised that Western Christians will find Orthodox Christianity to be "a new and unknown world" where not only the answers but even the questions are very different. Timothy Ware, himself a convert to Orthodoxy, draws attention to this insight from Khomiakov and suggests that Orthodoxy "is not just a kind of Roman Catholicism without the Pope [a badly mistaken judgment likely to be made by Protestants], but something quite distinct from any religious system in the west."[19] Would-be converts to Orthodoxy have been warned and even discouraged by Orthodox priests about the drastic differences between Eastern, Greek ways of thinking and Western, Latin patterns of Christian worship, life, and thought.

Thus most Christians in the West encounter Orthodoxy from the perspective of near total ignorance or mystification bordering on suspicion. Nor is this feeling merely a religious xenophobia or ethnocentrism; as Khomiakov observed, the differences between Eastern and Western Christianity are very real. If that is so, why, indeed, should Western believers even concern themselves with Orthodoxy?

The Case for Examining Orthodoxy

If we want to dispel the anonymity and mystery of Orthodoxy, we do not need to search very long or hard to discover a number of compelling reasons to enter into its world. First, as we have already mentioned, today Orthodoxy is recognized as the fourth major religion in America.[20] Despite its immigrant roots, limited social stature beyond its own ethnic communities, and the stigma of political prejudice, Orthodox Christians in America now number more than 6 million adherents.[21] If we enlarge our scope to consider the Orthodox believers worldwide, they number around 185 million. Russia alone is home to about 70 million Orthodox Christians, not including millions of other non-Orthodox Christians. These facts should give pause to American Christians tempted to neglect or spurn their Eastern counterparts. Such estimates have fluctuated, of course, because of such variables as the definition of an adherent, the

19. Ware, *Orthodox Church*, 9–10.

20. Arthur C. Piepkorn, *Profiles in Belief: The Religious Bodies of the United States and Canada*, 4 vols. (New York: Harper and Row, 1977–79), 1:52.

21. Doulis, *Journeys*, 7. The figures found in this paragraph are debated.

inclusion or exclusion of nominal members, the fortunes of Orthodoxy before and after the vicious onslaught of atheistic communism (e.g., by 1941 some 98 percent of Orthodox churches had been closed by the Communists), but by any measure Orthodoxy in the East and the West counts a considerable number of followers and on that basis alone merits study.

Second, Christians in the evangelical tradition, who have always been characterized by a strong defense of the fundamental truths of Christianity and a calculated rejection of such doctrinal modifications as the nineteenth-century liberalism of Friedrich Schleiermacher and the contemporary pluralism of John Hick, will find Orthodoxy to be a mutual friend and stalwart defender of the basic truths of Christianity. Indeed, "the greatest insult one could pay to any [Orthodox] theologian . . . would be to call him a 'creative mind.'"[22] Fidelity and an unwavering loyalty to the apostolic faith characterize Eastern Christianity. One of the most common reasons that converts to Orthodoxy give to explain their new allegiance is their frustration with liberal theology or faddish innovations found in their former churches. They have longed and sought for an authentic expression of New Testament Christianity. For many of these converts Orthodoxy provides a sturdy doctrinal anchor that they have missed.

Orthodoxy is so steeped in the traditions of the early church that it proudly identifies itself as the Church of the Seven Councils (see pp. 35–38). In fact, like evangelicalism it is sometimes criticized for being stuck in a static, backward-looking posture that is out of step with contemporary society. In some ways the criticism is just. But for Orthodoxy, intent on maintaining a direct link with its apostolic, patristic heritage, that criticism is a badge of pride, not of embarrassment. All good Orthodox Christians cherish the words of the great Eastern theologian John of Damascus (c. 675–749) that "we do not change the everlasting boundaries which our fathers have set, but we keep the traditions just as we received them."[23] There are some important areas where evangelicals will disagree with Orthodoxy (sacramentalism, the veneration of Mary), but upon close inspection one finds that on almost all the major doctrines of Christianity Orthodoxy places itself squarely within the tradition of what Vincent of Lérins said (c. 434) was believed by Christians "everywhere, always, and by all." This unquestioning loyalty to the boundaries of orthodox Christianity, an "unwavering devotion to the faith of the Ancient Church," provides a natural link between the Orthodox and evangelicals.[24] According to

22. Jaroslav Pelikan, *The Spirit of Eastern Christendom (600–1700)* (Chicago: University of Chicago Press, 1974), vii.

23. John of Damascus *On the Divine Images* 2.12.

24. John Morris, "My Voyage to Orthodoxy," in Doulis, *Journeys*, 49.

Gillquist, "there's a lot of overlay between the raw, hard doctrine of Ortho-doxy and the typical committed evangelical. The Trinity, the Resurrection, the Second Coming, it's all there."[25] Conferences held each fall by the Soci-ety for the Study of Eastern Orthodoxy and Evangelicalism bring together theologians from these two traditions to explore areas of agreement and dif-ference. Bradley Nassif, founder and president of the society, hopes that such meetings will encourage the natural similarities between the two groups.[26]

In addition to their mutual interest in defending the basic truths of Chris-tianity, evangelicals will also discover that the Orthodox church is often strongest where they are weakest, and this provides a third reason to acquaint ourselves with Orthodoxy. It responds to what some have experi-enced as a reductionism, barrenness, or minimalism in evangelicalism. A strong sense of the majesty and mystery of worship, joyful and confident cel-ebration of the gospel liturgy, a commitment to the role of tradition as a sup-plement to the Bible as a source for theology, a well-defined sense of Chris-tian identity that is rooted in a historical consciousness of the patristic fathers, a heritage of Christian perseverance tested by the terrible fires of persecution, and an emphasis on some overlooked biblical truths (such as the theme of deification in 2 Peter 1:4)—all of these are hallmarks of Ortho-doxy that could serve to strengthen Christians in evangelical traditions.

The breathtaking changes in Eastern Europe's history the last ten years offer a fourth reason why Western Christians need to study Eastern Ortho-doxy. Before 1985 (when Mikhail Gorbachev came to power) Eastern Christianity was closed to the West by the Iron Curtain of communism, by our Cold War cultural conditioning that programed Americans to see the former Soviet Union as only atheistic and not also as Christian (both were true), and by the fact that Orthodoxy itself continued to be sorely persecuted and oppressed. With the destruction of the Berlin Wall in 1989 and the disintegration of the Soviet Union two years later, Eastern Europe and Russia have been opened to the West as never before, and the Ortho-dox churches have been given new freedoms of worship that had been unknown for seventy-five years. Christians of the East and West now experience unprecedented opportunities to know, learn from, and interact with one another. My own experience in Russia is but one of many bizarre examples we could give: in what used to be called the Department of Sci-entific Atheism at Moscow State University, I as an evangelical theolo-gian have for three years taught Christian studies.[27]

25. "'New' Orthodox," 53.

26. "Peering over the Orthodox-Evangelical Crevasse," *Christianity Today* 36.13 (Nov. 9, 1992): 63.

27. See Daniel B. Clendenin, *From the Coup to the Commonwealth* (Grand Rapids: Baker, 1992).

One result of these historic changes in this part of the world has been a massive influx of Western Christians into Russia and Eastern Europe. As shocking as it might seem, almost seven hundred Western Christian organizations have been documented as now working in Eastern Europe and the former Soviet Union.[28] If Westerners are to minister in the East with any degree of cultural sensitivity and respect, it is imperative that they master the basics of Orthodox life, history, and thought. This is especially true given the well-documented theological and cultural xenophobia that Orthodoxy has exhibited toward the West and especially Western Christians. This xenophobia toward the West has ebbed and flowed over the past one thousand years in the life of Russia in general; in the last five years it has markedly increased within the Orthodox church. The Russian Orthodox Church, which with seventy million adherents is by far the largest Orthodox church in the world, has shown by word and deed that it is less than enthusiastic about the efforts of both Catholics and Protestants to evangelize and proselytize on its home turf, a land that from the Orthodox perspective has been home to Christianity for more than a thousand years. As one Orthodox priest stated in an interview, for the West to send missionaries to Russia to teach Christianity is like Russia's sending economists to the West to teach capitalism. "Resentment" of Western missionaries is not too strong a term, as was demonstrated by the "old" Russian Parliament, which just after being disbanded by Boris Yeltsin passed a law that greatly restricted foreign religious groups (July 14, 1993). Commenting on the Orthodox refusal to participate in an outreach in Russia, Leonid Kishkovsky, an American Orthodox priest, noted the presence of this negative attitude toward Western missionary efforts "even when they [Orthodox officials] see evidence that these efforts are not hostile."[29] Thus Westerners who go to Russia to live and work must bridge this unfortunate gap through a conscientious study of and appreciation for the rich heritage of the Orthodox tradition. Just how deep and rich this cultural influence of Orthodoxy is in Russia might surprise Westerners who have typically thought of Russia as atheist and America as Christian.

The fortunes of Orthodoxy in Eastern Europe and the former Soviet Union are almost the opposite of the fortunes of Orthodoxy in the West. In the West, Orthodoxy is an immigrant church on the periphery of American life and culture; but despite its small numbers, it nevertheless enjoys the protections of a political democracy. In the East, Orthodoxy has been perhaps the single greatest factor in shaping culture. Even seventy-five years of atheism could not

28. *East-West Christian Organizations: A Directory of Western Christian Organizations Working in East Central Europe and the Former Soviet Union*, ed. Sharon Linzey, Holt Ruffin, and Mark Elliott (Evanston, Ill.: Berry, 1993).

29. "Witnessing on the Volga," *Christianity Today* 36.12 (Oct. 26, 1992): 77.

erase the deep influence exerted over the course of a thousand years. When Russia's Prince Vladimir in A.D. 988 opted for Byzantine Christianity instead of Western Christianity, he "determined the destiny of Russia. . . . The whole Russian mind and heart were shaped by this Eastern mold."[30] Vladimir's faith spawned not merely a private faith for individuals but "a whole Christian culture and civilization."[31] Long before it became the center of atheism, Moscow was hailed as the "Third Rome," joining Rome and Constantinople as the chief defenders of Christianity. Librarian of Congress James Billington argues that by the sixteenth century Russia had experienced a "radical monasticization of society" that had virtually eliminated secular culture; "by the time of Ivan the Terrible (1533–1584), Muscovy had set itself off even from other Orthodox Slavs by the totality of its historical pretensions and the religious character of its entire culture."[32]

Westerners must not only learn to appreciate the numerical strength of Orthodoxy and the need to bridge the gap of xenophobic resentment at Western missionaries; they must also plumb the depths of the enormous cultural influence that one thousand years of Eastern Christianity has had in Eastern Europe and the former Soviet Union. For Russians in particular, as one of my students reminded me, Orthodoxy is much more than simply a church; it is an entire way of life and culture. In the words of a Russian proverb, "to be Russian is to be Orthodox." Imagine living in Italy without understanding Catholicism, traveling to Kuwait and ignoring Islam, or trying to understand the people of Utah without ever studying the history of Mormonism. That will give an idea of the catastrophic results of attempting to engage Eastern Europe and the former Soviet Union while neglecting the role of Orthodox Christianity.

There is a fifth reason why Western Christians should study Orthodoxy. Perhaps the greatest theological imperative spoken by Jesus Christ himself was the unity of his church. Near the end of his earthly life, Christ imparted a final word to his disciples, no doubt intent upon stressing the most essential truths about Christian identity. In the prayer of John 17 Jesus prayed three times that his disciples "may be one." He prayed that they might "be brought to complete unity to let the world know that you sent me" (v. 23). The apostle Paul likewise enjoined this imperative on all who would follow Christ: "Make every effort to keep the unity of the Spirit through the bond of peace. There is one body and one Spirit" (Eph. 4:3–4). Moreover, he sharply warned the Corinthians against divisions that would threaten oneness in Christ (1 Cor. 1:10–31). Unfortunately, despite

30. George P. Fedotov, *The Russian Religious Mind* (New York: Harper and Row, 1965), 21.

31. Ware, *Orthodox Church*, 86.

32. Billington, *Icon and the Axe*, 61, 69.

our Lord's mandate that love and unity be our chief identifying characteristic, Christians have, as we all know, all too often had a well-earned reputation for "mutual nastiness."[33]

Many Christians today find it difficult to see beyond the narrow confines of
their own particular experience of Christianity. Religious myopia and centrip-
etalism prevent us from experiencing and appreciating the full diversity of the
body of Christ. Some evangelicals, for example, can hardly bring themselves
to study, much less participate in, anything that smacks of being ecumenical.
Reformed and Wesleyan believers routinely neglect and in some cases even
spurn one another. Dispensationalists and charismatics or Pentecostals find
mutual cooperation almost impossible. Mainline and independent Bible
churches eye one another with unveiled suspicion. The Low Church and the
High Church would never be caught worshiping together. The rich tradition
of black Christianity in America is a complete unknown to most white Christians. Likewise, most of us have remained ignorant of Eastern Orthodoxy, as if
it were a rejected stepchild. If we are to follow the great imperative of our Lord,
we must recall the admonition of Paul that such a situation ought not to be.
The unity of the body of Christ is a necessity, not an option. Since the ecumenical councils at Ephesus in 431 and Chalcedon in 451, the Christian
church has affirmed its true marks to include not only holiness, catholicity,
and apostolicity, but also unity. For too long, however, both theology and politics have obstructed our field of vision.

On any given Sunday Protestant congregations may sing the classic
hymn "In Christ There Is No East nor West." Reality indicates otherwise.
Differences of theological outlook, so well expressed in the sentiment of
Khomiakov, have long hindered Christian unity. As for relations between
the Orthodox and Catholics, whom Protestants understandably but
wrongly lump together, the Orthodox rejection of both the papacy and
the doctrine that the Holy Spirit proceeds from the Father "and the Son"
(*filioque*) prevents any real movement toward oneness. And Orthodoxy's
sacramental and liturgical vision, the smells and bells so cherished by
Eastern believers, make it very difficult for Protestants, and especially
evangelicals, to believe there is a common ground that they can share with
Orthodox Christians. To be sure, Orthodoxy bears some responsibility for
this state of affairs. It spurned Catholic overtures for dialogue as recently
as late 1992, and Billy Graham, a Protestant insistent on garnering ecumenical support in the cities where he holds crusades, was received only

---

33. Ugolnik, *Illuminating Icon*, 6; cf. H. Richard Niebuhr, *The Social Sources of Denomi-
nationalism* (New York: H. Holt, 1929). According to the *World Christian Encyclopedia*, ed.
David B. Barrett (New York: Oxford University Press, 1982), v, at the beginning of the
twentieth century there were about 1,900 church denominations; today there are some
20,800.

lukewarmly by Russian Orthodox Patriarch Alexei II during the Moscow crusade of October 1992. Orthodoxy has insistently registered its displeasure at what it sees as unnecessary proselytization by both Catholics and Protestants who have moved into the former Soviet Union.

In addition to these theological obstacles to unity, Anthony Ugolnik demonstrates how the poison of political prejudice poses an even greater obstacle for American Christians. The problem, he notes, is that Russian believers "embrace a church that holds to its bosom hosts of those Russian people most Americans have been conditioned to view as the enemy."[34] Political allegiance to the West and ignorance of the strength and history of Christians in the East have frustrated the work of the gospel that should bind us together. Civil theology or phyletism (the identification of one's own nation and its values with the universal church) has inclined us, as we rejected Soviet politics, to reject Russian believers as well. Born in America to Russian immigrants, Ugolnik was ambivalent and confused in grade school when his teachers warned of the Red Menace (recall the rantings of Senator Joseph McCarthy). Ugolnik still remembers the vivid smells the night his parents burned some Russian literature in their backyard out of fear that their ethnic identity would be discovered; he also remembers the issue of *Newsweek* that contained a photo of a Russian priest with the caption "Puppet with Red Strings." There is no question that Orthodoxy too struggles with its own plagues of nationalism and phyletism. Fortunately, the end of the Cold War has blunted some of this mutual ideological suspicion. May we never again let the politics that have divided us for so long take precedence over the gospel that binds us together as one.[35]

Despite these theological and political barriers that would thwart Christ's imperative of the unity of the church, recent years have in fact witnessed encouraging signs of dialogue between the Orthodox and other Christian bodies. In spite of their ethnically centered identity and their insistence that they are the true visible church of Christ, the Orthodox have long participated in ecumenical exchanges. For many decades they have participated in the World Council of Churches, some of their priests even serving as its president.[36] In addition, a host of consultations, studies,

34. Ugolnik, *Illuminating Icon*, 4.

35. Ibid., chap. 1, esp. p. 8.

36. *The Orthodox Church in the Ecumenical Movement: Documents and Statements, 1902–1975*, ed. Constantin G. Patelos (Geneva: World Council of Churches, 1978); *The New Valamo Consultation: The Ecumenical Nature of Orthodox Witness* (Geneva: World Council of Churches, 1978). The Orthodox relationship with the WCC has at times been rocky. This was due in part to the liberal theology and politics of the WCC, which was soft on doctrinal rigor and Soviet abuse of human rights. On the other hand, Orthodoxy's own responsibility for the abuse of human rights has been pointed out by, among others, Hans Hebly.

and commissions have explored the relationship of Orthodoxy to Protestantism in general,[37] and even to Judaism.[38] Other joint studies have engaged Orthodoxy with particular denominations: Anglicans,[39] Reformed,[40] Lutherans,[41] Southern Baptists,[42] and even the Unification Church.[43] Until recently, evangelical-Orthodox dialogue lagged behind these substantial efforts. Almost nothing had been written by evangelicals about Orthodoxy, and the efforts of Orthodox thinkers in this area had all been short, popular attempts to introduce Orthodoxy to evangelicals and answer common questions.[44] There had been no full-fledged scholarly and dialogical encounter. However, the fall conferences of the Society for the Study of Eastern Orthodoxy and Evangelicalism, which now numbers about sixty scholars, are surely steps in the right direction.

37. See Derek Baker, *The Orthodox Churches and the West* (Oxford: Basil Blackwell, 1976); Carnegie S. Calian, *Icon and Pulpit: The Protestant-Orthodox Encounter* (Philadelphia: Westminster, 1968); idem, *Theology without Boundaries*; Apostolos Makrakis, *An Orthodox-Protestant Dialogue* (Chicago: Orthodox Christian Educational Society, 1966); and Wilhelm Niesel, *Reformed Symbolics: A Comparison of Catholicism, Orthodoxy, and Protestantism* (London: Oliver and Boyd, 1962).

38. See "The Greek Orthodox–Jewish Consultation," *Greek Orthodox Theological Review* 22.1 (1977).

39. See *Anglican-Orthodox Dialogue: The Moscow Agreed Statement of 1976* (London: S.P.C.K., 1977), and *Anglican-Orthodox Dialogue: The Dublin Agreed Statement of 1984* (Crestwood, N.Y.: St. Vladimir's Seminary Press, 1985). These two books summarize the results of years of meetings of the Anglican-Orthodox Joint Doctrinal Commission, which was founded in 1966.

40. See John Meyendorff and Joseph McLelland, eds., *The New Man: An Orthodox and Reformed Dialogue* (New Brunswick, N.J.: Agora Books, 1973); *The Orthodox Church and the Churches of the Reformation: A Survey of Orthodox-Protestant Dialogue*, Faith and Order paper 76 (Geneva: World Council of Churches, 1975); and *Theological Dialogue between Orthodox and Reformed Churches*, ed. Thomas F. Torrance (Edinburgh: Scottish Academic Press, 1985), a volume that comprises the papers read at three consultations between Orthodox and Reformed theologians (Istanbul, 1979; Geneva, 1981, 1983).

41. See John Meyendorff and Robert Tobias, eds., *Salvation in Christ: A Lutheran-Orthodox Dialogue* (Minneapolis: Augsburg, 1992).

42. See the *Greek Orthodox Theological Review* 22.4 (1977) and 27.1 (1982) for the papers presented at the Greek Orthodox–Southern Baptist consultations held in 1977 (Garrison, N.Y.) and 1981 (Bagdad, Ky.).

43. See *Orthodox-Unification Dialogue*, ed. Constantin N. Tsirpanlis (New York: Rose of Sharon Press, 1981).

44. Bajis, *Common Ground*; Paul O'Callaghan, *An Eastern Orthodox Response to Evangelical Claims* (Minneapolis: Light and Life, 1984); Gillquist, *Making America Orthodox*; and the Lausanne pamphlet "Witnessing to Nominal Orthodox Christians." Interestingly, both O'Callaghan and Gillquist were converts to Orthodoxy, from Catholicism and Protestantism respectively.

Requisites for Effective Dialogue with Orthodoxy

The imperative of Christian unity must somehow offset the theological and political barriers that have divided us. The study of Eastern Orthodoxy by Western Christians, which has so long been neglected, can help to make that divine command a reality. What else will it take for Orthodoxy and other Christian bodies to realize unity in Christ? On what basis should the recommended engagement with Orthodoxy, once its importance is finally appreciated, take place?

One of the greatest contemporary Orthodox theologians, Alexander Schmemann, former dean of St. Vladimir's Orthodox Theological Seminary in New York, has offered some judicious insights on this matter.[45] He registers the concern that too often no real encounter takes place in ecumenical discussions with the Orthodox. The primary reason is the fact that, as Khomiakov noted, there is a fundamentally different outlook between the East and the West. Christians in the West typically frame their ecumenical thinking in terms of the Catholic-Protestant split that Martin Luther precipitated when he nailed his ninety-five theses to the Wittenberg church on October 31, 1517. Christians in the East, on the other hand, see Protestants and Catholics as opposite sides of the same coin; Orthodox thinking is filtered through a more ancient prism, the much earlier division of 1054 when churches in the East and West split.

According to Schmemann, "For the Orthodox Church the fundamental opposition is that between the East and the West, understood as two spiritual and theological 'trends' or 'worlds' and it is this opposition that, in the Orthodox mind, should determine the initial framework of the ecumenical encounter. We must not forget that the only division or schism which the Orthodox Church remembers to speak of *existentially* as an event of her own past is precisely the alienation from her of the whole West."[46] John Meyendorff (died 1992), Schmemann's colleague at St. Vladimir's Seminary and perhaps the greatest contemporary Orthodox theologian in America, reiterates this important point: "In the light of what happened in the West throughout the Middle Ages and the Renaissance, the Orthodox historian considers the schism between Rome and Constantinople as the fundamental, the basic tragedy in the history of Christianity through which the whole of the Christian West lost its spiritual and theological balance."[47] Because the

---

45. The following discussion follows Stamoolis, *Orthodox Mission Theology*, 3–5.

46. Alexander Schmemann, "Moment of Truth for Orthodoxy," in Keith R. Bridston and Walter D. Wagoner, eds., *Unity in Mid-Career: An Ecumenical Critique* (New York: Macmillan, 1963), 50–51.

47. John Meyendorff, *Orthodoxy and Catholicity* (New York: Sheed and Ward, 1966), 133–34.

terms we use in theological debate have typically been framed in Western ways of thinking, ways that are foreign to the Eastern mind-set, Schmemann's first recommendation is that Western believers learn to appreciate the very different world of Eastern ways of thinking, so aptly described by Khomiakov, and in particular understand the significance of Orthodoxy's fixation on 1054 rather than 1517. At the very least interlocutors must acknowledge and traverse the chasm between these two different worldviews, which frame theological questions and answers in dissimilar ways.

Schmemann's second recommendation builds upon the first. Because the Orthodox insist that the primary schism in the Christian church is that between East and West (1054) rather than between Catholics and Protestants (1517), participants in dialogue need to employ a nonpartisan theological language that was in use before the split. The so-called terms of reference must reflect the early patristic tradition, a tradition that is not exclusively Eastern, but, as Schmemann insists, the common heritage of all believers. "This return to the sources," writes James Stamoolis, "is seen as a way out of the maze of Western controversies."[48] The recent efforts of evangelical theologians like Donald Bloesch of Dubuque Seminary, Thomas Oden of Drew University, and Robert Webber of Wheaton College to find a common theological language in the writings of the early church implement Schmemann's advice and demonstrate its potential for success.

The final recommendation of Schmemann is that Westerners reassert the sense of truth and error in theology, that is, they must recover the concept of heresy. This is necessary because "the only adequate *ecumenical method* from the Orthodox point of view [is] that of a total and direct doctrinal confrontation, with, as its inescapable and logical conclusion, the acceptance of truth and the rejection of error." Many ecumenical discussions blur or neglect the matter of truth and error and instead cater to the lowest common denominator of agreement. Because of the participants' respect for one another and modernism's fear of the very politically incorrect sins of intolerance, fanaticism, and narrow-mindedness, differences in theological propositions are sometimes considered to be of little consequence. That posture, insists Schmemann, is unacceptable, because ultimately the issues under consideration are not only intellectual ones about truth and error, but also salvific ones in which heresy can threaten the possibility of salvation itself. "It is therefore truth, and not unity, which in the Orthodox opinion and experience has to be the real goal of the Ecumenical Movement."[49] In short, far too much is at stake for us to tolerate error.

48. Stamoolis, *Orthodox Mission Theology*, 4.
49. Schmemann, "Moment," 52.

Reemphasis on truth and heresy need not end dialogue, as is sometimes thought, but can be its beginning. Christians of all three primary traditions (Orthodox, Catholic, Protestant) bear their share of responsibility for the failure to fulfill Christ's imperative of unity. With refreshing candor, for example, Meyendorff acknowledges that "the Orthodox East was often led to adopt toward the West an attitude of sufficiency, and this is undoubtedly our—very human—sin; for it belongs to the very essence of Catholicity to share in the brother's problems and to help him in resolving them before rushing into anathemas and condemnations."[50] Without disregarding our profound differences, unique perspectives, and the importance of repudiating heresy, it is past time for Christians to move forward toward unity in a spirit of mutual appreciation.

Two scholars, one Protestant and one Orthodox, have recently illustrated for us ways of fulfilling Christ's imperative. The personal biographies and scholarly publications of Carnegie Calian and Anthony Ugolnik evidence extensive and deeply personal boundary-crossings between Protestantism and Orthodoxy. Calian, who was baptized in the Eastern tradition but raised as a Protestant, is president and professor of theology at Pittsburgh Theological Seminary. He insists that it is "anachronistic" to make sharp distinctions between Eastern and Western ways of thinking, and that to continue this mentality will only fragment theology further:

> Today we are more aware than ever that each ecclesiastical tradition has written and followed its [own] rendition of the "Gospel according to Jesus Christ." Thus we have the gospel according to the Orthodox, Roman Catholics, and Protestants. Ecclesiastically we have created a synoptic exposition of the tradition personified in Jesus Christ. Each of the traditions, "gospel according to . . . ," highlights the mystery and glory of the Word made flesh. We are not so naive as to think that the sum of these ecclesiastical traditions is equal to *the* tradition. Tradition personified in Jesus Christ is greater than our grasp of him in our respective traditions. Such a statement may not please the Orthodox, Roman Catholics, or even many Protestants, but from the realistic viewpoint of the eschaton to claim any more would be presumptuous for any household of faith. We need a more relentless search into one another's ecclesiological heritage, asking embarrassing but honest questions of one another.
>
> We must ask these difficult questions, for all the traditions share in many of the same problems. . . . Christ himself calls us from our confessional caves and invites us to revamp our strategies from defense to offense, as we acknowledge one another's uniqueness and contribution in fulfilling the Christian mission and shortening the shadows surrounding the eschaton.

50. Meyendorff, *Orthodoxy and Catholicity*, 134.

According to Calian we must refuse to idolize our own respective traditions and must see ourselves, not only our neighbors, as in need of reform. In short, we need to embrace a methodology of reconciliation instead of rejection, an era of "cooperative didactics" that listens, learns, theologizes, and works together.[51] Seeing ourselves as debtors to our believing neighbors and not just as creditors will facilitate the imperative of unity.

Ugolnik, a Greek Orthodox priest of Russian heritage and professor of ethics and humanities at Franklin and Marshall College, shows how such a posture, far from diluting our sense of and commitment to a denominational tradition, can actually enrich and solidify our theological identity: "We Christians of America and Russia, simply by reaching a greater understanding of how each of us envisions and lives the gospel, can live that gospel more fully. If we cut ourselves off from that understanding, reject it or mutilate it through our suspicion or hatred, we are turning ourselves away from God's grace." Far from isolating us from one another, Christian faith urges us to "loving association":

> It is natural, then, that Christians should value their specific communities as distinct, precious expressions of their Christian life. What is more, Christians would not be honest with themselves if they did not see their own perspectives as normative; I understand Orthodoxy to be the fullest expression of the Christian life, or I would not be Orthodox. Yet the Christian identity is also "relational." Our separate Christian identities contain the anthropological expression of our Christianity. In my engagement with other Christians I have come to a fuller understanding of what it means to be Orthodox. In engaging other expressions of the Christian life and in coming into relation with those who live them, I have fulfilled an injunction of the gospel. I have come to love the image of Christ as they perceive it, and thus I have come to know Christ more fully.[52]

What will it take to fulfill the nonnegotiable of Christian love and unity? Schmemann, Calian, and Ugolnik point us in the right direction. At a minimum Western believers must begin with a knowledge of the history of Eastern Christianity. To that history we now turn.

51. Calian, *Theology without Boundaries*, 98–99, 103.
52. Ugolnik, *Illuminating Icon*, 264, 266–67.

The Forgotten Family
A Brief History

Orthodoxy is the Church of Christ on earth. The Church of Christ is not an institution; it is a new life with Christ and in Christ, guided by the Holy Spirit.

—Sergius Bulgakov

The Orthodox Church understands itself to be the one, holy, catholic, and apostolic Church, the true Church of Christ on earth . . . and claims [that] there is an absolute identity and continuity of this Church from the time of the apostles to the present day.

—Thomas Hopko

When Peter Gillquist and his followers were shedding their Protestant past, they did not know exactly where their fifteen-year quest would lead them. They did, however, have a growing sense of what it was that they sought. Above all, they nurtured the dream of finding the true church, the church of the New Testament, the church as it existed before centuries of accretions and distortions. They sought a pure and unvarnished expression of Christianity, an unadulterated and distilled essence of the faith purged of centuries of moral and theological impurities. In short, they longed for "a twentieth century expression of the first century church."[1] In a very real sense they wanted to link themselves in an identifiable way with the apostolic testimony and the first believers.

---

1. Peter E. Gillquist, *Becoming Orthodox: A Journey to the Ancient Christian Faith* (Brentwood, Tenn.: Wolgemuth and Hyatt, 1989), 29; see also 25–26.

It is no surprise that after years of prayer and study toward their stated goal Gillquist and his followers came home to Orthodoxy. To an extent matched by no other Christian communion, Orthodoxy claims that it alone has maintained an unbroken continuity with the apostolic faith of the New Testament, that it alone is the true visible church, and that salvation outside of the Orthodox church is a questionable assumption: "Orthodoxy, believing that the Church on earth has remained and must remain visibly one, naturally also believes itself to be that one visible Church. This is a bold claim, and to many it will seem an arrogant one; but this is to misunderstand the spirit in which it is made. Orthodox believe that they are the true Church, not on account of any personal merit, but by the grace of God. . . . While claiming no credit for themselves, Orthodox are in all humility convinced that they have received a precious and unique gift from God; and if they pretended to men that they did not possess this gift, they would be guilty of an act of betrayal in the sight of heaven."[2]

The questions of Gillquist and his followers and the answer of Orthodoxy were made for each other. The pilgrimage that began in San Bernardino ended at Antioch. Departing from California, the spiritual travelers arrived at Constantinople. In this chapter we will explore the rich history and heritage of this Eastern church which, as irony would have it, claims to be the one true church yet remains shrouded in obscurity and anonymity for Western believers. Before doing so, however, we must paint a broad picture of the Orthodox ethos and compare it with churches in the West.

Mapping the Orthodox Terrain

Many readers will have encountered a number of similar-sounding referents that describe the world of Orthodoxy: Greek Orthodox, Russian Orthodox, Eastern Orthodox, the Orthodox Catholic Church, and so on. The full and official title is "The Holy Orthodox Catholic Apostolic Eastern Church." In fact, all of these names are at the same time both helpful and potentially misleading.

The historical roots and strength of Orthodoxy certainly sink deep into Greek and Russian soil, but by no means do all Orthodox believers belong to one or the other of these two ethnic groups. Employing the adjective *Catholic* accurately captures the Orthodox sense of self-identity, but it is likely to be confused with *Roman* Catholicism—an unfortunate confusion. And although Orthodoxy originated and flourished in the Eastern and Mediterranean regions, nearly all of those lands have since fallen

2. Timothy Ware, *The Orthodox Church* (Baltimore: Penguin, 1964), 250–51.

under Muslim or atheistic control, while conversely a sizable number of Orthodox believers today live in the West. For these reasons the simple terminology *Orthodoxy* or the *Orthodox church* is the best way to refer to a rather large and diverse family of believers from around the world who share the same faith.

The so-called Orthodox church is actually not one church but a family of thirteen autocephalous or independent, self-governing churches. Though united in their understanding of the sacraments, discipline, doctrine, faith, government, and worship, these thirteen churches administer their internal affairs separately. As independent churches, they are not bound together by any central organization, nor do they owe allegiance to one particular person, as Roman Catholics do to the pope. Rather, each Orthodox church has its own head, who is variously referred to as the patriarch, archbishop, or metropolitan.

The table on page 32 lists the thirteen autocephalous Orthodox churches with rough estimates of their respective sizes. To be more nearly exact, we would have to distinguish between nominal and committed adherents as well as specify whether the figures reflect conditions before, during, or after Orthodoxy's struggles with Islam and atheism. Although small in size, the first four patriarchates are normally accorded special honor because of their antiquity and unique history. The patriarch of Constantinople is esteemed as the ecumenical or universal patriarch. As such he enjoys a special honor, but has no prerogative to interfere with the other Orthodox bodies. Small bodies of Orthodox Christians also live in Finland, Japan, the Czech and Slovak republics, Sinai, and China. Although the churches in these lands are autonomous, they are not autocephalous. The Orthodox Church in America, according to Thomas Doulis, numbers more than 6 million adherents.[3]

The Eastern church is distinct from its Western counterpart on several general levels. First, to be "Orthodox" is above all to stake a theological claim, for the word *Orthodoxy* has the double sense of "correct belief" and "correct worship." The Orthodox "regard their Church as the Church which guards and teaches the true belief about God and which glorifies Him with right worship, that is, *as nothing less than the*

3. But see the *Yearbook of American and Canadian Churches, 1992*, ed. Kenneth Bedell and Alice Jones (Nashville: Abingdon, 1992), which gives figures of 2 million members in the Greek Orthodox Archdiocese of North and South America, and 1 million members in the Orthodox Church in America (the two largest Orthodox bodies in the United States). On the wider group of churches within "Eastern" or "Oriental" Christianity, see Ronald Roberson, *The Eastern Christian Churches*, rev. 3d ed. (Chicago: Loyola University Press, 1990). For additional bibliography see Timothy Ware, *The Orthodox Church* (Baltimore: Penguin, 1993), 330–31. The figures in the table are taken from p. 6.

The Autocephalous Orthodox Churches

Constantinople	6,000,000
Alexandria	350,000
Antioch	750,000
Jerusalem	60,000
Russia	50–75,000,000
Romania	17,000,000
Greece	9,000,000
Serbia	8,000,000
Bulgaria	8,000,000
Georgia	5,000,000
Cyprus	450,000
Poland	750,000
Albania	210,000 in 1944

Church of Christ on earth."[4] This claim carries the moral implication that the East has kept the faith while the West has diverged from it. According to Orthodoxy, the Roman Catholic Church deviated from the true apostolic faith when it introduced the innovations of the papacy and the *filioque* doctrine. And Protestantism is, in Alexei Khomiakov's description (see p. 15), essentially the same Western datum as Catholicism; the basic difference is that in Protestantism the datum is preceded by a negative sign (rejection), in Catholicism by a positive sign (affirmation). We will explore the theological distinctives between the East and West in the following four chapters.

Second, there is a geopolitical distinction. Christians in the West look variously to Rome (Catholics), Wittenberg, and Geneva (Protestants); those in the East follow the lead of Constantinople (modern-day Istanbul). Early on, the life of the church was divided between the Greek-speaking East, with its center in Alexandria, and the Latin-speaking West, centered in Carthage. After his conversion in 313 Constantine moved the political capital of his empire from Rome to Con-

4. Ware, *Orthodox Church*, 1964 ed., 16.

stantinople in the East, a move that had ramifications for the ecclesiastical status of both cities and exacerbated the strained relations
between Christians of the two regions.

At the Council of Constantinople in 381, which was the second ecumenical council, the new capital of the empire was acknowledged as
"the New Rome" (Canon 3), an honor reaffirmed by Canon 28 of the
Council of Chalcedon in 451.[5] Furthermore, stated Canon 28, Old
Rome was accorded its special ecclesiastical status not because it was
theologically significant, but because it was the imperial city. "Equal
privileges" and "equal rank in ecclesiastical matters" were accorded
Constantinople, the New Rome. Not until the Lateran Council of 1215
did the Latin church recognize this status of Constantinople. While the
political fortunes of Rome, and with it the Roman church, waned in the
late fifth century, Constantinople enjoyed eleven hundred years of relative political and theological continuity until it was sacked in 1453 by
the Turks. Even today this basic geopolitical distinction has continued
to separate Eastern and Western churches. Western churches look to
Rome. While Protestants define their identity with reference to Roman
Catholicism, they usually make no reference at all to Eastern Christianity. Orthodox churches, concentrated primarily in Eastern Europe, the
old Byzantine Empire, the Balkans, and Russia, trace their heritage to
Constantinople.

Third, there is a linguistic distinction. The Eastern churches follow the
Greek-speaking tradition. Even though most Orthodox believers today do
not speak Greek (the Russian Orthodox Church is by far the largest
Orthodox body), their church is solidly anchored in the Greek tradition.
Greek was the language of the New Testament, the Septuagint (a translation of the Hebrew Old Testament), the first apologists and theologians,
the seven ecumenical councils (all of which were held in or near Constantinople), and the creeds issued by those councils. The Western, Roman
tradition, on the other hand, has always been Latin. With the Reformation of the sixteenth century churches began to use the vernacular for
worship and theological reflection, a change hastened this century with
the Second Vatican Council (1962–65), but even today some readers will
remember hearing a Catholic mass in Latin. Contemporary theological
scholars still make the linguistic distinction between the great patristic
theologians of the Greek-speaking East (Clement of Alexandria, Origen,
Athanasius, Basil the Great, Gregory of Nazianzus, Chrysostom, and John

5. John Meyendorff, "The Council of 381 and the Primacy of Constantinople," in *Catholicity and the Church* (Crestwood, N.Y.: St. Vladimir's Seminary Press, 1983), 121–42.

of Damascus) and the Latin-speaking West (Tertullian, Cyprian, Ambrose, Augustine, Jerome, and Gregory the Great).[6]

Thus, on a general level theological, geopolitical, and linguistic factors combine to differentiate the Orthodox ethos from Western patterns of Christianity. In the following chapters we will explore more specific and particular differences in the way these two bodies envisage the Christian tradition. None of these differences between Eastern and Western Christians occurred overnight, of course; they are the combined result of centuries of historical, political, sociological, and theological factors.

Classical Orthodoxy: To 787

The present chapter cannot attempt anything like a complete history of Orthodoxy. Others have done that well enough.[7] Nevertheless, we will introduce some of the main contours, events, and people of Orthodox Christianity.

Historians are always eager to locate chronological signposts by which to schematize history. A specifically Byzantine Christianity might be dated from the Council of Chalcedon (451) to the fall of Constantinople to the Turks (1453).[8] For our purposes we will divide the history of Orthodoxy into its early or classical period, ending with the death of John of Damascus in 754 and the seventh and last ecumenical council at Nicea (787), which upheld the use of icons; a middle period, ending with the fall of Constantinople to Islam; and a modern period that is marked by Orthodoxy's life under Islam and subsequently atheism.

In its first few centuries of existence the Christian community faced serious threats on a number of fronts. Until the Edict of Toleration issued by the Emperor Galerius in 311, Christians suffered horrible persecutions.[9] In the second century intellectual challenges came from within and without the church. Celsus (refuted by Origen) and Marcion's Gnosticism (refuted by Irenaeus) posed external, pagan challenges. The

6. Philip Sherrard, *The Greek East and the Latin West* (New York: Oxford University Press, 1959); John E. L. Oulton and Henry Chadwick, eds., *Alexandrian Christianity* (Philadelphia: Westminster, 1954); S. L. Greenslade, ed., *Early Latin Theology* (Philadelphia: Westminster, 1956); and the two works by Hans von Campenhausen, *Fathers of the Greek Church* (New York: Pantheon, 1959), and *Fathers of the Latin Church* (Stanford, Calif.: Stanford University Press, 1963).

7. See the works by Atiya, Benz, Bratsiotis, Ellis, French, Tarasar, Ware, and Zernov that are listed in the bibliography. Ware's *Orthodox Church*, on which this chapter is heavily dependent, is an especially helpful summary of the history and theology of Orthodoxy.

8. John Meyendorff, *Byzantine Theology: Historical Trends and Doctrinal Themes* (New York: Fordham University Press, 1974), 3.

9. Eusebius *Ecclesiastical History* 8.17.6–10.

internal threat of heresy from fellow Christians was another problem. It is to the Greek Christians that all believers owe a debt of gratitude for their indispensable role in forging the basic doctrines of the Trinity, and for expressing those beliefs in creeds that are recited today by believers East and West.

Around the year 321, a prestigious and popular priest from Alexandria, Arius, had a dispute with his bishop over the relationship of Jesus Christ to God the Father. Was Jesus Christ a created being, as Arius taught, or uncreated and coeternal with the Father, as Bishop Alexander maintained? In a letter to one of his advocates, Eusebius of Nicomedia, Arius complained that "we are persecuted because we say that the Son has a beginning, but God is without beginning." Before he was created, Arius taught, Christ did not exist. At issue was the full deity of Christ, for if Christ was a created being with a beginning, then he was not fully God.

When Emperor Constantine first learned of the matter, he dismissed it as "an unprofitable question"; but when theological division threatened political stability, he decided to take action. After his emissary Hosius of Cordova (Spain) failed to resolve the problem in 322, Constantine summoned some three hundred bishops, mostly from the Greek-speaking East where the controversy was concentrated, to his summer palace to settle the matter. Thus was born the first ecumenical council, the Council of Nicea (modern Isnik, Turkey).

It was Athanasius (296–373), bishop of Alexandria from 328 until his death, who played the leading role in securing the orthodox conclusions of the Council of Nicea. Athanasius stood unyielding in his refutation of Arianism, a stance that cost him dearly during his stormy period as bishop of Alexandria, for he was exiled five different times. At the council, which was convened in 325, Athanasius was a young deacon under Bishop Alexander (whom he eventually succeeded in 328). He helped to secure and then later defended uncompromisingly the important distinction that Christ was not simply "similar in substance" (*homoiousios*) to the Father, as the Arians had taught. According to the Nicene Creed, Jesus Christ was "true God of true God, begotten not made, of one substance (*homoousios*) with the Father."

In the fourth century three theological giants of the East loom large in the defense of the trinitarian orthodoxy that was enunciated at Nicea and subsequently ratified and refined at the second ecumenical council, the Council of Constantinople (381). Together with Athanasius, the three Cappadocian fathers are indispensable for understanding Eastern Christianity. Seldom has the church had four such theological titans simultaneously.

Basil the Great (329–79) and his brother Gregory of Nyssa (330–95) were born into a wealthy Christian family. In the year 370 Basil succeeded

Eusebius as the bishop of Caesarea, a post he held until his death. As an ascetic Basil is often considered the father of Eastern monasticism. With his friend Gregory of Nazianzus he founded a monastic community for which he wrote a rule of order. By all accounts Basil was a loving and exemplary Christian, selling all his possessions to finance the elaborate network of schools and hospitals he created to meet the needs of the poor, and modeling loving service by undertaking the most lowly and disagreeable of tasks. As a theologian Basil repudiated the continuing Arian influence (*Against Eunomius*), defended the deity of the Holy Spirit (*On the Holy Spirit*), and crafted the crucial theological phrase that the Trinity is "three persons in one essence."

Gregory of Nyssa incurred his brother Basil's displeasure when he took up a secular career as a teacher of rhetoric, but later, after his wife died, he entered a monastery founded by Basil. In 371 he became the bishop of Nyssa. Like Basil, Gregory was a vigorous defender of Nicene orthodoxy (he was deposed in 376 by Arian bishops, but reinstated two years later). Despite his love for obscurity and retirement, Gregory gave the opening address at the Council of Constantinople in 381.

Gregory of Nazianzus (329–89), who became friends with Basil when they both studied in Athens, joined the latter in monastic life. Although elected the bishop of Constantinople at the second ecumenical council, Gregory resigned when his nomination created a controversy. His most important theological work, the *Theological Orations*, is yet another defense of the orthodox trinitarian theology first enunciated at Nicea.

The fourth and fifth centuries saw the continuing importance of ecumenical councils. In the year 381 Emperor Theodosius I called the second ecumenical council. The canons of the Council of Constantinople ratified the Nicene faith and anathematized heretics; they also affirmed the primacy of Constantinople after that of Rome. After the Council of Ephesus (431), which banned the use of any creed other than that of Nicea, comes perhaps the most important ecumenical council of all, that of Chalcedon (451). Summoned by Marcian, the Eastern emperor, the council convened five hundred bishops to settle the matter of the relationship between the two natures of Christ. Against the Eutychian and Nestorian heresies, which respectively fused the two natures of Christ into one nature (Eutyches) and divided them between two persons (Nestorius), the Chalcedonian definition insisted that Christ is one person, that he has two natures (divine and human), that each nature is complete and maintains its integrity, and that the two natures are united in such a way that a third nature is not formed. Jesus Christ, the formulation of 451 confesses, existed "in two natures, without confusion, change, division, or separation; the distinction of natures in no way annulled by the union, but rather the characteristics of each nature being preserved and coming together to form one person and subsistence, not as parted or separated into two persons, but one and the same Son, and only begotten God the Word, Lord Jesus Christ."

The late fourth to the end of the eighth century marked an important period of fruitful development for Orthodox Christianity. Eastern monasticism, which began in the deserts of Egypt, flourished.[10] By the time of Chalcedon the so-called pentarchy had been established. That is, five great jurisdictions of the church were held to have special honor because of their apostolic foundations and political significance (except for Jerusalem, which as the city of our Lord was also included). The bishops of each city were recognized as patriarchs: Rome, Constantinople, Alexandria, Antioch, and Jerusalem. In Orthodoxy these five sees were accorded special honor, but their authority was merely equal to that of all the other bishops around the world. While granting the see of Rome a primacy of honor, and esteeming the pope as first among equals, Orthodoxy, unlike Catholicism, refused to accord Rome any supremacy of authority.

Key Greek theologians were instrumental in the maturation of Eastern Christianity during these centuries. John Chrysostom (c. 345–407), literally John "the golden-mouthed," gained a well-deserved reputation as an eloquent biblical expositor, emphasizing the historical and literal meaning of the text, and as a popular defender of the faith. After years of service at Antioch in Syria, in 398 John unwillingly became the patriarch of Constantinople. It has been said that next to Augustine, no theologian was more popular with the sixteenth-century Reformers than was Chrysostom.

Maximus the Confessor (580–662) dominates the seventh century and is considered by many to be the real father of Byzantine theology,[11] while John Climacus (579–649) produced one of the most widely read manuals of mystic spirituality, his *Ladder of Divine Ascent*. In the eighth century it is John of Damascus (675–754) that dominates the landscape. John gave to Orthodoxy its first, most important, and, by some accounts, only systematic theology (*The Orthodox Faith*). John was also the primary defender of the use of icons.

The fifth and sixth ecumenical councils convened in 553 and 680 (both in Constantinople). The great controversy over the use of icons, which we shall discuss at length in chapter 4, was finally settled by the ecumenical council of 787, which upheld their veneration. The seven councils are of

10. See, e.g., Athanasius, *Life of Antony* (New York: Paulist, 1980). The chief center of Orthodox monasticism is the "Holy Mountain" of Athos in northern Greece, which is said to have been at one time home to forty thousand monks. See Philip Sherrard, *Athos: The Holy Mountain* (New York: Overlook, 1985).

11. Meyendorff, *Byzantine Theology*, 37.

enormous importance to Orthodox Christianity, so much so that it often refers to itself as the Church of the Seven Councils. In the words of John II, the metropolitan of Russia (1080–89), "all profess that there are seven holy and ecumenical councils, and that these are the seven pillars of the faith of the Divine Word on which He erected His holy mansion, the catholic and ecumenical Church."[12] That is, Orthodoxy considers the seven ecumenical councils to be in theological importance second only to the Bible. With the death of John of Damascus (754) and the legitimization of icons at the seventh ecumenical council (787), the first great period of Orthodox Christianity came to a close.

New Opportunities, New Challenges: To 1453

Conversion of the Slavs

The major milestones of Orthodoxy's middle ages are the conversion of the Slavic people (988), the final split with Western Christianity (1054), and the fall of Constantinople (1453). The beginnings of Christian Russia are recorded in the *Russian Primary Chronicle* of the twelfth century, the earliest historical record of Kiev. Determined to find the one true religion, Prince Vladimir of Kiev sent out a team of emissaries. The delegation first encountered the Bulgar Muslims of the Volga, but found them uncouth and hysterical: "There is no joy among them, but mournfulness and a great smell; and there is nothing good about their system." The Western expressions of Christianity were no better; in Germany and Rome, the chronicle reports, Vladimir's emissaries "beheld no beauty." Worship at Constantinople, however, was a different matter altogether. There the delegation attended the Divine Liturgy of Saint John Chrysostom (the normal liturgy for Sundays and weekdays) at the Church of the Holy Wisdom (Saint Sophia). They were spellbound by the liturgical splendor they witnessed. They did not know whether they were in heaven or on earth, the chronicle records; they were "at a loss to describe it."[13]

In 988 Prince Vladimir was baptized, and in 1988 Russia celebrated a millennium of Orthodox Christian heritage. By all accounts Vladimir led Kievan Russia (today Ukraine) along a path of zealous reform: mass baptisms took place; cathedrals were built; priests, relics, sacred vessels, and liturgies were imported; monasteries flourished; pagan idols were toppled; church courts were started; and tithes were instituted. In rejecting paganism for a specifically Eastern form of Christianity, Vladimir "determined

12. Quoted in Ware, *Orthodox Church*, 1964 ed., 26.
13. James H. Billington, *The Icon and the Axe: An Interpretive History of Russian Culture* (New York: Random House, 1966), 6–7.

the destiny of Russia. . . . The whole Russian mind and heart were shaped by this Eastern Christian mold."[14] In their wake, the waters of Vladimir's celebrated baptism left not only an Orthodox faith for individuals, but "a whole Christian culture and civilization."[15]

What began in Kiev continued in Moscow—the development not simply of an economic or political civilization, but of a specifically Christian culture. In this regard scholars often refer to a well-documented sense of manifest destiny, a Muscovite or Russian messianism—that is, the people thought of themselves as chosen by God for a mission to the world. At its rise to greatness in the twelfth century, Moscow was something of a revivalist camp. By the late sixteenth century, while the West was in the early throes of the Reformation, a "radical monasticization of society" had already virtually eliminated secular culture in Russia: "By the time of Ivan the Terrible [1533–84] Muscovy had set itself off even from other Orthodox Slavs by the totality of its historical pretensions and the religious character of its entire culture."[16]

While Westerners often think of Moscow as the center of an atheistic, evil empire, the truth of the matter is that it was long considered the Third Rome of Christianity. When Constantinople, the center of Eastern Orthodoxy, fell to the Turks in 1453 after eleven hundred years as the New Rome, Moscow was heir to the title of protector of Christianity. Historians trace this idea to the monk Philotheus of the Eleazar Monastery in Pskov, who in 1510 wrote a letter to Tsar Basil III in which he heralded Moscow as the Third Rome: "The church of ancient Rome fell because of the Apollinarian heresy; as to the second Rome—the church of Constantinople—it has been hewn by the axes of the Hagarenes. But this third, new Rome, the Universal Apostolic Church under thy mighty rule, radiates forth the Orthodox Christian faith to the ends of the earth more brightly than the sun. . . . In all the universe thou art the only Tsar of Christians. . . . Hear me, pious Tsar, all Christian kingdoms have converged in thine alone. Two Romes have fallen, a third stands, a fourth there shall not be."[17] The marriage of Ivan the Great in 1472 to Sophia, niece of the last Byzantine emperor, had earlier helped to secure Moscow's status as the legitimate successor to Constantinople.

By 1914, just before the Russian Revolution, Russia was home to more than one thousand monasteries. Even during the seventy long years of virulent atheism, a half dozen magnificent churches dating back to the fif-

14. George P. Fedotov, *The Russian Religious Mind* (New York: Harper and Row, 1965), 21.
15. Ware, *Orthodox Church*, 1964 ed., 86.
16. Billington, *Icon and the Axe*, 61, 69.
17. Ibid., 58; Ware, *Orthodox Church*, 1964 ed., 113.

teenth century stood inside the Kremlin walls adjacent to the Palace of Congresses (the former seat of the atheist Soviet government), silent witnesses to one thousand years of Christian identity.[18]

The Split between East and West

Prince Vladimir's tenth-century delegation had recognized major differences between the Christians of the East and the West. Despite efforts by both sides to protect the unity of the church, by the eleventh century it had become inevitable that an acrimonious split would separate Greek and Latin Christians. Since the Great Schism of 1054 the Orthodox churches have had their own identity, separate from both Protestants and Catholics. Schisms had already occurred in the church (e.g., the Donatist controversy of the fifth century in North Africa), and others would occur in the future (the Papal Schism from 1378 to 1417 and the Protestant Reformation), but the Great Schism was the first division of such major consequence. To this day the wound has not healed.

Much like a marital divorce, the schism was a problem that brewed for years. The year 1054 marks only the denouement of a long and tragic estrangement. In that year Pope Leo IX dispatched his legate, Cardinal Humbert, to the Church of the Holy Wisdom in Constantinople. There on June 16 Humbert delivered a papal bull of excommunication that anathematized the Orthodox patriarch Michael Cerularius and with him Eastern Christians. Rome accused the "Greek heretics" of trying to "humiliate and crush the holy catholic and apostolic church," while for his part Cerularius entreated Orthodox believers to "flee the fellowship of those who have accepted the heretical Latins."[19] In the centuries leading up to 1054, political, cultural, and theological factors combined to insure the eventual divorce.

As early as the fourth century the political empires of the East and West were drifting apart. Constantine, we saw, moved the capital of his empire to Constantinople in 330, where for the next millennium relative political and religious stability reigned. Meanwhile, the barbarian invasions of Rome in the late fifth century hastened the demise of its political prestige

18. On Russian Christianity see Nicolas Zernov, *The Russians and Their Church* (Crestwood, N.Y.: St. Vladimir's Seminary Press, 1978); George P. Fedotov, *A Treasury of Russian Spirituality*, 2 vols. (Belmont, Mass.: Nordland, 1975); idem, *Russian Religious Mind*; and Jane Ellis, *The Russian Orthodox Church: A Contemporary History* (Bloomington: Indiana University Press, 1986).

19. Jaroslav Pelikan, *The Spirit of Eastern Christendom (600–1700)* (Chicago: University of Chicago Press, 1974), 170–71. On the schism of 1054 see Yves Congar, *After Nine Hundred Years* (New York: Fordham University Press, 1959); Steven Runciman, *The Eastern Schism* (New York: Oxford University Press, 1955); and Francis Dvornik, *The Photian Schism: History and Legend* (New York: Cambridge University Press, 1948).

and severed the unity once enjoyed by the citizens of the two regions. Language posed another, most practical problem. By the end of the sixth century neither group could speak the other's language. The rise of Islam after Muhammad (died 632) was checked by Charles Martel at the Battle of Tours in 732, but by that time most of the Eastern Mediterranean had fallen under Muslim control. While Constantine had once controlled the lands around the entire perimeter of the Mediterranean and Christianity had as a result flourished in these regions, the expansion of Islam severed Byzantine Christians and their capital at Constantinople from their counterparts in the West. When Pope Leo III turned a deaf ear to the objections from the Greek East and crowned Charlemagne emperor of the West on Christmas Day in the year 800, the Byzantines refused to recognize him. They considered the formation of his Holy Roman Empire an act of political sabotage and Leo's complicity in the coronation an act of schism. Charlemagne's cultural renaissance, in fact, was marked by a strong anti-Greek sentiment, while in the theological realm he reproached Orthodox Christians for failing to adopt the version of the Nicene Creed that contained the term *filioque*.

Other theological matters joined with political and cultural factors to rend the fabric of Christian unity in two. For example, a number of general practices differentiated Greek and Latin Christians and added to the growing sense of alienation. The East allowed some clergy to marry; the West required celibacy. In the East the local parish priest could administer the sacrament of confirmation; in the West only the bishop could. When celebrating the Eucharist, Catholics mixed the wine with water, while the Orthodox did not. The West used unleavened bread, the East leavened. Differences over clerical beards, the tonsure, and fasting also contributed to the deterioration of unity.

Two controversies, however, were far and away more important than all the others combined. Together they drove the final wedge between Catholic and Orthodox Christians: papal supremacy and the *filioque* doctrine. The barbarian invasions of Rome and the haplessness of the emperors that followed created a power vacuum that was filled by the Roman papacy. Eastern Christians, who with their concept of a pentarchy were much more inclined to appeal to ecumenical councils than to a single ecclesiastical figure to settle matters of debate, resented and resisted the encroaching power of the papacy and likewise the theological scaffolding built to justify it. They acknowledged that the pope deserved a primacy of honor, but at the same time they insisted that he was only first among equals. The so-called Photian Schism brought the matter to a head.

In 858 Photius was appointed as Orthodoxy's new patriarch at Constantinople, replacing Saint Ignatius, who had been exiled and later resigned his duties. Ignatius's followers, however, refused to acknowledge the transition, and eventually both Ignatius and Photius appealed to Pope Nicholas I (858–67) in Rome for support. After investigating the matter, Nicholas reversed the decision of his legates to support Photius, reinstated Ignatius, and deposed Photius. From the perspective of Orthodox Christians in the East, Nicholas's decision was yet another example of the proverbial camel's nose in the tent, an infringement of their own autonomy. Moreover, in a letter in 865 Nicholas declared that he sought to extend the power of the papacy "over all the earth, that is, over every church." Eastern Christians would hear nothing of it.

Photius then branded the entire Latin church as heretical for inserting the term *filioque* into the Nicene Creed. Originally the creed read that the Holy Spirit proceeded "from the Father"; a later Western interpolation (why, where, and by whom are not known), ratified at the Council of Toledo (589), added *filioque* to indicate that the Spirit proceeded from the Father "and the Son." Charlemagne, we have just seen, upbraided Eastern Christians for not including the interpolation.

Orthodox Christians considered the *filioque* amendment to be contrary to explicit instructions by the past ecumenical councils not to change the creeds; it was a usurpation of the inviolable wisdom of the Fathers. Worse, they considered the *filioque* addition to be theologically untrue and a threat to the doctrine of the Trinity. Exacerbating the whole affair, in 1009 the Orthodox Patriarch Sergius refused to include the name of the Catholic pope (Sergius IV) on the diptychs, the official list of bishops acknowledged as orthodox. Thus in effect ended communion between the East and West.

The final act of the tragedy began when Cardinal Humbert placed Leo IX's bull of excommunication on the altar in Constantinople while Patriarch Cerularius prepared to celebrate the liturgy. It ended with a blow that Eastern Christians have never forgotten. During the Fourth Crusade, Western forces stormed Constantinople (1204) and ransacked the Church of the Holy Wisdom, an unimaginable act of desecration from the viewpoint of Orthodoxy. Any vestiges of hope that remained after the bull of 1054 were dashed with the pillage of 1204. Despite efforts at reunification between Catholics and the Orthodox at Lyon (1274) and Florence (1438–39), to this day the two bodies remain estranged. As recently as 1991 the Orthodox patriarchy refused an invitation to participate at a synod of Catholic bishops from Europe.[20]

20. On Catholic-Orthodox differences see John Meyendorff, ed., *The Primacy of Peter in the Orthodox Church* (Crestwood, N.Y.: St. Vladimir's Seminary Press, 1992).

The Threat of Islam

The threat of Islam which began in the seventh century exploded with lightning speed. Timothy Ware observes that when Muhammad died in 632 his influence was limited, but within only fifteen years Syria, Palestine, and Egypt were under Muslim control. By the turn of the century Muslims almost captured Constantinople. Only a hundred years after Muhammad died Islam had "swept across North Africa, advanced through Spain, and forced western Europe to fight for its life at the Battle of Poitiers."[21] Constantinople held out for another seven hundred years, but eventually it too fell.

The fall of Constantinople to the Turks in 1453 brought to a close a millennium of Byzantine Christian civilization. Henceforth Orthodox Christians were under the control of the infidels. How the Christians fared under Islam is a matter of some debate. On the one hand, the Muslims treated the Orthodox with remarkable generosity; in fact, they were more tolerant of Christians than Protestants and Catholics were of each other during the sixteenth and seventeenth centuries. Islam honored Jesus Christ as a prophet and the Bible as a holy book. Sultan Muhammad II, who had conquered Constantinople, treated the patriarchy with due respect; Christians were distinguished from pagans and allowed to practice their worship. On the other hand, toleration under the sultan meant a position of guaranteed inferiority. "Christianity under Islam was a second-class religion, and its adherents second-class citizens. They paid heavy taxes, wore a distinctive dress, were not allowed to serve in the army, and were forbidden to marry Moslem women. The Church was allowed to undertake no missionary work, and it was a crime to convert a Moslem to the Christian faith. From the material point of view there was every inducement for a Christian to apostatize to Islam."[22] Furthermore, the entire ecclesiastical hierarchy came under the direct control of the government. Christians found themselves on the defensive theologically: the doctrine of the Trinity led to charges of tritheism, the veneration of icons to charges of idolatry. That Orthodoxy survived at all during these demoralizing and trying times is a fulfilment of the words of Christ to Peter about the gates of hell (Matt. 16:18).[23]

21. Ware, *Orthodox Church*, 1964 ed., 37.
22. Ibid., 97–98.
23. On Orthodoxy under Islam see Pelikan, *Spirit*, 227–42; and Steven Runciman, *The Great Church in Captivity: A Study of the Patriarchate of Constantinople from the Eve of the Turkish Conquest to the Greek War of Independence* (New York: Cambridge University Press, 1968).

The Modern Period: After 1453

From the late seventh century onward, the Orthodox church of the Mediterranean region had found itself swimming against the rising tide of Islam. In Russia and Eastern Europe, Orthodoxy took a different path after Moscow succeeded Constantinople as the New (the Third) Rome, a path that was by no means an easy one.

In 1237 pagan Mongol forces had invaded, sacking Kiev and then ruling parts of Russia until 1480. Under Peter the Great (1689–1725), whom the Old Believers (a conservative sectarian group within Russian Orthodoxy) considered the Antichrist, the Orthodox patriarchate was abolished and replaced with the so-called Holy Synod. The synod, which ruled the church until 1917, was in fact an arm of the state whose members were nominated by the emperor. From the perspective of Peter's pro-Western program of secularization, the Russian church was a backward-looking, nationalistic, and bothersome impediment to reform; it had to be subjugated in the name of progress. Peter's *Spiritual Regulations* (1721) not only eliminated the patriarchate, but effectively smothered the vitality of church life. Priests were obligated to spy on their parishioners and needed special permission to leave their churches. Existing monasteries were closely monitored, and new ones could not be started without state permission. The church fared no better in the post-Petrine period under tsarinas Elizabeth (1741–62) and Catherine the Great (1762–96), who closed over half of the country's monasteries. Although Orthodoxy had its true saints during these dark days, spiritual giants like Saint Nicodemos of Athos in Greece (1748–1809) and Saint Seraphim of Sarov in Russia (1759–1833), in general this period under the Holy Synod was marked by compromise of integrity, secularization, and obsequiousness toward the state.

On November 5, 1917, the Russian Orthodox bishops finally freed themselves from the synodal government imposed two hundred years earlier by Peter and restored the patriarchate. At long last a new day had dawned for the church, but one much different from what they had expected. An ominous new foe had appeared on the horizon. Just two weeks before the new patriarch, Tikhon, was elected from three nominees, Nikolai Lenin and the Bolsheviks had taken control of Petrograd; only two days before Tikhon's election they overpowered Moscow. As if the Eastern threat of Islam was not enough, now Orthodoxy faced a new foe—the Western heresy of radical Marxism. Moscow, once the Third Rome, now became the most powerful purveyor of a new religion—scientific atheism.

That a calculated hostility to all religion is endemic to consistent Marxist Leninism is beyond debate.[24] The facts speak for themselves.

24. Daniel B. Clendenin, *From the Coup to the Commonwealth* (Grand Rapids: Baker, 1992), 129–34.

Under Lenin, Joseph Stalin, and Nikita Khrushchev unspeakable horrors were unleashed upon the church. As many as fifty million people were killed during the Soviet period. Between the 1917 Revolution and the outbreak of World War II nearly fifty thousand priests vanished. A thousand monasteries and sixty seminaries were closed.[25] By 1933 all but one hundred of Moscow's six hundred churches had been closed; by 1941, 98 percent of all Orthodox churches in Russia were closed.[26] By another estimate, before the Revolution of 1917 some fifty thousand Orthodox churches existed; by 1985 that number had dwindled to seven thousand.[27] A bishop of the catacomb church declared that the Bolsheviks' announcement of their intentions to liquidate the church was "probably the only honest act in their entire political activity."[28] Beyond the tragedy of fifty million deaths and the closure of thousands of churches and monasteries, matters of fact that historians like Roy Medvedev and Robert Conquest have documented, people living in the former Soviet Union can testify anecdotally to the multifaceted dimensions of this atheistic terror. It is not an exaggeration to say that very few people living there today have not lost a family member to this evil.

The last five hundred years have not been easy ones for Orthodoxy. Unlike most of the Protestants and Catholics in the world, a vast majority of Orthodox Christians have had to live with the challenges of either Islam or atheism. With the recent political upheavals, of course, Russian Orthodoxy faces new opportunities and challenges. In 1992, for the first time since the 1917 Revolution, Easter bells chimed in the Kremlin from the bell tower of Ivan the Great. In early 1993 Patriarch Alexei II met with Russian President Boris Yeltsin to discuss the return of the Kremlin churches to the Orthodox fold. With a one-thousand-year history, seventy years of atheism, present-day religious revival among seventy million adherents, and pronounced nationalism that is often hostile to Protestant and Catholic incursions into Russia, contemporary Russian Orthodoxy is an unusual mixture of problems and potential in the kingdom of God. Where all this will lead remains to be seen.

25. Mikhail Heller and Aleksandr Nekrich, *Utopia in Power* (New York: Summit Books, 1986), 407.

26. Kent R. Hill, *The Soviet Union on the Brink: An Inside Look at Christianity and Glasnost* (Portland: Multnomah, 1991), 84.

27. Elisabeth Rubinfien, "Orthodox Revival," *Wall Street Journal Europe*, 11 December 1991, p. 7.

28. Dimitry V. Pospielovsky, *The Russian Church under the Soviet Regime, 1917–1982*, 2 vols. (Crestwood, N.Y.: St. Vladimir's Seminary Press, 1984), 1:163.

The Mystery of God
Apophatic Vision

God cannot be grasped by the mind. If He could be grasped, He would not be God.

—Evagrios of Pontus

The true knowledge and vision of God consist in this—in seeing that He is invisible, because what we seek lies behind all knowledge, being wholly separated by the darkness of incomprehensibility.

—Gregory of Nyssa

No one has ever seen God.

—John 1:18; 1 John 4:12

God . . . who lives in unapproachable light, whom no one has seen or can see.

—1 Timothy 6:15–16

Every theology begins with presuppositions or principles that are accepted rather than proven. These presuppositions, which in the best theologies are clearly enunciated, help to guide and frame the task of theology. Even more basic than these presuppositions, however, is the posture, attitude, or orientation that exists before any systematic attempt to theologize. Anyone who attempts to think about God begins with a fundamental demeanor, a certain perspective or mind-set, that will control both one's presuppositions and the entire theological process. Two students of mine at Moscow State University helped me to understand the importance of one's orientation, and the different perspectives that theologians of the East and the West bring to the task of thinking about God.

47

During my first semester as a visiting professor of theology at Moscow State University I led a seminar of graduate and undergraduate philosophy of religion students in a critical reading of C. S. Lewis's *Mere Christianity*. I chose this book because of the significant impact it has had in the West among intellectuals, its careful delineation of basic Christianity, and its availability in Russian translation for my students. Lewis was a sure bet, I thought, to impact these students who were enrolled in what only a few years ago was called the Department of Scientific Atheism. I launched the seminar with high expectations, but as we progressed from week to week, I began to have the disappointing feeling that the students were rather unimpressed with Lewis. He did not seem to jog their thinking as I had hoped. How could this be, when the book had been so powerful for so many people in the West? I kept wondering what the problem was until a graduate student, my good friend and nontheist Vasily Vasilevich, registered his main criticism of Lewis with a remark that startled me. His problem with Lewis was not so much the content of his book; it was more basic than that. Vasily objected to his entire methodological orientation: "Lewis is too logical and rational."

A year later, the students in my seminar on the problem of evil read another book by Lewis, *The Problem of Pain*, which too was available in Russian translation. As with the first seminar, I could tell that one student especially had a major problem with Lewis's entire mind-set. But this time I anticipated the problem, and it turned out that I was right. Maxim, who was a believer, was exasperated with our class text: "I don't like Lewis's position that we must use logic to discuss the question of evil. It isn't right to use logic to discuss questions of the noumenal realm. In discussing the phenomenal realm, the world of creation and nature, logic is good and proper, but not with metaphysical questions. Problems relating to God transcend human logic."

Too logical? Too rational? How is it possible for an author to be too logical? Is not rationality a virtue to cultivate rather than a vice to avoid? The remarks by Vasily and Maxim, and my own initial shock, point to a major difference of perspective in the theological posture of Orthodox theologians of the East and their counterparts in the West.

The Western Enthronement and Eastern Distrust of Rationalism

Following the legacy of the Enlightenment, the West has enthroned reason and logic as the final arbiters of all matters of truth, so much so that it is not uncommon for scholars to speak of the autocracy of reason in Western culture. In the West, all truth claims must pass the test of rational intelligibility that is administered at the bar of reason. Many trace this orientation back to the Christian philosopher René Descartes (1596–1650) and his two works *Discourse on Method* (1637) and *Meditations on First Philosophy* (1641), which attempted to ground all philosophic and religious thinking in a new and solid starting point. In those two works Descartes set forth his famous criterion of methodical doubt, insisting that he would accept nothing as true unless he perceived it as very clear and distinct, indubitable, or very certain. His philosophic conclusions, he claimed, would be even more certain than geometrical proofs. This tradition of Cartesian or Continental rationalism (which included Gottfried Wilhelm von Leibniz, Benedict Spinoza, and Christian von Wolff), then, exhibits supreme confidence in and optimism about the mind's capacity, and even obligation, to unravel any and all mysteries. Methodical doubt suspends all belief until the imprimatur of reason is duly obtained and acknowledged. Rationalism lives by the motto *credo quia intelligo* (I believe because I understand) and regards "absolute precision as necessary for the fulfillment of meaning."[1] Truth claims that cannot be justified by reason are rejected as false or even meaningless. Working from this presupposition, rationalists like Descartes, Spinoza, Leibniz, and Immanuel Kant conceive of God in ways very different from the Orthodox tradition.[2]

In contrast to its enthronement of logic, the rationalistic orientation has a positive distrust of, even a disdain for, concepts like myth and mystery. The rationalist mind-set is intolerant of, embarrassed by, and condescending toward the whole category of mystery. In his perceptive study of the differences between Eastern and Western ways of thinking, Anthony Ugolnik observes that our educational training actually teaches us to distrust and eliminate mystery. Citing the anthropologist and structuralist Claude Levi-Strauss as an example of this orientation, Ugolnik points out that rationalism's precondition for all belief, its "mission in modernity," is to expunge mystery, "to make the unknown known." Levi-Strauss acknowledged that myth functions as an organizing principle for the mind, but, Ugolnik notes, he did so only in a patronizing sense; what he gave with the right hand he took away with the left. "Myth," wrote Levi-Strauss, "gives man, very importantly, the illusion that he can understand the universe and *does* understand the universe. It is, of course, only an illusion."[3] This "devastating qualifier" that myth (i.e., mystery) is only an illusion, Ugolnik contends, symbolizes "both the arrogance and tragedy of modern rationalism."[4] Supremely confi-

1. Donald Bloesch, *A Theology of Word and Spirit* (Downers Grove, Ill.: Inter-Varsity, 1992), 58, 103.

2. Vladimir Lossky, *Orthodox Theology: An Introduction* (Crestwood, N.Y.: St. Vladimir's Seminary Press, 1978), 19; Jordan Bajis, *Common Ground: An Introduction to Eastern Christianity for the American Christian* (Minneapolis: Light and Life, 1991), vi, 6.

3. Claude Levi-Strauss, *Myth and Meaning* (New York: Schocken, 1979), 17.

4. Anthony Ugolnik, *The Illuminating Icon* (Grand Rapids: Eerdmans, 1989), 144.

dent in its own powers, convinced of its duty to explain the inscrutable, and intolerant of mystery, rationalism typifies the mentality of many, if not most, thinkers in the West.

Our theology in the West is not immune from this epistemological orientation; an identifiable tradition in theology enshrines human rationality as the decisive criterion of theological truth. Any number of examples could be given to illustrate this perspective. In his work *The Reasonableness of Christianity* (1695) John Locke (1632–1704) insisted that all truths of biblical revelation must be proven by the ultimate criterion of reason before they can be accepted by faith. Theological statements that are contrary to reason and logic are to be rejected. Bishop Joseph Butler (1692–1752), a leading opponent of deism in his day, wrote in his influential work *Analogy of Religion,* "Let reason be kept to; and if any part of the Scripture account of the redemption of the world by Christ can be shown to be really contrary to it, let the Scripture, in the name of God, be given up."[5] According to contemporary writer Norman Geisler, the law of noncontradiction is inviolable; it must "reign sovereignly and universally over all thinking and speaking about God . . . . [Human logic] controls all our thoughts about reality all the time or we are left with some thoughts and statements about reality that are contradictory."[6] One of the most influential theologians writing today, Wolfhart Pannenberg of Munich, evinces a similar commitment to make theology conform to the canons of Enlightenment rationality. The truth of revelation must be proven to be reasonable. Religious statements, writes Pannenberg, "must positively prove themselves worthy of belief if they are to be able to claim universal acceptance." That is to say, "every theological statement must prove itself on the field of reason, and can no longer be argued on the basis of unquestioned presuppositions of faith."[7]

Eastern thinkers, by contrast, begin their thinking about God with a very different mind-set. As the examples of my students Vasily and Maxim show, Eastern thinkers typically exhibit a skepticism toward Western rationalism; some have even suggested that such distrust of rationalism is endemic to

5. Joseph Butler, *The Analogy of Religion, Natural and Revealed, to the Constitution and Course of Nature* (New York: Robert Carter and Brothers, 1858), 224.

6. Norman Geisler, "Avoid *All* Contradictions: A Surrejoinder to John Dahms," *Journal of the Evangelical Theological Society* 22.2 (June 1979): 159, 155.

7. Wolfhart Pannenberg, *Basic Questions in Theology,* trans. George H. Kehm, 2 vols. (Philadelphia: Westminster, 1983), 2:102, 54. The examples of Locke, Butler, Geisler, and Pannenberg come from Bloesch, *Theology of Word.* Bloesch also finds theological rationalism in B. B. Warfield, James Oliver Buswell, John Gerstner, R. C. Sproul, John Warwick Montgomery, and Gordon Clark (pp. 253–54). See also Nicholas Gier, *God, Reason and the Evangelicals* (Lanham, Md.: University Press of America, 1987). On Protestantism's confidence in the power of human reason to validate the claims of Christianity, see Jaroslav Pelikan, *From Luther to Kierkegaard* (St. Louis: Concordia, 1950), 49–75.

Orthodoxy. Conversely, Orthodoxy fosters a positive appreciation for mystery.[8] Any number of Orthodox thinkers could be cited to verify this characterization. An anti-Western posture is particularly strong in the so-called Slavophile movement. Thinkers like Alexei Khomiakov (1804–60) and Lev Shestov (1866–1938) were sharply critical of Peter the Great's Westernizing program and the concomitant influence of rationalism in particular.

Shestov's rejection of rationalism was one of the most uncompromising and categorical to appear in Russian thought. He insisted that Kant's demand that theology justify itself before the bar of reason would inevitably lead to an "autocracy of reason"; reason would be the master, placing the cause of religion "in a bad way."[9] In Shestov's thought, biblical faith and philosophic reliance on logic were two very different and incompatible vantage points.

Khomiakov, the chief advocate of the Slavophile movement, sees Protestantism and Catholicism as two versions of the same incipient rationalism; both are completely incompatible with Eastern Orthodoxy. In Khomiakov's thought, these two Western expressions of Christianity are rooted in the soil of rationalism and do not even deserve the appellation of faith. Orthodoxy "stands on completely different soil" and must be vigilant lest the "ruinous legacy" of Western rationalism, which contains "the embryo of death," kill the spiritual life of Eastern Christianity. Rooted in this fundamentally different perspective regarding reason and faith, Khomiakov insists that "the difference [between East and West] is so great that it is hardly possible to find one point on which they might agree."[10]

It is important to note, however, that Eastern thinkers do not reject reason as a necessary component of human knowledge and experience. A reading of the *Philokalia*, the most important collection of Orthodox religious texts, will show the central role of the intellect in Eastern spirituality. Orthodoxy does not embrace a crass irrationalism that believes something because it is absurd (*credo quia absurdum est*). It was, after all, the Latin father Tertullian (c. 160–215) who made this extremist posture famous when he wrote that he believed in the death and resurrection of Christ precisely because they were absurd and impossible,[11] and that the

8. Frederick C. Copleston, *Philosophy in Russia* (Notre Dame: University of Notre Dame Press, 1986), 16; Sergius Bulgakov, *The Orthodox Church*, rev. ed. (Crestwood, N.Y.: St. Vladimir's Seminary Press, 1988), chap. 11, "Orthodox Mysticism."

9. Lev Shestov, *Speculation and Revelation*, trans. Bernard Martin (Athens, Ohio: Ohio University Press, 1982), 41, 21. On Shestov see Frederick C. Copleston, *Russian Religious Philosophy* (Notre Dame: University of Notre Dame Press, 1988), chap. 6.

10. Alexei S. Khomiakov, "On the Western Confessions of Faith," in Alexander Schmemann, ed., *Ultimate Questions: An Anthology of Modern Russian Religious Thought* (Crestwood, N.Y.: St. Vladimir's Seminary Press, 1977), 29–69.

11. Tertullian "On the Flesh of Christ," in *The Ante-Nicene Fathers*, ed. Alexander Roberts and James Donaldson, 10 vols. (Grand Rapids: Eerdmans, 1950), 3:525.

worlds of Athens and Jerusalem, the philosophic academy and the Christian church, had nothing whatsoever in common.[12] Further, not all Eastern thinkers are as dogmatic as Shestov and Khomiakov, just as the four examples of Western theologians given above do not represent all theologians of the West. John Wesley, for example, has been shown to have a number of affinities with Eastern Orthodox thought.[13]

While Eastern thinkers do not reject reason, they do reject what they see as the hubris of reason that now typifies Western culture. They resist any tendency that would allow or encourage reason to expunge theological mystery and appoint itself as the only criterion of truth. Ivan Kireevsky (1806–56) is a case in point. Kireevsky, who according to Ugolnik coined the term *secular humanism*, laments the narrowness of analytic abstractions so common in the West, but he is careful not to fall into a triumphalist condemnation of reason per se. Instead, Kireevsky wants to moderate the Western impulse that views reason as the only mediator of truth: "If [Western rationalism] would only recognize its own limitations, and see that, in itself, it is only one of the instruments by means of which truth is known, and not the sole way to knowledge, then it would also view its conclusions as only conditional and relative to its point of view, and would expect other, supreme and most truthful conclusions from another supreme and most truthful mode of thinking."[14]

As seen from the Eastern perspective, Westerners need to move beyond their propensity to reductionistic rationalism and gain a positive appreciation for the categories of myth and mystery, categories which, the Orthodox are eager to remind us, inhere in our Christian profession and have been historically emphasized by Eastern Christendom. Ugolnik captures the essentially mysterious nature of Christianity and the West's tendency to avoid it rather than adore it:

> We [Christians in the West] confess to doctrines profoundly mysterious by their nature—that a man should be God, that one God should be at the same time three persons, that we of corruptible flesh should also be temples of the living God. So we believe, but so we cannot comfortably *think*. For as

12. Tertullian "Prescription against Heretics," in *Ante-Nicene Fathers*, 3:246.

13. Randy Maddox, "John Wesley and Eastern Orthodoxy: Influences, Convergences, and Differences," *Asbury Theological Journal* 45.2 (Fall 1990): 29–53; and Howard Snyder, "John Wesley and Macarius of Egypt," *Asbury Theological Journal* 45.2 (Fall 1990): 55–60.

14. Ivan Kireevsky, "Of the Necessity and Possibility of New Principles for Philosophy," in *Polnoe sobranie sochinenii*, vol. 2 (Moscow: Theological Academy, 1861), 318 (cited by Ugolnik, *Illuminating Icon*, 193). Cf. Vladimir Weidlé, "Russia and the West," in Schmemann, *Ultimate Questions*, 11–27, who argues that the differences between Russia and the West have been exaggerated and that Europe as well as Byzantium has deeply influenced Russia.

"thoughts," these are in essence mystery. Mystery is what many contemporary minds are hungry for; it is what they seek far afield, in the non-Christian realms and such Eastern, Asiatic sources as the Bhagavad Gita and the Tibetan Book of the Dead. We Christians in the West have not shared what we possess. We have mystery in plenty, yet our discourse averts it, avoids it as if in embarrassment. For mystery is what we have been taught through our education to extinguish.[15]

Eastern theology does not prescribe a leap into the irrational, but instead (1) a recognition of the radical limitations of human cognition and of conceptual language, and (2) celebration of the mystery so inherent in the story of Christianity. It points us to a way beyond the arid rationalism that threatens much of our Western secular culture and even some of our theologies.

Orthodoxy's attitude toward systematic theology, its historic credal statements of the Trinity and Christology, and its concept of God's self-revelation all illustrate the basic difference between Eastern and Western ways of theologizing. The history of theology in the East reveals a striking lacuna. Except for the monumentally important work *Exposition of the Orthodox Faith* (*De fide orthodoxa*) by John of Damascus (675–754), almost no Eastern theologians have written what we in the West have come to know as systematic theologies. In Eastern theology we find nothing at all that would compare with Aquinas's *Summa theologica*, Calvin's *Institutes of the Christian Religion*, or Karl Barth's *Church Dogmatics*. Even works that appear to be quite systematic, like the *Treasury of Divine Knowledge* and *Twenty-four Discourses* by Peter of Damascus (c. 1100), lack any coherent line of thought and contain many digressions and repetitions. But Peter's monastic readers were not seeking abstract intellections; they wanted practical spiritual counsel, and so the lack of systematization would have been of little concern to them.

Many of the conciliar statements and ecumenical creeds that are so important for Eastern Christianity are framed in negative language, telling us what God is not rather than trying to plumb the depths of his nature. The great mysteries of the faith are for the East matters of adoration rather than analysis. The creeds describe rather than dissect the great truths of Christianity, such as the nature of the Trinity (three persons in one essence) and the relationship between the divine and human natures in Christ.

In the East the doctrine of the Trinity has always been a matter for faith and practical experience rather than for abstract speculation by "unimaginative and pedestrian souls who are incapable of rising above rational concepts."[16] The doctrine of the Trinity is inaccessible by rational demon-

15. Ugolnik, *Illuminating Icon*, 92.
16. Vladimir Lossky, *The Mystical Theology of the Eastern Church* (Crestwood, N.Y.: St. Vladimir's Seminary Press, 1976), 47.

stration; faith alone can "embrace these mysteries, for it is faith that makes real for us things beyond reason and intellect (Heb. 11:1)."[17] Simple dogmatic description rather than philosophic solution typifies Eastern trinitarian theology.

As for Christology, most instructive here is the Chalcedonian Creed of 451, which in describing the union of the divine and human natures of Christ employs a series of four negative words: the two natures of Christ exist "without confusion, change, division, or separation." In other words, the creed states the fact of the union of Christ's two natures in one person, and does so in such a way that we avoid theological error, but it resists any temptation to provide a rational explanation of how this can be. Eastern theology remains constantly aware of the conceptual inadequacies of human language, the severe limitations of the human mind, and the incomprehensibility of the very being of God—all of which means that Eastern theology is far removed from the theological abstractions common in the West.[18] Adoration, contemplation, and vision, not rational intellection, characterize the Eastern tradition.

Eastern theology likewise tends toward a different conception of the nature of God's self-revelation. John Meyendorff acknowledges that Byzantine theology proposes a view of revelation that is substantially different from that in the West. In the West, theology is typically viewed as rational deductions from revealed premises or intellectual abstractions from cognitive propositions, while in the East theology and revelation are viewed much more experientially, as contemplation or vision. In this view, *theologia* and *theoria* (contemplation) are inseparable. In the *Philokalia*, for example, theology is a level of spiritual experience reached by only a precious few ascetics, not intellectual discourse. Rational deduction is not unimportant for the East, Meyendorff suggests, but it is clearly an inferior level of theology. Rather than separating reason and experience, theology and spirituality, cognition and mystery, Eastern theology joins the two realms together:

> The really important implication of this attitude concerns the very important notion of Truth, which is conceived, by the Byzantines, not as a concept which can be expressed adequately in words or developed rationally,

17. Maximus the Confessor *Two Hundred Texts on Theology* 2.36, and *Various Texts on Theology* 1.13, in *Philokalia*, trans. and ed. G. E. H. Palmer, Philip Sherrard, and Kallistos Ware, 3 vols. (London: Faber and Faber, 1979–90), 2:146, 167.

18. John Meyendorff, *Byzantine Theology: Historical Trends and Doctrinal Themes* (New York: Fordham University Press, 1974), 4–5, 128, 180–81; Lossky, *Mystical Theology*, 143; Stanley Harakas, "Creed and Confession in the Orthodox Church," *Journal of Ecumenical Studies* 7.4 (1970): 783; and Carnegie S. Calian, *Theology without Boundaries: Encounters of Eastern Orthodoxy and Western Tradition* (Louisville: Westminster/John Knox, 1992), 39.

but as God Himself—personally present and met in the Church in His very personal identity. Not Scripture, not conciliar definitions, not theology can express Him fully; each can only point to some aspects of His existence, or exclude wrong interpretations of His being or acts. No human language, however, is *fully* adequate to Truth itself, nor can it exhaust it. . . . This is the authentic message maintained most explicitly by the Byzantine "mystical" tradition of Maximus the Confessor, Symeon the New Theologian, and Gregory Palamas.[19]

John Climacus (579–649) contrasts the experiential emphasis with a mere conceptual or linguistic view of God's revelation: "Do you imagine plain words can precisely or truly or appropriately describe the love of the Lord . . . and assurance of the heart? Do you imagine that *talk* of such matters will mean anything to someone who has never *experienced* them? If you think so, then you will be like a man who with words and examples tries to convey the sweetness of honey to people who have never tasted it. He talks uselessly. Indeed I would say he is simply prattling."[20] Similarly, Simeon the New Theologian (949–1022) objected strongly to theology that was little more than rational discourse. He urged a conscious awareness of the primacy of experience as confirmation of the power of the Holy Spirit. So too Gregory Palamas (1296–1359), who insisted that true theology is wedded to actual experience and not relegated solely to the intellect.

Thus, in the Eastern conception of revelation, theological rationalism does not dissect truth, much less attempt to explain its every concept; instead, in Eastern thought theology and mystery walk hand in hand as the closest of friends. In the history of theology Byzantine Christianity is heir to the apophatic tradition, in which contemplation and vision, not intellection and analysis, characterize the theological task. In this apophatic orientation the mystery of God leads to mystical union with him.

The Apophatic East

If Orthodox theology is characterized by any single trait, that would surely be the apophatic orientation of its entire theological vision. All true Orthodox theology is at root apophatic;[21] apophaticism is "the fundamental characteristic of the whole theological tradition of the Eastern Church."[22] This negative orientation (*apophasis*, denial) of unknowing (*agnosia*) or of

19. Meyendorff, *Byzantine Theology*, 11; see also 9–13, 139–40; Calian, *Theology without Boundaries*, 51.

20. John Climacus, *The Ladder of Divine Ascent* (New York: Paulist, 1982), step 25, p. 218. See also Kallistos Ware's introduction to the text, 7–8.

21. Timothy Ware, *The Orthodox Church* (Baltimore: Penguin, 1964), 215.

22. Lossky, *Mystical Theology*, 26.

learned ignorance begins with the celebration, rather than the rationalistic extermination or explanation, of divine mystery. In the most important patristic work on this subject, *Mystical Theology*, Pseudo-Dionysius the Areopagite (c. 500) distinguished apophatic or negative theology from positive or cataphatic theology. The former is a theology of denial in contrast to the cataphatic theology of affirmation. When we begin to describe God affirmatively (he is omnipotent, loving, just, etc.), we must remember that human language is woefully inadequate to the task and that it always falls short of its object. "Having made an assertion about God, we must pass beyond it: the statement is not untrue, yet neither it nor any other form of words can contain the fullness of the transcendent God."[23] According to Pseudo-Dionysius, negative theology, being ideally suited to its Subject, who is beyond all existence, is superior to the limited benefits of positive theology. According to Maximus the Confessor (580–662), "negative statements about divine matters are the only true ones."[24] Thus apophatic theology begins with a conscious awareness of God's radical transcendence and the total inadequacy of linguistic concepts to apprehend his essential nature.

In view of the finitude of human categories and the infinity of the living God, true knowledge of God, according to Orthodoxy, requires a combined spiritual and intellectual catharsis or cleansing, a purification of the mind that rids us of all false ideas about God. Vladimir Lossky (1903–58), alluding to an important text from Gregory of Nyssa (330–95), describes this process: "The negative way of the knowledge of God is an ascendant undertaking of the mind that progressively eliminates all positive attributes of the object it wishes to attain, in order to culminate finally in a kind of apprehension by supreme ignorance of Him who cannot be an object of knowledge. We can say that it is an intellectual experience of the mind's failure when confronted with something beyond the conceivable."[25] Elsewhere Eastern theologians refer to this intellectual purification or catharsis in terms of repentance (*metanoia*), a conscious turning away from our natural ideas about God.

When we approach God, we must begin with a sense of awe and astonishment. In his book *The Idea of the Holy* the German theologian Rudolf Otto spoke of the "numinous," a combined sense of tremendous mystery, dread, and fascination, an overwhelming feeling of one's own inadequacy before the

23. Timothy Ware, *The Orthodox Way* (Crestwood, N.Y.: St. Vladimir's Seminary Press, 1990), 17.

24. Maximus the Confessor *Book of Ambiguities* 20 (cited by Jaroslav Pelikan, *The Spirit of Eastern Christendom [600–1700]* [Chicago: University of Chicago Press, 1974], 32–33).

25. Vladimir Lossky, "Apophasis and Trinitarian Theology," in Vladimir Lossky, *In the Image and Likeness of God* (Crestwood, N.Y.: St. Vladimir's Seminary Press, 1974), 13. For Gregory's text see Meyendorff, *Byzantine Theology*, 12.

infinite. Rather than direct description, Eastern theologians often employed pictures, images, and metaphors in an attempt to portray the human encounter with him who defies every human description. Simeon the New Theologian compared the divine-human encounter to a blinding flash of light:

> Think of a man standing at night inside his house, with all the doors closed; and then suppose that he opens a window just at that moment when there is a sudden flash of lightning. Unable to bear its brightness, at once he protects himself by closing his eyes and drawing back from the window. So it is with the soul that is enclosed in the realm of the senses; if ever she peeps out through the window of the intellect, she is overwhelmed by the brightness, like lightning, of the pledge of the Holy Spirit that is within her. Unable to bear the splendor of unveiled light, at once she is bewildered in her intellect, and she draws back entirely upon herself, taking refuge, as in a house, among sensory and human things.

For Gregory of Nyssa a hiker facing a dangerous precipice symbolized the position of a person before the transcendent God:

> Imagine a sheer, steep crag with a projecting edge at the top. Now imagine what a person would probably feel if he put his foot on the edge of this precipice and, looking down into the chasm below, saw no solid footing nor anything to hold on to. This is what I think the soul experiences when it goes beyond its footing in material things, in its quest for that which has no dimension and which exists from all eternity. For here there is nothing it can take hold of, neither place, nor time, neither measure nor anything else; our minds cannot approach it. And thus the soul, slipping at every point from what cannot be grasped, becomes dizzy and perplexed and returns once again to what is connatural with it, content now to know merely this about the Transcendent, that it is completely different from the nature of the things that the soul knows.

Brilliant light, an infinite chasm—when people encounter the living God, Orthodoxy insists, dizziness, bewilderment, blindness, and "shattered assumptions" are the necessary beginning point.[26] Such is the apophatic way. It acknowledges "the breakdown of human thought before the radical transcendence of God. . . . The apophaticism of Orthodox theology is . . . a prostration before the living God, radically ungraspable, unobjectifiable and unknowable, because He is personal, because He is the free plenitude of personal existence. *Apophasis is the inscription in human language, in theological language, of the mystery of faith.*"[27]

26. The quotations are taken from Ware, *Orthodox Way*, 11, 29–30.
27. Lossky, *Orthodox Theology*, 24–25.

In his classic work on this entire theme Lossky summarizes the nature and importance of Orthodox apophaticism and the entire Eastern theological epistemology that shuns rational abstractions in favor of mysterious communion. Rather than being a part of theology, or even a presupposition or prolegomenon of theology, apophaticism signifies an entire orientation that transforms theology:

> Negative theology is not merely a theory of ecstasy. It is an expression of that fundamental attitude which transforms the whole of theology into a contemplation of the mysteries of revelation. It is not a branch of theology, a chapter, or an inevitable introduction on the incomprehensibility of God from which one passes unruffled to a doctrinal exposition in the usual terminology of human reason and philosophy in general. Apophaticism teaches us to see above all a negative meaning in the dogmas of the Church: it forbids us to follow natural ways of thought and to form concepts which would usurp the place of spiritual realities. For Christianity is not a philosophical school for speculating about abstract concepts, but is essentially a communion with the living God. That is why, despite all their philosophical learning and natural bent towards speculation, the fathers of the eastern tradition in remaining faithful to the apophatic principle of theology, never allowed their thought to cross the threshold of the mystery, or to substitute idols of God for God Himself.[28]

Eastern theologians base their apophatic orientation in a series of Old and New Testament texts. They point to texts in the Old Testament that remind us that no person can see God and live. Though acknowledging that God spoke to Moses face to face, as a man speaks with his friend, they point out that when Moses asked to see the glory of the living God, he responded, "You cannot see my face, for no one may see me and live." So it was that as he passed by, God covered the face of Moses, so that Moses would see only his back and not his face (Exod. 33:11, 18–23).

Other examples include Isaiah, who feared death because of his vision of God; even the seraphim shielded their eyes from his very presence (Isa. 6:1–5). Isaiah also saw a radical abyss between the mind of God and our minds: as the heavens are higher than the earth, so are his ways and thoughts higher than ours (55:8–9). Gideon and Manoah feared death at the sight of God (Judg. 6:22; 13:22). And when God appeared to Elijah, the prophet covered his face with a mantle (1 Kings 19:13). The Psalms, Eastern thinkers point out, are filled with references to the utterly transcendent God. "Clouds and thick darkness surround him" (Ps. 97:2), a theme that perhaps recalls the experience of Moses at Sinai. The very

28. Lossky, *Mystical Theology*, 42.

name of God is majestic and wonderful (Ps. 8:1), causing Gregory of Nyssa to observe that "God's name is not known; it is wondered at."[29]

Moses, in fact, is a favorite Old Testament paradigm of the apophatic posture of the Eastern fathers. Moses, we recall, encountered the holy God in the burning bush (Exod. 3:2), in the pillar of cloud and fire, and in the thick darkness of Sinai where God descended in violence, smoke, thunder, lightning, cloud, earthquake, and fire, threatening to "break out against" the people. Moses approached the thick darkness (Exod. 20:21), while the people were warned to distance themselves lest they perish (Exod. 19:20–22).

Reflecting on these texts, Gregory of Nyssa devoted an entire treatise to the *Life of Moses*; he suggests that Moses' ascent into the darkness of Sinai represents an approach to God that is superior to the encounter at the burning bush, for there he saw God in the light, while at Sinai God revealed himself in darkness.[30] Gregory of Nazianzus (329–89) likewise drew upon the Moses narrative: "I was running to lay hold on God, and thus I went up into the mount, and drew aside the curtain of the cloud, and entered away from matter and from material things, and as far as I could I withdrew within myself. And when I looked up, I scarce saw the back parts of God; although I was sheltered by the Rock, the Word that was made flesh for us. And when I looked a little closer, I saw, not the first and unmingled nature known to itself—to the Trinity, I mean; not that which abideth in the first veil, and is hidden by the cherubim; but only that nature which at last reaches even to us."[31] Maximus the Confessor wrote that when "Moses pitches his tent outside the camp (Exod. 33:7)—that is, when he establishes his will and mind outside the world of visible things—he begins to worship God. Then entering into the darkness (Exod. 20:21)—that is, into the formless and immaterial realm of spiritual knowledge—he there celebrates the most sacred rites."[32] The *Spiritual Homilies* of Macarius of Egypt (300–390); *To the Shepherd* by John Climacus, who in fact was a monk who lived in the desert of Mount Sinai; and Clement of Alexandria's *Stromata* (c. 150–215)—all draw upon the Mosaic accounts of blinding light and cloudy darkness to describe the apophatic knowledge of God.[33]

29. Quoted in Ware, *Orthodox Way*, 16.

30. Lossky, *Mystical Theology*, 35.

31. Gregory of Nazianzus "Second Theological Oration" 3 (Oration 28), in *The Nicene and Post-Nicene Fathers*, 2d series, ed. Philip Schaff and Henry Wace, 14 vols. (Grand Rapids: Eerdmans, 1989 reprint), 7:289. Gregory also refers to Moses in Oration 32.16.

32. Maximus the Confessor *Two Hundred Texts on Theology* 1.84; see also 1.85 (in *Philokalia*, 2:133).

33. Macarius of Egypt *Spiritual Homilies* 5, 8 (cited by Vladimir Lossky, *The Vision of God* [Crestwood, N.Y.: St. Vladimir's Seminary Press, 1963], 114); John Climacus *To the Shepherd* 15 (in Ware's introduction to Climacus, *Ladder*, 55); Clement of Alexandria *Stromata* 5 (cited by Lossky, *Mystical Theology*, 34).

Finally, Pseudo-Dionysius also compares Moses' ascent of Sinai and the ascent of the mind to the knowledge of God. Moses, after purifying himself and separating himself from all uncleanness, hears the trumpets and sees the flashing lights. In so doing

> he reaches the height of the divine ascent. Even here he does not associate with God, he does not contemplate God (for He is unseen), but the place where He is. I think this means that the highest and most divine of the things which are seen and understood are a kind of hypothetical account of what is subject to Him who is over all. Through them is revealed the presence of Him who is above all thought, a presence which occupies the intelligible heights of His holy places. It is then that Moses is freed from the things that see and are seen: he passes into the truly mystical darkness of ignorance, where he shuts his eyes to all scientific apprehensions, and reaches what is entirely untouched and unseen, belonging not to himself and not to another, but wholly to Him who is above all. He is united to the best of his powers with the unknowing quiescence of all knowledge, and by that very unknowing he knows what surpasses understanding.[34]

In this passage Pseudo-Dionysius has captured the spirit of Eastern negative theology.

Like the Old Testament, the New Testament emphasizes the radical incomprehensibility of God. No person can see God (John 1:18; 1 John 4:12). He dwells in unapproachable light (1 Tim. 6:15–16). On the Damascus road Paul, like Moses, encountered God in blinding light. In recounting his vision of God (2 Cor. 12:2–4), Paul twice tells us that he does not know, but only God knows exactly what it was that he experienced. Caught up into paradise, he had a vision of God that was beyond words; it was "inexpressible" (v. 4). In the majestic doxology at the end of Romans 11 Paul draws upon Isaiah 40:13 and Jeremiah 23:18 to remind us that God's ways are unsearchable, "his paths beyond tracing out." No one can fully know the mind of the Lord, Paul says. For the Corinthians Paul draws a distinction between God's transcendent wisdom and the frailty of all human thought (1 Cor. 1:18–31; 3:18–23). Thus in both the Old and New Testaments there is a solid basis for the Eastern understanding of theology as an apophatic task. The entire Eastern tradition of unknowing, of learned ignorance, is rooted in Scripture.

In a sense all theology is mystical in that it deals with the data of revelation. The West has its own tradition of Christian mysticism, of course. Indeed, it is not uncommon for theologians in the West to take some note of the apophatic boundaries of theology. We can cite passages in Augus-

---

34. Pseudo-Dionysius *Mystical Theology* 1.3, trans. C. E. Rolt (London: S.P.C.K., 1920).

tine or Aquinas, for example, that affirm apophaticism, and we can study Western mystics like Meister Eckhart or Jakob Böhme. But in the West acknowledgments of apophaticism tend to be just that—acknowledgments, a tip of the hat, an introductory admission limited to theological prolegomena before long and rigorous intellectual abstractions. The West—Protestantism more than Catholicism—also tends to relegate the mystics to sectarian extremes. In the East, by contrast, apophaticism and mystery are not just passing admissions for theology, nor even characteristics of theology; in the East apophaticism and mystery *are* theology. Orthodox thought removes all boundaries that would separate theology and spirituality. At this point it is important to note just how thoroughly the apophatic tradition pervades almost all of the key Eastern theologians. The breadth and depth of Orthodox theological history would allow us to cite passages almost indefinitely. John Climacus's failure to mention negative theology, though not mystical experience, is perhaps the sole exception to this general rule.

Although the *Mystical Theology* of Pseudo-Dionysius is generally credited as the most comprehensive and influential statement of apophaticism in the early church, the Eastern fathers of the fourth century already had a clearly defined apophatic orientation. A notable example is found in the Liturgy of John Chrysostom (c. 345–407), the bishop of Constantinople. Before the words of the Lord's Prayer, the supplicant prays, "Grant us, O Lord, to dare to invoke Thee with confidence and without fear by calling Thee Father." In fact, the Greek text of the liturgy reads literally, "Thou, God on high whom one cannot name, the apophatic God, [grant us] to name Thee Father and to dare to invoke Thee." As Lossky observes, "one prays to have the audacity and the simplicity to say 'Thou' to God."[35]

During the fourth century Eunomius (died 395) had taught that it is possible for a person to know the essential nature of God through human reason. With one voice the three Cappadocian fathers, all of whom wrote treatises against Eunomius, insisted that God is above and beyond any human definition and comprehension. According to Basil the Great (329–79), the final essence of God is beyond knowledge and explanation: "It is by His energies that we can say we know our God; we do not assert that we can come near to the essence itself, for His energies descend to us, but His essence remains unapproachable."[36] Gregory of Nazianzus, who we have already seen compared his own search for God to Moses' experience at Sinai, declared that "it is difficult to conceive God, but to define Him

35. Lossky, *Orthodox Theology*, 32; see also Chrysostom's twelve homilies "On the Incomprehensibility of God."
36. Quoted in Lossky, *Mystical Theology*, 72; see also 33; idem, *Vision*, 78.

in words is an impossibility. . . . It is impossible to express Him, and yet more impossible to conceive Him. For that which may be conceived may perhaps be made clear by language, if not fairly well, at any rate imperfectly, to anyone who is not quite deprived of hearing or slothful of understanding. But to comprehend the whole of so great a Subject as this is quite impossible and impracticable, not merely to the utterly careless and ignorant, but even to those who are highly exalted, and who love God."[37] In his homilies on the Beatitudes, Gregory of Nyssa, like Basil, affirms that the essence of God, unlike his energies, is unknowable: "Now the divine nature, as it is in itself, according to its essence, transcends every act of comprehensive knowledge, and it cannot be approached or attained by our speculation. Man has never discovered a faculty to comprehend the incomprehensible; nor have we ever been able to devise an intellectual technique for grasping the inconceivable."[38]

More than any early thinker it is the sixth-century Greek Pseudo-Dionysius who is credited with giving the classic comprehensive expression of apophatic theology. Once thought to be a convert of Paul (see Acts 17:34), this anonymous author composed the *Mystical Theology*, a work whose "importance for the whole history of Christian thought cannot be exaggerated."[39] Maximus the Confessor composed commentaries on Dionysius's writings, and a fourteenth-century writer observed that the *Mystical Theology* "ran through England like the wild deer."[40]

Dionysius, we have seen, argues that negative, apophatic theology is superior to positive, cataphatic theology. One must renounce the ways of human reason and seek a purification or catharsis from all speculative idols; that is, one must proceed by unknowing. In his final chapter Dionysius concludes that God is beyond both affirmation *and* negation. He is beyond any and all human comprehension. God as final cause eludes our grasp: "When we make affirmations and negations about the things that are inferior to it, we affirm and deny nothing about the Cause itself, which, being wholly apart from all things, is above all affirmation, as the supremacy of Him who, being in His simplicity freed from all things and beyond everything, is above all denial."[41]

In the seventh and eighth centuries Maximus the Confessor and John of Damascus dominated the landscape of Eastern theology. Maxi-

37. Gregory of Nazianzus "Second Theological Oration" 4.
38. Gregory of Nyssa *On the Beatitudes* 6. See also Thomas Hopko, *All The Fulness of God: Essays on Orthodoxy, Ecumenism and Modern Society* (Crestwood, N.Y.: St. Vladimir's Seminary Press, 1982), 18.
39. Lossky, *Mystical Theology*, 23.
40. See Ware, *Orthodox Church*, 73.
41. Cited in Lossky, *Mystical Theology*, 29.

mus observed that "a perfect mind is one which, by true faith, in supreme ignorance knows the supremely unknowable one." And in his commentary on Pseudo-Dionysius's *On the Divine Names* he wrote that "the ignorance about God on the part of those who are wise in divine things is not a lack of learning, but a knowledge that knows by silence that God is unknown."[42] The radically transcendent God is beyond definition and human comprehension; only silence befits those who would approach him.

John of Damascus devotes an entire section of the first part of his *Exposition of the Orthodox Faith*, the standard Eastern theological textbook of the period, to "The Nature of Deity: That It Is Incomprehensible." There we find a mature expression of the long-standing apophatic tradition: "It is plain, then, that there is a God. But what He is in His essence and nature is absolutely incomprehensible and unknowable." Even our attempts to talk about God, our statements, for example, that he is unbegotten, without beginning, changeless, and imperishable, are, according to John, merely apophatic conveniences. They do not tell us what God is like, but what he is not, for in fact "it is impossible to explain what He is in His essence, and it befits us the rather to hold discourse about His absolute separation from all things. For He does not belong to the class of existing things: not that He has no existence, but that He is above all existing things, nay even above existence itself. . . . God then is infinite and incomprehensible; and all that is comprehensible about Him is His incomprehensibility."[43]

We could amass any number of similar citations from the wealth of Orthodox literature. We will use the examples of Simeon the New Theologian and Gregory Palamas as two case studies to complete our survey. But we already have sufficient witness to warrant our thesis about the deep and abiding influence of apophaticism in Orthodox thought. For Eastern theologians God is radically transcendent, above time and space, beyond human description. Human sin, linguistic limitations, the very nature of God himself—all of these force us to use negative language, a language that tells us only what God is not, for we can never know his essential nature.

But having made their point, the Eastern theologians raise an important question. How is it possible to know God? Can anyone experience him; or is he so ineffable, so beyond any affirmation, that, as the Neoplatonist philosopher Plotinus declared, no one can know or experience him? Can we

---

42. Maximus the Confessor *Four Hundred Texts on Love* 3.99, and *"On the Divine Names" of Dionysius the Areopagite* 7.1 (in Pelikan, *Spirit*, 33–34).

43. John of Damascus *Exposition of the Orthodox Faith* 1.4, in *The Nicene and Post-Nicene Fathers*, 2d series, ed. Philip Schaff and Henry Wace, 14 vols. (Grand Rapids: Eerdmans, 1989 reprint), 9:3–4.

say or think absolutely nothing at all about God? Have the Eastern theologians stressed the divine transcendence to the point that they must deny his immanence, his nearness, his personal interaction with us? In fact, it seems that we have to answer in the affirmative. But if we left the Eastern fathers at this point we would do them a great disservice, for in addition to affirming the mystery of God, they equally insist on the necessity of mystical union with him, and draw our attention to the many biblical statements about our knowing God in a personal way: The "negations which draw attention to the divine incomprehensibility are not prohibitions upon knowledge: apophaticism, so far from being a limitation, enables us to transcend all concepts, every sphere of philosophical speculation. It is a tendency toward an ever-greater plenitude, in which knowledge is transformed into ignorance, the theology of concepts into contemplation, dogmas into experience of ineffable mystery. It is, moreover, an existential theology involving man's entire being, which sets him upon the way of union, which obliges him to be changed, to transform his nature that he may attain to the true *gnosis* which is the contemplation of the Holy Trinity."[44] Here it is only the one who prays who is truly a theologian, for the true theologian prays truly.[45]

Two Case Studies: Simeon the New Theologian and Gregory Palamas

In chapter 6 we will focus at length on Orthodoxy's crucial doctrine of union with the living God (*theosis*, divinization). For now, the two case studies of Simeon the New Theologian and Gregory Palamas will demonstrate how in the Orthodox tradition one moves from theological mystery to experiential mysticism, from theological abstractions to the very vision of God wherein one communes with the loving Holy Trinity.

Of all the Orthodox fathers who viewed the life of theological reflection as intensely practical mystical communion with the living God, few stand out more than Saint Simeon the New Theologian. For Simeon, a conscious awareness of the indwelling Holy Spirit was the necessary sign of true Christian identity. It would be no exaggeration to think of him as a charismatic theologian in terms of both his personality and his doctrine. Throughout his writings, including his accounts of his own visions of God, Simeon stresses the idea of God as mystical light. Simeon's entire purpose is to lead his reader into a direct experience of the living God, who is light, an experience in which "one has to destroy idols, go beyond words and ideas, and live in

44. Lossky, *Mystical Theology*, 238.
45. Evagrios *On Prayer: One Hundred and Fifty-Three Texts* 61 (in *Philokalia*, 1:62).

the awesome darkness of mystery that becomes a light to those who have become purified." That is, Simeon leads us from the darkness of the apophatic mystery of God to the light of mystical union with him.

Other than his own writings, the primary resource for the life of Simeon is the biography written by Nicetas Stethatos, a younger disciple of Simeon. Born in Galatia in 949, Simeon entered the monastery of Studion when he was twenty-seven. After a few months he relocated to the nearby monastery of Mamas where in a few years he was elected abbot at the age of thirty-one, a position he held until his exile in 1009. There he initiated a strong ministry of monastic renewal, and in general earned a reputation as a zealous and pious reformer. As so often happens with people of his stature and reforming zeal, Simeon encountered some resistance, both within his monastery and, more importantly for our purposes, outside the monastery in a famous encounter with Stephen of Nicomedia.

Stephen, a former metropolitan of Nicomedia, was the official court theologian at Constantinople. A sophisticated thinker, he was well connected with both the church and state. Nicetas Stethatos tells us that "in speech and knowledge [Stephen] was superior to the masses. Not only was he influential with the patriarch and the emperor, but he was able to present a solution to unexpected problems to anyone who consulted him. He possessed an abundance of words, a ready tongue. . . . He remained close to the patriarch and enjoyed a great reputation with everyone for his learning."[46] The clash between Simeon and Stephen was between two strong personalities no doubt, and Nicetas tells us that Stephen's jealousy of Simeon's popularity played no small part.

During a meeting at his home Stephen "assumed the mask of friendship," Nicetas writes, and attempted to embarrass Simeon with a difficult theological question. The latter responded the next day with a sophisticated theological treatise (Hymn 21) that put to rest any doubts about his theological acumen. Simeon used the occasion and the bulk of the treatise to lecture Stephen on the nature of true Christianity, and therein lies the essence of their conflict.

The controversy involved matters of practical spirituality rather than intellectual doctrine. Simeon was a charismatic person who offended the ecclesiastical hierarchies with his belief that authority resides in the

46. Nicetas Stethatos Life of Simeon the New Theologian 74.5–12. For the text by Nicetas see Un Grand Mystique byzantin: Vie de Syméon le Nouveau Théologien (949–1022) par Nicetas Stethatos, ed. and trans. I. Hausherr and G. Horn, Orientalia Christiana 12, fasc. 45 (Rome, 1928), 1–128. The best English text on Simeon is that by Basil Krivocheine, In the Light of Christ: St. Symeon the New Theologian—Life, Spirituality, Doctrine (Crestwood, N.Y.: St. Vladimir's Seminary Press, 1986). The citations of Nicetas's Life are taken from Krivocheine.

power of the indwelling Holy Spirit rather than in church structures. In fact, his response to Stephen scolded him for trying to do theology apart from a conscious experience of the indwelling Spirit: "The Spirit who proceeded from the Father, in a way that cannot be expressed, has been sent by the Son to men; not to the unbelieving, nor to the patrons of glory, not to actors, not to scholars, nor to those who have studied the pagan writings, nor to those who do not know our Scriptures, nor to those who have played a role on the world's stage, nor to those who utter abundant, mannered speech, nor to those who have made a great name, nor to those who have succeeded in being friends with famous people, but to those who are poor in their spirit and their life, to those who are pure of heart and of body, to those whose words are unadorned and whose thoughts are simpler still."[47] It is through the indwelling Spirit, not rational reflection or ecclesiastical teaching, that the pure encounter God: they "have no need of human knowledge because they have the Spirit for their teacher; awakened by the light of this Spirit they see the Son, they behold the Father and adore the Trinity of Persons, the one God, who by nature is one in a manner that cannot be expressed."[48]

After a protracted struggle with Stephen, Simeon was exiled from his monastery on January 3, 1009. In a letter after his exile, Simeon argued that the conflict was over his theology of mystical experience. His detractors, wrote Simeon, "view themselves as self-ordained Apostles without having received, like the Apostles, the grace of the Holy Spirit, without being illumined by the light of knowledge, without having seen the God of whom they speak and who reveals Himself in His undeceitful message." The reason for the denunciation, wrote Simeon, is that "I teach everyone to seek grace from on high and the conscious advent of the Holy Spirit."[49] Although he was later recalled to the monastery, he refused the invitation and died on March 12, 1022.

What Simeon illustrates for us is the great contrast between a heady, scholastic, abstract, and ecclesiastically approved rational reflection about God—a theology which Stephen embodied, but with which Simeon had little empathy—and his own vigorous efforts to meld theology

47. Simeon the New Theologian *Hymn* 21.51–86. An English translation of the hymns is available in *Hymns of Divine Love*, trans. George A. Maloney (Denville, N.J.: Dimension Books, 1975). My citations follow the translation made by Krivocheine from J. Koder, *Hymnes*, in *Sources Chrétiennes* 156 (hymns 1–15, 1969), 174 (hymns 16–40, 1971), and 196 (hymns 41–58, 1973) (Paris: Editions du Cerf).

48. Simeon *Hymn* 21.102–7.

49. Simeon the New Theologian *Epistle* 4.181–96, 392–99 (cited by Krivocheine, *St. Symeon*, 57–58).

with spirituality—a dynamic, personal, and direct mystical experience of God. Stephen represented a "head-trip scholastic theology," while Simeon urged an apophatic, mystical approach. "Basically his argument is that they err who insist that no one living at that time can truly experience God mystically, directly, and intensely."[50] Basil Krivocheine captures both the apophatic yet intensely practical spirit of Simeon and the essence of his debate with Stephen: theirs was "a conflict between a learned, scholastic theology removed from the spiritual life yet still formally Orthodox and conservative, and a theology that was understood as expressing the Holy Spirit, one that emphasized how the mystery of God was beyond understanding yet was disclosed through the mystic experience of the saints."[51]

True to the long-standing tradition of apophaticism, Simeon began his *Theological Discourses* on the Trinity with the warning that it is presumptuous to speak about God "as though that which is incomprehensible were comprehensible." But, as Jaroslav Pelikan observes, while this negative approach characterized Eastern theology, Simeon exemplified an important counterpart, "the identification of personal religious experience as an epistemological principle in theology."[52] The apparent conflict between the apophatic insistence on a transcendent God who is incomprehensible and direct consciousness of him such as Simeon the New Theologian experienced came to a head in the fourteenth century in the so-called hesychast controversy.

The controversy centered on the Eastern monastic life devoted entirely to prayer, whose practitioners had become known as hesychasts (*hesychia*, silence, stillness) because of their precise method of prayer. Hesychastic prayer is expounded most fully in an anonymous treatise that is erroneously attributed to Nicephorus the Hesychast and entitled *Method of Holy Prayer and Attention*. As many texts in the *Philokalia* show, this science of stillness, coupled with constant invocation of the name of Jesus, had been important in Eastern monasticism for at least a thousand years. Viewed as a literal obedience to Paul's injunction to pray without ceasing (1 Thess. 5:17), it consisted of a series of precisely defined prayer techniques: a prescribed body posture, carefully regulated breathing, inward reflection, and constant mental repetition of the Jesus Prayer ("Lord Jesus Christ, Son of God, have mercy on me"). Gregory of Sinai (1255–1346), to whom some ascribe the *Method of Holy Prayer and Attention*, taught his disciples the hesychastic method of prayer:

50. George A. Maloney, introduction to *Symeon the New Theologian: The Discourses* (New York: Paulist, 1980), 3–4.
    51. Krivocheine, *St. Symeon*, 43.
    52. Pelikan, *Spirit*, 258–59.

From early morning sit down on a low stool, about eight inches; compress your mind, forcing it down from your brain into your heart, and keep it there. Laboriously bow yourself down, feeling sharp pain in your chest, shoulders and neck, and cry persistently in mind and soul, "Lord Jesus Christ, have mercy on me." Then, because of the constraint and labor, and also perhaps because of the feelings of distaste that result from this effort . . . transfer your mind now to the second half and say, "Son of God, have mercy on me." Repeat this many times, and do not from laziness change frequently from one half to the other; for trees which are continually transplanted do not grow roots. Control the drawing in of your breath so that you do not breathe at your ease. For the current of air that rises from the heart darkens the mind and agitates the intelligence, keeping it far from the heart. . . . Hold back the expulsion of your breath, so far as possible, and enclose your mind in your heart, continually and persistently practicing the invocation of the Lord Jesus.[53]

In addition to this individual method of prayer Gregory prescribed a daily and even hourly regimen that was graded for beginners, intermediates, and advanced disciples.

By the fourteenth century the hesychastic method of prayer had come under attack. Of course, it would be easy to criticize the apparently materialistic and psychosomatic techniques of prayer as artificial and mechanical, but all of the hesychasts affirmed that these methods were means to an important end—vision of and unity with God himself. The hesychasts had joined negative theology with mystical experience to claim a direct encounter with the incomprehensible and unknowable God. This resulted in a more fundamental criticism. How can one maintain at the same time the apophatic insistence that God is beyond knowing and the hesychastic insistence that we can know him directly and immediately through prayer?

It was Barlaam the Calabrian, a Greek scholar from Italy, who attacked the hesychasts at this very point. Barlaam ridiculed the hesychasts for their materialistic methods of prayer and, more importantly, charged that they had violated the apophatic principle that we cannot know God directly. In response Gregory Palamas, the archbishop of Thessalonica, defended the hesychasts, providing a solid dogmatic basis for their tradition of prayer. His *Defense of the Holy Hesychasts* gives extended treatment to the implications of theology as spirituality and spirituality as theology.

In his *Theophanes* Gregory tackled the apparent contradiction between transcendent apophaticism that stresses the incomprehensibil-

53. Quoted in Kallistos Ware, "The Jesus Prayer in St. Gregory of Sinai," *Eastern Churches Review* 4.1 (Spring 1972): 14–15.

ity of God and the biblical affirmation that we can enjoy direct mystical communion with him: "The divine nature must be said to be at the same time both exclusive of, and, in some sense, open to participation. We attain to participation in the divine nature, and yet at the same time it remains totally inaccessible. We need to affirm both at the same time and to preserve the antinomy as a criterion of right devotion."[54] On the one hand, Gregory insistently maintained the long tradition of apophatic theology: "The super-essential nature of God is not a subject for speech or thought or even contemplation, for it is far removed from all that exists and more than unknowable, being founded upon the uncircumscribed might of the celestial spirits—incomprehensible and ineffable to all for ever. There is no name whereby it can be named, neither in this age or in the age to come, nor word found in the soul and uttered by the tongue . . . if this be not that perfect incomprehensibility which one acknowledges in denying all that can be named. None can properly name its essence or nature if he be truly seeking the truth that is above all truth."[55] On the other hand, to affirm the reality of experiencing God, Palamas drew upon an important distinction made a thousand years earlier by the Cappadocian fathers. In his essence or fundamental nature, we cannot know God, says Palamas; he remains inaccessible to us. But in his energies or actions, in his grace and divine operations, God communicates himself to us. "To say that the divine nature is communicable not in itself but through its energy, is to remain within the bounds of right devotion."[56]

As we suggested earlier in this chapter, the distinction between the energy and essence of God had already been made by people like Basil the Great, Gregory of Nyssa, Gregory of Nazianzus, John of Damascus, and Pseudo-Dionysius. For example, Gregory of Nyssa's comment on Ecclesiastes 3:7 simultaneously affirmed and denied the possibility of human speech about God: "In speaking of God, when there is a question of His essence, then is the time to keep silence. When, however, it is a question of His operation . . . that is the time to speak."[57] According to Basil, as we saw earlier, "It is by His energies that we can say we know our God; we do not assert that we can come near to the essence itself, for His energies descend to us, but His essence remains unapproachable."[58] In councils at Constantinople in 1341, 1351, and 1368 the Orthodox church endorsed Palamas's distinction between the essence and energies of God, and as a

54. Quoted in Lossky, *Mystical Theology*, 69.
55. Ibid., 37.
56. Ibid., 70.
57. Quoted in Meyendorff, *Byzantine Theology*, 14.
58. Quoted in Lossky, *Mystical Theology*, 72.

result both the divine transcendence and immanence were affirmed. "It was Gregory's achievement to set Hesychasm on a firm dogmatic basis, by integrating it into Orthodox theology as a whole, and by showing how the Hesychast vision of Divine Light in no way undermined the apophatic doctrine of God."[59]

59. Ware, *Orthodox Church*, 76. For further study of Gregory Palamas see John Meyendorff, *St. Gregory Palamas and Orthodox Spirituality* (Crestwood, N.Y.: St. Vladimir's Seminary Press, 1974); idem, *A Study of Gregory Palamas* (Crestwood, N.Y.: St. Vladimir's Seminary Press, 1964); and Gregory Palamas, *The Triads in Defense of the Holy Hesychasts*, ed. John Meyendorff, trans. Nicholas Gendle (New York: Paulist, 1983).

The Image of Christ
Theology in Color

Supported by the Holy Scriptures and the Fathers, we declare unanimously in the name of the Holy Trinity that there shall be rejected and removed and cursed out of the Christian Church every likeness which is made out of any material whatever by the evil art of painters. Whoever in the future dares to make such a thing or venerate it, or set it up in a church or in a private house, or possess it in secret, shall, if bishop, priest, or deacon, be deposed, if monk or layman, anathematized and become liable to be tried by the secular laws as an adversary of God and an enemy of the doctrines handed down by the Fathers.

—Iconoclastic Council of 754

We retain, without introducing anything new, all the ecclesiastical traditions, written or not written, which have been established for us. One of these is the representation of painted images, being in accord with the story of the biblical preaching, because of the belief in the true and non-illusory Incarnation of God the Word for our benefit . . . .

Since this is the case, following the royal path and the teaching divinely inspired by our holy Fathers and the Tradition of the catholic Church . . . we decide in all correctness and after a thorough examination that, just as the holy and vivifying cross, similarly the holy and precious icons painted with colors, made with little stones or with any other matter serving this purpose, should be placed in the holy churches of God, on vases and on sacred vestments, on walls and boards, in houses and on roads, whether these are icons of our Lord God and Savior, Jesus Christ, or of our spotless Sovereign Lady, the holy Mother of God, or of the holy angels and of holy and venerable men. For each time that we see their representation

71

in an image, each time, while gazing upon them, we are made to remember the prototypes, we grow to love them more, and we are even more induced to worship them by kissing them and by witnessing our veneration, not the true adoration which, according to our faith, is proper only to the divine nature, but in the same way as we venerate the precious and vivifying cross, the holy Gospel and other sacred objects which we honor with incense and candles according to the pious custom of our forefathers. For the honor rendered to the image goes to the prototype, and the person who venerates an icon venerates the person represented on it. . . . Thus, we decide that those who dare to think or teach differently, following the example of the evil heretics; those who dare to scorn the ecclesiastical traditions, to make innovations or to repudiate something which has been sanctified by the Church, whether it be the Gospel or the representation of the cross, or the painting of icons, or the sacred relics of martyrs, or who have evil, pernicious and subversive feelings towards the traditions of the catholic Church; those, finally, who dare give sacred vases or venerable monasteries to ordinary uses: we decide that, if they are bishops or priests, they be defrocked; if they are monks or laymen, they be excommunicated.

—Ecumenical Council of 787

I will always remember my first visits to Orthodox worship services in Nizhni Novgorod, Saint Petersburg, and Moscow. Two vivid impressions, indelibly stamped on my mind, remain with me even today.

First, the Orthodox services were a sensory extravaganza of sight, sound, and smell unlike anything I had ever experienced. The effect began outside the church with the glittering gold onion domes sparkling in the blue sky, and continued inside with the service itself—the chanted liturgy, bells, a cappella choirs, wafting incense, elaborate priestly vestments, and frescoes, mosaics, and icons that covered, quite literally, every inch of ceiling and wall space in the church, hundreds of burning candles in the dimly lit sanctuary, and worshipers who stood for the entire two-hour service (there are no seats in Orthodox churches). The experience was above all things aesthetic, a liturgy celebrated through calculated beauty. It was all foreign, even exotic, to one used to a church with four whitewashed walls, a slightly out-of-tune piano, and a leader whose expressed intent is "to share just a few thoughts from the Word." Even today as one walks through the Kremlin churches one has the feeling of being in a beautiful art museum. I identified with those first emissaries of Prince Vladimir who in 988 had been awestruck at the unforgettable beauty that they had encountered in the Church of the Holy Wisdom in Constantinople.

The second impression during my initial visits was of the sacred and liturgical nature of the aesthetic act. Aesthetic splendor had an intended purpose. It was anything but art for art's sake, or even art to adorn the church and its rites. Here aesthetic beauty was employed as the means of sacred worship. Earlier I mentioned that during an Orthodox service I was told to remove my hands from my pockets, and on another occasion to remove myself from a special piece of carpet where a lectern stood. Orthodox worship is not a gathering for small talk, not the time to "share a cup of coffee together." It is instead a sacred moment, a liturgical reenactment of heaven on earth in all its beauty and transcendence, an aesthetic attempt to incarnate the present reality of the future kingdom of God.[1] It is a bold affirmation of the incarnation of God that, as John of Damascus put it in his defense of icons, "sanctifies the senses," especially the "noblest sense of sight," and permits the "glorification of matter."[2]

Sights, Sounds, and the Sacred

Little did I know during my first visits that synthesis of the liturgical with the aesthetic is a primary characteristic of Orthodox Christianity. As I read, studied, and worshiped more within the Orthodox world, I began to understand why some Orthodox authorities complain of what they consider the tacky evangelistic methods and the lack of culture among Protestant Christians working in Russia. An Orthodox priest once told me that Orthodox Christianity is like music made in a conservatory, whereas Protestant Christianity is akin to honky-tonk music. He complained that the Baptists have no culture. Even though that priest was wrong, his comment pointed to a unique feature of Orthodoxy—its fusion of the aesthetic with the theological.

It has been suggested that each of the major branches of Christianity has received a special gift or characteristic to contribute to the universal church: "Catholicism has received the gift of organization and administration, Protestantism the ethical gift of probity of life and of intellectual honesty, while on the Orthodox peoples—and especially Byzantium and Russia—has fallen the gift of perceiving the beauty of the spiritual world."[3] Without question Orthodoxy "exults in beauty" and seeks to experience and express spiritual truth in the concrete, tangible forms of color and design and in music rather than in books or discourse.[4]

It is no accident that the title of Orthodoxy's greatest collection of spiritual texts, the *Philokalia*, means, literally, "love of the beautiful." Early

1. Sergius Bulgakov, *The Orthodox Church*, rev. ed. (Crestwood, N.Y.: St. Vladimir's Seminary Press, 1988), 129.

2. John of Damascus *On the Divine Images* 1.17; 2.14 (Crestwood, N.Y.: St. Vladimir's Seminary Press, 1980); see also the commentary, p. 39.

3. Bulgakov, *Orthodox Church*, 129.

4. Nicolas Zernov, *The Russians and Their Church* (Crestwood, N.Y.: St. Vladimir's Seminary Press, 1978), 5.

Orthodoxy sought to convey the Christian message through the concrete beauty of Byzantine cathedrals with their bells and icons rather than through abstract ideas. The experience of Vladimir's emissaries, which led to the conversion of the Slavs, points directly to the centrality of beauty in Orthodoxy. Their words as recorded in the *Russian Primary Chronicle* are quite instructive on this point: "The Greeks led us to the buildings where they worship their God, and we knew not whether we were in heaven or on earth. For on earth there is no such splendor or such beauty, and we are at a loss to describe it. We know only that God dwells there among men, and their ceremonies are fairer than the ceremonies of other nations. For we cannot forget that beauty." Vladimir's delegation did not respond to any rational apologetic by theologians, but to the aesthetic splendor of the liturgy, a feature which was sorely lacking in the Western churches they visited (where they "beheld no beauty"). One might even say that this aesthetic apologetic has been the paradigm for Orthodox conversion ever since. Orthodoxy, Sergius Bulgakov observes, "does not persuade or try to compel; it charms and attracts."[5] The stories of modern-day conversions to Orthodoxy in Thomas Doulis's *Journeys to Orthodoxy* also bear out the point that it is through its aesthetic splendor that the Orthodox liturgy witnesses to the gospel.[6]

In the Orthodox liturgical scheme, deliberate attention is given to the employment of all five of the senses. One might even call this a Christian materialism: the eyes behold the icons, frescoes, and mosaics; the smell of incense symbolizes the prayers of the saints and the coming kingdom; the sense of taste is satisfied in the Eucharist; the sense of touch finds expression in the anointing of chrismation, and in kissing the Gospel, the cross, and icons; and the sense of hearing savors the chanted liturgy and a cappella choirs.[7]

The icon, as we shall see and study at length in this chapter, epitomizes the employment of the aesthetic in the service of the sacred. The icon,

5. Sergius Bulgakov, "The Orthodox Church," in James Pain and Nicolas Zernov, eds., *A Bulgakov Anthology* (Philadelphia: Westminster, 1976), 12.

6. Thomas Doulis, ed., *Journeys to Orthodoxy: A Collection of Essays by Converts to Orthodox Christianity* (Minneapolis: Light and Life, 1986); see also James J. Stamoolis, *Eastern Orthodox Mission Theology Today* (Maryknoll, N.Y.: Orbis, 1986), 99.

7. Michel Quenot, *The Icon: Window on the Kingdom* (Crestwood, N.Y.: St. Vladimir's Seminary Press, 1991), 47; and Jaroslav Pelikan, *Imago Dei: The Byzantine Apologia for Icons* (Princeton: Princeton University Press, 1990), 108–11. On the Orthodox analysis of the five senses see Nicodemos of Athos, *Handbook of Spiritual Counsel* (New York: Paulist, 1989), chaps. 3–8 (an entire chapter is devoted to each of the five senses, and one chapter to the senses in general, along with their relation to the mind, heart, and imagination); and John of Damascus *Exposition of the Orthodox Faith* 2.18 ("Concerning Sense Perception") and *Divine Images* 1.16–17.

"the most revered form of theological expression" in early Russian Christianity, is the prime example of Orthodoxy's tendency to "crystallize in images rather than ideas." Indeed, in Orthodox Christianity "seeing is better than hearing,"[8] and sight is the "noblest of the senses."[9]

Aesthetic Images and Scholarly Texts (East versus West)

The Eastern emphasis on the aesthetic is likely to strike the Western Protestant as rather foreign. In fact we have here another fundamental characteristic of Eastern Christianity that distinguishes it from its Western counterpart. This difference is not so much one of doctrine or faith, but of what Anthony Ugolnik terms "sensibility."[10] Whereas most Protestants would discover large areas of doctrinal agreement with Orthodoxy, especially regarding the essential teachings of Christianity, they would nevertheless likely feel quite estranged in an Orthodox worship service.

In Eastern Christianity beauty is a fundamental and essential category; it is "not an ephemeral issue but a lasting one, not a peripheral concern but a central one."[11] In the West Christians typically regard aesthetics as having no importance for their Christian identity; aesthetics is, rather, a matter of private preference or peripheral concern. Western Christians would have little empathy for a social aesthetic, much less a pastoral aesthetic (the idea that aesthetics can instruct us and urge us toward the good) as advocated by the influential Orthodox thinker Pavel Florensky (1881–1949).[12] The references by John of Damascus and Theodore the Studite to the "sanctification of the sense of sight" as the "noblest among the senses," the priority of visual over verbal images, and the "glorification of matter" strike us as odd.[13] In some instances Western Christians even view beauty in a negative light, as something evil, soft, vulnerable, feminine, and fragile, rather than as something tough, disciplined, and rational. Beauty is sometimes considered a distraction to avoid or an unneces-

8. James H. Billington, *The Icon and the Axe: An Interpretive History of Russian Culture* (New York: Random House, 1966), 6–9, 28–38.

9. John of Damascus *Divine Images* 1.17. For general studies on icons see Eugene Trubetskoi, *Icons: Theology in Color* (Crestwood, N.Y.: St. Vladimir's Seminary Press, 1973); and Paul Evdokimov, *The Art of the Icon: A Theology of Beauty* (Torrance, Calif.: Oakwood, 1990).

10. Anthony Ugolnik, *The Illuminating Icon* (Grand Rapids: Eerdmans, 1989), 42.

11. Ibid., 187.

12. V. Ivanov, "The Aesthetic Views of Father Pavel Florensky," *Journal of the Moscow Patriarch* 9 (1982): 75 (cited by Ugolnik, *Illuminating Icon*, 208–15).

13. Theodore the Studite *On the Holy Icons* 1.13, 17; 3.A.2 (Crestwood, N.Y.: St. Vladimir's Seminary Press, 1982); John of Damascus *Divine Images* 1.16–17; 2.13–14 (and the commentary on p. 39). See also Pelikan, "The Senses Sanctified," in *Imago*, 99–119.

sary luxury. That mind-set, as Ugolnik notes, "is foreign to the Slavic sensitivity. Among Russians beauty is a powerful constituent of theology and the culture of which religion is a part."[14] The difference between East and West is most evident in the comparative importance assigned to two different epistemological prisms through which Christianity is both understood and experienced—aesthetic images and written texts.

We have noted that the conversion of the Slavs to Christianity had an identifiable aesthetic component. The emissaries of Prince Vladimir were repelled by Western and Muslim forms of worship which lacked beauty. Their encounter with Orthodoxy at Constantinople's Church of the Holy Wisdom was something altogether different. It was above all things an aesthetic experience that was resplendent, almost ineffable, and heavenly.

Consider the magnitude of the sensory grandeur that Vladimir's emissaries witnessed at Constantinople. Built under Justinian I, the last great Roman emperor of the East, and dedicated in 537, the Church of the Holy Wisdom was the main cathedral of the capital city of the empire. "In sheer size it is one of the largest manmade structures in the world; its great vaulted nave easily surpasses all the vaulted interiors of antiquity and the Middle Ages for space enclosed within a single clear span. In engineering it is as puzzling today as it was terrifying to Procopius, to whom it appeared to soar aloft without reliable support, threatening the safety of those within."[15] Serving in this magnificent structure was an army of attendants befitting its splendor. In the year 612, the staff of the Church of the Holy Wisdom numbered 80 priests, 150 deacons, 40 deaconesses, 70 subdeacons, 160 readers, 25 cantors, and 100 doorkeepers.[16] It is little wonder that Vladimir's emissaries were overwhelmed.

The passage from the *Russian Primary Chronicle* about the conversion of the Slavs illustrates several important features of Orthodoxy—the inextricable connection between material beauty and spiritual truth, the primacy of liturgy rather than doctrine, and the deliberate attempt in the Orthodox liturgy to prefigure heaven on earth.[17] Stressing that the Eastern orientation is different from the Western, James Billington notes that "the early Russians were drawn to Christianity by the aesthetic appeal of its liturgy, rather than by the rational shape of its theology."[18]

14. Ugolnik, *Illuminating Icon*, 187.

15. Thomas F. Mathews, *The Byzantine Churches of Istanbul: A Photographic Survey* (University Park: Pennsylvania State University Press, 1976), 263.

16. Timothy Ware, *The Orthodox Church* (Baltimore: Penguin, 1964), 270; see also Pelikan, *Imago*, 12, on the architectural magnitude and splendor of Hagia Sophia.

17. Ware, *Orthodox Church*, 270–72; John Meyendorff, *Byzantine Theology: Historical Trends and Doctrinal Themes* (New York: Fordham University Press, 1974), 115–16; and Bulgakov, *Orthodox Church*, 138.

18. Billington, *Icon and the Axe*, 9.

As an instructive contrast to this Orthodox conversion we can juxtapose another conversion account, equally symbolic and important, this one from the West. Ugolnik has suggested that the conversion of Saint Augustine in 386 serves as a model or paradigm for the Western Christian experience, much as the Slavic conversion story typifies Orthodoxy. In his *Confessions* Augustine records how he heard the voice of a little child that commanded him to "take up and read" the Bible, which lay open at Romans 13:13. His conversion, based upon the reading of a text, is a "primary epistemological model" for the Western understanding of Christianity.[19] While images mediate the Word of God for the East, in the West books, texts, and words are the fundamental vehicle of the knowledge of God. What began with Augustine's conversion through the reading of a text found its fullest expression in the Reformation and ensuing Protestant tradition. We might say that Western Christians have been reading ever since.

The first medieval pope, Gregory the Great (590–604), insisted that "icons are for the unlettered what the Sacred Scriptures are for the lettered" ("Letter to Serenus"). The Second Council of Nicea (787), which ratified the use of icons, went even further, declaring in its canons that iconographic representations were "of an equal benefit to us as the gospel narrative." For their part, almost to a person the Reformers and the Protestant tradition have categorically rejected that idea. While the East was fixed on aesthetic images, the West had a preference for the written word.[20]

While the East wanted to see the Word in images, the West insisted on hearing it in the spoken word. Begun by a "cadre of intellectuals," the Reformation placed a premium on the role of the intellect in the erudite exposition of Scripture.[21] In 1523 Ulrich Zwingli the pastor donned the gown of the secular scholar. A few years later Martin Luther exchanged his monk's cowl for the scholar's robe. As Wilhelm Pauck explains, this change in dress was anything but incidental; the "scholar's gown was *the* garment of the Protestant minister. It symbolizes all the changes wrought by the Reformation in the nature and the work of the ministry."[22] Whereas in the Catholic and Orthodox traditions the priestly functions were primarily sacerdotal in character, in the Reformation and subsequent

19. Ugolnik, *Illuminating Icon*, 49.

20. On the following analysis see the two chapters by Edward L. Long, "Ministry and Scholarship in the Reformed Tradition," and Bard Thompson, "Incidence of Renaissance Culture in Early Protestantism," in Daniel B. Clendenin and W. David Buschart, eds., *Scholarship, Sacraments, and Service: Essays in Honor of Bard Thompson* (Lewiston, N.Y.: Edwin Mellen, 1990), 1–28, 29–58.

21. Jaroslav Pelikan, *The Christian Intellectual* (New York: Harper and Row, 1965), 17.

22. Wilhelm Pauck, "Ministry in the Time of the Continental Reformation," in H. Richard Niebuhr and Daniel Day Williams, eds., *The Ministry in Historical Perspectives* (New York: Harper and Row, 1956), 147.

Protestant tradition the pastor's use of the scholar's robe symbolized an extraordinary and inextricable link between ministry and scholarship, so much so that it comes as no surprise when we read Alexei Khomiakov complaining that in Protestantism "a scholar has taken the place of the priest."[23] In this Western tradition erudition and learning were deemed essential to effective Christian life and work, so that in describing the Reformed tradition one must speak about "The Life of the Mind as the Service of God."[24] The Puritans epitomize this conception of the ministry, having founded schools like Harvard and Yale to cultivate a learned clergy. In Jonathan Edwards, a parish preacher and one of the greatest intellectuals in all of American history, we have the quintessential model of the pastor as scholar, one who leads his flock by rational exposition of the written text. So it is that Bulgakov describes Protestant Christianity as a "professorial" religion in which the central figure is the scholar-professor rather than the priest.[25]

The Reformation witnessed the general denigration of the image and the rise of a text-oriented cultus. Frescoes and paintings in Catholic churches were whitewashed.[26] Books replaced icons. Gregory's dictum notwithstanding, John Calvin objected that "images cannot stand in the place of books." The sermon, spoken in the vernacular and directed to the listener's intellect, upstaged the Eucharist as the defining moment of the liturgy and constituted the sine qua non of Protestant worship.[27] The newly invented printing press replaced the iconographer's pallet and was the engine that drove the Reformation.[28] According to the Puritan John Foxe, "God conducted the Reformation not by the sword, but by 'printing, writing, and reading.'" On the title page of his *Acts and Monuments* (1563), Foxe depicted two congregations at worship—the Catholics fingering their rosaries, the Protestants reading books in their laps. Luther insisted that the Reformers spread the gospel by emphasizing "speaking, reading, and writing." His protégé Philipp Melanchthon argued that "reading is the beginning of Christian doctrine."

23. Alexei S. Khomiakov, "On the Western Confessions of Faith," in Alexander Schmemann, ed., *Ultimate Questions: An Anthology of Modern Russian Religious Thought* (Crestwood, N.Y.: St. Vladimir's Seminary Press, 1977), 52.

24. See John H. Leith, *An Introduction to the Reformed Tradition: A Way of Being the Christian Community* (Atlanta: John Knox, 1977), 77–79.

25. Sergius Bulgakov, "A Professorial Religion," in Pain and Zernov, eds., *Bulgakov Anthology*, 73–76.

26. Quenot, *Icon*, 74.

27. Bulgakov, *Orthodox Church*, 135. Consider also Carnegie S. Calian's symbolic title *Icon and Pulpit*, but see Stamoolis's caveat in *Orthodox Mission Theology*, 88.

28. See Elizabeth Eisenstein, *The Printing Revolution in Early Modern Europe* (Cambridge: Cambridge University Press, 1983).

This text-oriented characteristic of the Reformation evidenced itself in any number of ways—the collection and study of ancient manuscripts (*ad fontes*— to the sources!), the compilation of critical editions of texts (Erasmus's Greek New Testament in 1516), the mastery and employment of ancient languages, the insistence upon public education (Luther's 1524 letter to German government officials), the demand for an educated clergy, and the utilization of the new technology of the printing press to enlighten an increasingly literate public (between 1517 and 1520 Luther's pamphlets sold over three hundred thousand copies). All told, these important examples of the Reformation's love of text and word document what Ugolnik refers to as a "primary epistemological model" for Protestant Christianity even today.[29]

Our two conversion stories (Augustine and the Slavs) and the respective emphases on scholarly texts and aesthetic images symbolize and illustrate the different prisms through which Christians in the East and West view the gospel. The story is told of a Protestant who asked an Orthodox priest exactly what it was that his church believed. The priest responded that "it would be better to ask not what we believe but how we worship." In Eastern Christianity theology and doctrine originate and find their ultimate expression in the aesthetic images of liturgy and worship, in intuition and contemplation rather than in rational discourse. The rule of prayer (*lex orandi*) is the basis, origin, and fullest expression of the rule of faith or belief (*lex credendi*). In the West theology is the scholarly exposition of a text (which is why one evangelical seminary invited prospective students to come "study with the scholars who write the books"). Eastern theology originates in the sanctuary, Western theology in the scholar's study or university library. The one employs candles, frescoes, mosaics, bells, icons, and incense, the other a word processor. For Orthodoxy "sights and sounds point the way to God, not philosophic speculation or literary subtlety."[30] Consequently, much of Eastern theology takes place within the context of the liturgy.[31] In short, in the West theology takes the form of scientific wisdom; in the East it is sacramental worship.

29. On all of these matters see Thompson, "Incidence of Renaissance Culture"; George Marsden, quoted in Jordan Bajis, *Common Ground: An Introduction to Eastern Christianity for the American Christian* (Minneapolis: Light and Life, 1991), 41. The promulgation of the mechanical dictation theory of inspiration is another example of this emphasis on the written word.

30. Billington, *Icon and the Axe*, 38.

31. This observation is made by numerous people: Schmemann, *Ultimate Questions*, 5; Meyendorff, *Byzantine Theology*, 6; Jaroslav Pelikan, *The Spirit of Eastern Christendom (600–1700)* (Chicago: University of Chicago Press, 1974), 275; Stamoolis, *Orthodox Mission Theology*, 86; Ugolnik, *Illuminating Icon*, 125–26; and the entire book by Alexander Schmemann, *Introduction to Liturgical Theology* (Crestwood, N.Y.: St. Vladimir's Seminary Press, 1986). In a personal letter John Breck cautioned that it is very difficult to apprehend the essence of Orthodoxy by reading theological treatises. On the Orthodox liturgy see Hugh Wybrew, *The Orthodox Liturgy* (Crestwood, N.Y.: St. Vladimir's Seminary Press, 1989).

The Iconoclastic Controversy

The icon is not only the most obvious but perhaps the most important symbol of the difference between the East and the West. With the icon we move from Orthodoxy's general love of beauty to its specific deployment in the service of the church. In the life, liturgy, and history of Orthodoxy, the icon is not simply sacred art or church decoration; it is above all things "theology in color."

For a number of interrelated reasons, the bitter controversy over the propriety of icons in Christian life and worship provides a fascinating case study in the history and theology of the church. First, we have noted that icons are essential to the very identity of Orthodoxy. Icons are rooted in the entire religious psychology of Eastern Christianity, and mark nearly every important milestone of an Orthodox Christian's life. At baptism the believer often receives an icon of the saint whose name he or she takes; at marriage the fathers of the couple bless them with icons; and at burial icons are at the front of the funeral procession. A Christian life without icons would be unthinkable for an Orthodox believer.

Second is the theological consideration. According to the Second Council of Nicea (787), icons are of equal benefit and mutually revelatory with the written Gospel. What the Gospel proclaims to us by words, declared the Council of 869–70, the icon also proclaims and renders present to us by color. Moreover, the defense of icons was for Orthodoxy an affirmation of and even litmus test for Chalcedonian Christology. To repudiate icons was to question the true humanity of Christ in the incarnation and by implication the entire basis of Christianity. If Christ cannot be represented by an image, said Theodore the Studite, he was not incarnate, "but this contradicts the whole divine economy of our salvation."[32]

Third is the liturgical consideration. On the first Sunday of Lent is commemorated the final victory over the iconoclasts on March 11, 843. Every year during this special celebration of the Triumph of Orthodoxy the *Synodicon* is read as part of the liturgy, proclaiming "the reaffirmation of true devotion, the security of the worship of icons, and the festival that brings us everything that saves." Conversely, those who reject icons are anathematized: "To those who reject the Councils of the Holy Fathers, and their traditions which are agreeable to divine revelation, and which the Orthodox Catholic Church piously maintains, ANATHEMA! ANATHEMA! ANATHEMA!"[33]

32. Theodore the Studite *Icons* 3.B.3.
33. Pelikan, *Spirit*, 145; Ware, *Orthodox Church*, 39. On the *Synodicon* see Leonid Ouspensky, *Theology of the Icon*, 2 vols. (Crestwood, N.Y.: St. Vladimir's Seminary Press, 1991), 1:164 n. 23.

Thus, in Orthodoxy, the "icon is not just a simple image, nor a decoration, nor even an illustration of Holy Scripture. It is something greater. . . . The Church sees in its holy image not simply one of the aspects of Orthodox teaching, but the expression of Orthodoxy in its totality, the expression of Orthodoxy as such."[34] The defense of icons, then, was not simply a defense of their artistic merit or even their teaching function for the illiterate; for Orthodoxy the defense of icons was tantamount to the defense of Christianity itself. Because of this central importance of icons for Eastern Christianity, the defeat of the "image smashers" and the final vindication of icons might be called the "distinctive genius" of Orthodoxy.[35]

Fourth, the iconographic controversy is also fascinating for Christian historians because of the fragmented nature of the evidence we have. To the witness of the written records we must add the artistic evidence itself—that is, what is left of it. The image smashers did their work so well that, sadly, the combination of their iconoclastic zeal, the Crusade of 1204, the sack of Constantinople in 1453, and the ravages of time have destroyed almost all of the icons that antedated the debate. The earliest extant icons now date from the sixth and seventh centuries. Conversely, just as the iconoclasts destroyed the aesthetic evidence, the iconodules who eventually won the debate destroyed many of the writings of their opponents. The important iconoclastic treatise written by emperor-turned-theologian Constantine V, for example, is no longer extant except in the records of the victors. Thus the evidence with which we must deal—both written and artistic—is incomplete.

Fifth, lasting for some 120 years, the iconoclastic controversy was the first and most sustained polemic by Christians over the deployment of art in the service of the sacred. It was the church's first full-fledged effort to hammer out a Christian aesthetic that explored the nature and function of art in the overall Christian worldview. When the dust had settled, it was clear that for Orthodoxy, unlike Christianity in the West, art and theology were inseparable.

By contrast, during the first centuries of Christianity and before any formal theological justification of aesthetics in Christian life and thought, a rather complex and widespread practical piety had surrounded liturgical art. For example, not even the most brazen iconoclast would have denied veneration to a physical cross; and Christians everywhere had long used the symbols of the fish and the lamb to depict our Lord. But until the icon-

34. Ouspensky, *Theology*, 1:8; see also Quenot, *Icon*, 43; Bulgakov, *Orthodox Church*, 139–40; John Meyendorff, *Christ in Eastern Christian Thought* (Crestwood, N.Y.: St. Vladimir's Seminary Press, 1975), 173.
35. Pelikan, *Imago*, 182.

oclastic controversy no one had ever explored the specificities and ramifications of a wide-ranging Christian aesthetic. Theological discourse followed rather than preceded practical piety; only later did it provide that piety with a nuanced apologetic.

Sixth, the debate over images in the eighth and ninth centuries was an intra-Eastern controversy, centered primarily in Constantinople. The Western popes in Rome during the time of the controversy (including Gregory II, Gregory III, Paschal I, and Gregory IV) all supported the use of images in worship. The bulk of Western iconoclasm would come later, particularly with the Crusades and the Protestant Reformation. Furthermore, we should note that the understanding of art in Catholicism is quite different from that in Orthodoxy.[36]

Finally, we must note a double irony or paradox regarding the metaphysics of matter in the worldviews of both Christians and pagans. On the one hand, the pagan metaphysic (e.g., Plato, Gnosticism, and Manicheanism) held that physical matter was evil, and yet material idols and images symbolized the very essence of paganism in the Greco-Roman world. Paul, we recall, was greatly provoked when he saw how full of idols the city of Athens was (Acts 17:16), while Demetrius and his fellow artisans knew that the apostolic preaching threatened the handsome profits from their handmade gods (Acts 19:24–27). This explains why Christians were especially sensitive to the charge that icons were tantamount to pagan idols. On the other hand, while it would be easy to compile a long litany of Christian texts (Clement of Alexandria, Athenagoras, Origen, etc.) strongly condemning the pagan use of physical images, the iconodules' defense of icons ultimately triumphed at the Council of Nicea in 787. Thus, pagans held that matter was evil, but they multiplied their images; Christians declared the goodness of all created matter, but shunned the pagan practice of idol worship, only later to anathematize anyone who denied the legitimacy of icons. We must explain this curious twist of history whereby Christians turned the prohibition of images into "permission, and permission into command."[37]

The History

There is abundant evidence of early Christian use of art. Long before the use of icons, and despite Old Testament prohibitions and pagan practices, Christians employed art to express the gospel. Tertullian tells us that as early as the second century Christians were accused of "rendering superstitious adoration to the cross."[38] Presumably they had physical crosses of

36. Ouspensky, *Theology*, 1:9–12; Quenot, *Icon*, 72–79.
37. Pelikan, *Imago*, 2; see also 54–55, 57, 61; Meyendorff, *Christ*, 173–76.
38. Tertullian *Apology* 16.6 (in Pelikan, *Imago*, 57).

some sort. The catacombs (frescoes, funeral inscriptions, relief sculptures on sarcophagi), a broad array of artistic symbols (fish, bread, lambs, doves, arks, ships, Old Testament themes), statues, tapestries, and the like all witness to a didactic use of art in the early church. With Constantine's conversion political patronage of the arts became important, as the Church of the Holy Sepulchre (Jerusalem), built by Constantine, and the Church of the Holy Wisdom, built by Justinian, both testify. Eusebius of Caesarea (c. 265–339) verifies that in the early fourth century there was widespread use of painted representations of Christ and the apostles.[39] And in his three apologies for icons John of Damascus appends dozens of patristic testimonies to the use of painted images dating from the fourth century on. It seems that by the fifth century the veneration of icons as we know them today was well established in the church.

Except for the small and local synod at Elvira, Spain, in the early fourth century, the first official pronouncement by the church on the use of art came at the Quinisext Council that convened on September 1, 692. Canon 82 specifies that whereas Christ had traditionally been portrayed symbolically as a lamb, "today we prefer grace and truth themselves as a fulfilment of the Law. Therefore, in order to expose to the sight of all, at least with the help of painting, that which is perfect, we decree that henceforth Christ our God be represented in His human form and not in the ancient form of the lamb. We understand this to be the elevation of the humility of God the Word, and we are led to remembering His life in the flesh, His passion, His saving death, and, thus, deliverance which took place for the world." Whereas indirect symbolism befitted the Old Testament Era, the incarnation of God demanded direct representation. Canon 82 thus established a direct link between Christology and the didactic character of icons.

How then did such a violent iconoclasm arise in the East? Scholars debate the issue, but several points are clear. Despite the theoretical justification, practical abuses of icon veneration no doubt encouraged iconoclastic objections. Crude superstitions such as adding flecks of icon paint to the Eucharist wine or using icons as godparents at baptism tended to verify the charge that icon veneration was little more than pagan idolatry. There was also the dubious technical merit of some icons which falsified the historical representation of Christ with subjective artistic imagination. Indeed, Canon 100 of the Quinisext Council censors "misleading paintings which corrupt the intelligence by arousing shameful pleasures." Further, it is likely that the campaign of Leo III (717–41) against icons was motivated by desire to reduce the influence of the monastic community,

39. Eusebius *Ecclesiastical History* 7.18; 9.11.

confiscate their property, and consolidate his own political power. Finally, and most important, was the growing threat of Islam. Claiming to possess a purer and higher form of revelation, Muslims accused Christians of both polytheism because of their doctrine of the Trinity and idolatry because of their veneration of icons. In 717 Muslims invaded Constantinople, only to be repelled by Leo III a year later. In 723 Caliph Yazid II ordered that all icons be removed from Christian churches.[40]

By the early eighth century, iconoclastic sentiment was strong enough that Germanus I, the patriarch of Constantinople (715–30), had to defend the long-standing practice of icon veneration as an affirmation of the incarnation.[41] It was to no avail, however, and in 726 Leo III provoked the iconoclastic controversy with his edict that prohibited the use of icons. Patriarch Germanus in Constantinople and Pope Gregory II in Rome both rejected the decree. Germanus was deposed and replaced by the iconoclastic Patriarch Anastasius (730–53). Violent persecutions of the iconodules and widespread destruction of icons ensued.

Writing in defense of icons during Leo III's reign, John of Damascus makes it clear that part of the controversy was political. The iconodules resented Leo's caesaropapist tendencies to combine the powers of the temporal throne and the eternal altar in his one person: "I am an emperor and priest," Leo wrote to Pope Gregory II in Rome.[42] Emperors had no business meddling in church councils, John objected, for the power to bind and loose was given to apostles and not kings: "Political prosperity is the business of emperors; the condition of the Church is the concern of the shepherds and teachers. Any other method is piracy, brothers. . . . We will obey you, O emperor, in those matters which pertain to our daily lives: payments, taxes, tributes; these are your due and we will give them to you. But as far as the government of the Church is concerned, we have our pastors, and they have preached the Word to us; we have those who interpret the ordinances of the Church. We will not remove the age-old landmarks which our fathers have set, but we keep the tradition we have received."[43]

Emperor Constantine V (741–75) was even more fanatical than his father Leo III. Proving himself to be no mean theologian, he wrote a treatise summarizing the iconoclastic position, violently persecuted those who venerated icons, and convened the famous Iconoclastic

---

40. On these points see Alexander Schmemann, *The Historical Road of Eastern Orthodoxy* (Crestwood, N.Y.: St. Vladimir's Seminary Press, 1977), 203–4; Ouspensky, *Theology*, 1:101–6; and Meyendorff, *Byzantine Theology*, 42–43. See also A. A. Vasiliev, "The Iconoclastic Edict of Caliph Yazid II, A.D. 721," Dumbarton Oaks Papers (1956).

41. Meyendorff, *Christ*, 178; *Byzantine Theology*, 45.

42. See Ouspensky, *Theology*, 1:109.

43. John of Damascus *Divine Images* 2.12.

Council of 754. At that council priests were deposed, monks and lay people were anathematized, and Germanus and John of Damascus were excommunicated, the former posthumously. It was only at the Second Council of Nicea (787), under Empress Irene, that iconoclasm was defeated and the christological justification of icon veneration was promulgated (see the quotations at the beginning of this chapter for statements by both councils).

After a brief respite, a second period of iconoclastic persecution erupted under Emperor Leo V (813–20). During this period Patriarch Nicephorus I (806–15) and the monk Theodore the Studite remained uncompromising in their support of icons. Nicephorus was deposed, exiled, and replaced with the iconoclastic Patriarch Theodotus I (815–21). Under Theodora, who was regent for her underage son, Emperor Michael III, a council was convened in March 843. It reconfirmed the decision of 787, excommunicated the iconoclasts, and established the first Sunday of Lent as a holy day to celebrate the Triumph of Orthodoxy. For over a thousand years now, Orthodoxy has gloried in this its ultimate triumph, the official sanctioning of the veneration of icons.

The Theology

Having briefly sketched the history of the iconoclastic controversy, we must now examine the theology that was involved. The Orthodox defense of icons was based on four interrelated arguments.

1. Both John of Damascus and Theodore the Studite began their apologetics by refuting the charges that icon veneration violated the Old Testament prohibitions of idolatry (Exod. 20:4; Deut. 4:15–18; and 5:7–9), and that it was a devilish reintroduction of paganism into the church (a charge made at the Iconoclastic Council of 754). The iconoclasts argued that when God spoke at Sinai, Moses had "heard the sound of words but saw no form; there was only a voice" (Deut. 4:12). They also pointed to the words of Christ himself: true worship of God is necessarily spiritual rather than material (John 4:23–24). In fact, the appeal to Scripture was not as clear or simple as either side might have wished.

First of all, claimed John and Theodore, the iconoclasts misapplied the Old Testament prohibitions. Pagan idols were one thing, but Christian icons another: "If you speak of pagan abuses, these abuses do not make our veneration of images loathsome. Blame the pagans, who made images into gods! Just because the pagans used them in a foul way, that is no reason to object to our pious practice."[44]

44. Ibid., 1.24, 26; 2.17; Theodore the Studite *Icons* 1.2.6–7; 3.A.55.

Secondly, John and Theodore admitted that to fashion an image of the invisible God would have been either impossible or blasphemous during the Old Testament Era. Nevertheless, even in that period the prohibition against images was relative and not absolute, for God commanded a whole array of material artifacts to be venerated as aids to worshiping him—the elaborately appointed tent of meeting (Exod. 35:4–19), the cherubim, the mercy seat, the brazen serpent, the Spirit-inspired artistic creations of Bezalel (Exod. 31:1–11), and so on. Thus John speaks of a "glorification of matter" even within the Old Testament Era, and Theodore presses the analogy that if God condescended to be symbolized by a brazen serpent, "how could it not be pleasing to Him and appropriate to set up the image of the bodily form which has been His since He became man?"[45]

Most important of all was the christological argument. The Old Testament material images were types, figures, or shadows that befitted the age of the law (Gal. 3:25). Whereas God spoke in a certain way in the age of law, in the age of grace he has spoken in a decisively new way (Heb. 1:1–2). The once invisible God assumed a human body and in so doing became circumscribable: "It is obvious that when you contemplate God becoming man, then you may depict Him clothed in human form. When the invisible One becomes visible to flesh, you may then draw His likeness. . . . In former times, God, who is without form or body, could never be depicted. But now, when God is seen in the flesh conversing with men, I make an image of the God whom I see. I do not worship matter, I worship the Creator of matter who became matter for my sake, who willed to take His abode in matter, who worked out my salvation through matter. Never will I cease honoring the matter which wrought my salvation!"[46] Theodore observes that in their "insanity" the iconoclasts had confused the doctrine of "theology," according to which God remains beyond all human knowledge and description, and the doctrine of "economy," according to which the invisible God became incarnate and consequently circumscribable.[47]

Finally, John and Theodore drew attention to the obvious, that in this age of visible incarnation not every Old Testament prescription is obligatory for New Testament ethics. Christians, they noted, no longer observed Old Testament dietary laws and the requirement of circumcision, nor, to take an instance from the Decalogue itself, the observance of the Sabbath on Saturday (1 Cor. 16:2; Rev. 1:10). In like manner the commandment against graven images was construed as a temporal rather than a universal prohibition, one that was appropriate to the age of pagan idols but has now been superseded by the incarnation of God himself.

45. Theodore the Studite *Icons* 1.6; John of Damascus *Divine Images* 1.16.
46. John of Damascus *Divine Images* 1.8, 16; see also 2.5.
47. Theodore the Studite *Icons* 2.4; 3.C.15.

2. A major element of the iconoclastic charge of idolatry rested on Constantine V's insistence that an image is of the exact same nature or essence as its prototype, even as Christ the image of God is of the same essence as the Father (2 Cor. 4:4; Col. 1:15). In view of this definition, argued the iconoclasts, the Eucharist, in which Christ is held to be literally and physically present, is the only permissible icon of Christ,[48] and to venerate any other image is to treat as God something that is not God, and to commit idolatry. The iconodules responded to this charge in two ways.

First, they made an etymological distinction regarding the nature of worship. Both John and Theodore distinguished between different kinds or degrees of worship. Absolute worship or adoration (*latreia*) is unique and due to God alone, while relative worship, reverence, veneration, or respect (*proskynesis, douleia*) can and in fact should be paid to any number of people and objects. Although relative veneration has the same outward form, says Theodore, it has a different intention. Both apologists made a number of comparisons. Servants honor their masters, citizens honor their king, and children honor their parents. More important, and impossible for the iconoclasts to deny, were several examples from liturgical practice. Christians rightly venerated the Gospel texts, which were given to them not only for hearing but for seeing.[49] So too the cross: "If that which is inferior and less honorable [a cross] is correctly considered [worthy of veneration], it is stupid to say that the greater and more honorable [an icon of Christ] is not also correctly considered. For what closer comparison does the icon of Christ have than the symbol of the cross, when the icon has the same relation with its prototype as the symbol has?"[50] The relative veneration given to Mary, the saints, relics, and books were further liturgical proofs of the etymological distinction: "Either do away with the honor and veneration these things deserve, or accept the tradition of the Church and the veneration of images."[51] Thus, by offering relative veneration but not absolute worship to an icon, the iconodules could claim that they were not violating the commandment against graven images, but simply following a well-established practice.[52]

Second, both John and Theodore made an ontological distinction between the nature of the image and the nature of its prototype. "We say that Christ is one thing and His image is another thing by nature,

48. Ibid., 1.10; see also Pelikan, *Imago*, 58–59, and *Spirit*, 109–10.
49. Theodore the Studite *Icons* 1.19; 2.34.
50. Ibid., 2.23.
51. John of Damascus *Divine Images* 1.16.
52. Ibid., 1.8, 14. John even distinguished between five types of absolute worship and seven types of relative honor (3.27–39). See also Theodore the Studite *Icons* 1.19; and for a similar distinction see Augustine *City of God* 10.1.

although they have an identity in the use of the same name."[53] To refute
the iconoclasts' insistence that the Eucharist is the only permissible image
of Christ, John and Theodore pointed out that the prototype and its image
are not identical in every way.[54] The relationship between the artificial
form of the material image (the icon), which is only a copy or shadow, and
the actual prototype (Christ himself) is analogical rather than univocal.
The charge of idolatry, then, they insist, is invalid: "It is not the essence
of the image which we venerate, but the form of the prototype which is
stamped upon it, since the essence of the image is not venerable. Neither
is it the material which is venerated, but the prototype is venerated
together with the form and not the essence of the image."[55] The prototype
and the image share the same name, and so we speak of them in the same
way, but in the case of the prototype the attributes are applied properly,
while in the case of the image they are applied figuratively. This principle,
writes Theodore, "applies to Christ and His icon. For Christ is called 'very
God' and also 'man' because of the signification of the names and because
of the natures of divinity and humanity. His image, on the other hand, is
called 'Christ' because of the signification of the name, but not because
it has the nature of divinity and humanity. . . . It shares the name of its
prototype, as it shares also the honor and veneration; but it has no part
in the nature of the prototype. . . . So what is said applies to the name
only and the identity of veneration, not to an identity of material
between the prototype and the image; for the material cannot participate
in the veneration, although he who is depicted appears in it for veneration."[56] The authoritative principle in this regard, repeatedly invoked by
both John and Theodore, is found in a text from Basil (and similar ones
from Athanasius, Pseudo-Dionysius, and Cyril): "The honor given to the
image passes over to the prototype."[57]

3. The appeal to patristic authority, particularly the *consensus quin-
quesaecularis* (the basic position held in the first five centuries), was no
less important, no less obligatory, and, unfortunately, no less ambiguous
than the appeal to scriptural texts. Both sides appealed to tradition,
both hurled the venomous epithet of "novelty-mongering" at their
opponents,[58] and both were hard-pressed to find unequivocal support for
their positions.

53. Theodore the Studite *Icons* 1.11.
54. John of Damascus *Divine Images* 1.8; 3.16; Theodore the Studite *Icons* 1.12.
55. Theodore the Studite *Icons* 3.C.2.
56. Ibid., 2.17–18.
57. John of Damascus *Divine Images* 1.21; Theodore the Studite *Icons* 1.8; 2.24; Basil *On the Holy Spirit* 18.45.
58. Pelikan, *Imago*, 41.

Theodore declared that time would never permit him to unroll "the great swarm of texts available from both ancient and recent authorities concerning the venerable icons."[59] John insisted that his position accorded with the "single stream" of scriptural and patristic testimony, and that icon veneration was "no new invention, but the ancient tradition of the Church."[60] He cites Leontius of Cyprus, who had argued that "this tradition begins with the Law and not with us."[61] Nevertheless, complains Theodore, the iconoclasts have charged that "the Scriptures say nothing" on this subject, and that icon veneration "is not included in the traditional confession of our faith."[62]

The iconoclastic indictment had force. In some respects the "main authority" of the iconoclasts was "an appeal to antiquity. . . . This was possibly the strongest point of their attack and their self-defense."[63] For a practice reputed to be widespread in the ancient church, the iconodules could not produce from the first three hundred years of Christian literature a single unambiguous text that mandated icon veneration. Conversely, the iconoclasts could "multiply at will" an "almost unbroken succession" of early apologists who equated the use of external images with Greek paganism. The "sheer mass of the explicit evidence" seemed to favor the iconoclasts.[64] One example is Canon 36 from the local synod at Elvira, Spain (c. 305): "It seemed good to us that paintings should not be found in churches, and that which is venerated and adored not be painted on the walls."

Debate persisted over two fourth-century texts. First was a letter, no longer extant, from Eusebius of Caesarea to Empress Constantia (the sister of Constantine I), who had requested an icon of Christ. In his response to her request Eusebius categorically repudiated the use of icons: "I do not know what has impelled you to command that an image of our Saviour be drawn. Which icon of Christ do you mean? That which is true and unchangeable and which bears the characteristics of his divine nature, or that which he assumed for us, the figure, that is, that he took 'in the form of a slave'?"[65] Either answer seemed to entrap the iconodules: to portray Christ's divine nature was impossible, while to separate the two natures and portray only his human form was heretical (Nestorianism).

59. Theodore the Studite Icons 2.40.
60. John of Damascus Divine Images 2.20; see also 3.41 (and the commentary on pp. 45–47).
61. John of Damascus Divine Images, commentary, p. 97.
62. Theodore the Studite Icons 2.5–6.
63. George Florovsky, "Origen, Eusebius, and the Iconoclastic Controversy," Church History 19 (1950): 81; see also idem, Christianity and Culture (Belmont, Mass.: Nordland, 1974), 105.
64. Pelikan, Imago, 54, 57, 68; Spirit, 97–99.
65. For the text see Pelikan, Spirit, 101.

If the letter had not come from a theologian unanimously recognized as having semi-Arian tendencies, it might have carried weight; but ironically, the iconodules turned it to their own advantage. They noted that in six centuries of patristic texts the most explicit rejection of the Christian (and not simply pagan) use of images was that of a theologian whose own Christology was acknowledged by everyone to be heretical. Furthermore, if the patristic tradition had uniformly equated icons with idols, why were the first six ecumenical councils of the church silent on such a critical matter? To be sure, the councils had addressed other liturgical and practical abuses.[66]

The second text was even more uncompromising and explicit in its rejection of icons, and it came, the iconoclasts reminded their opponents, not from some "heretical interpolator" but from one "prominent and renowned among the saints." A work reputedly written by Epiphanius (c. 315–403), the bishop of Cyprus and a zealous orthodox dogmatist, equated images with pagan idolatry; he even anathematized anyone who appealed to the incarnation to justify venerating icons "painted with earthly colors." In their rejoinders John, Theodore, and Patriarch Nicephorus of Constantinople all rejected the text as spurious. Its authenticity continues to be a matter for scholarly debate even today.[67] Leonid Ouspensky has noted that the churches in Cyprus under Epiphanius were decorated with paintings.

Even more intriguing than the texts by Eusebius and Epiphanius is a tactical move made by the iconodules. Invoking Pauline authority, both John and Theodore urged believers to "stand firm and hold to the teachings . . . passed on to you, whether by word of mouth or by letter" (2 Thess. 2:15). Irenaeus had referred to the authority of unwritten tradition quite early,[68] but it was the venerable Basil whom the iconodules cited. In his work *On the Holy Spirit* Basil observed that "among the carefully guarded teachings and doctrines of the Church, there are some teachings we received from written documents, while others we receive secretly, for they have been handed on to us from the apostolic tradition. Both sources have equal power to lead us to righteousness. No one who values the seasoned discipline of the Church will dispute this, for if we neglect unwritten customs as not having much force, we then bury much of the Gospel that is

66. John of Jerusalem *Against Constantine* V, 5 (cited by Pelikan, *Imago*, 60).

67. John of Damascus *Divine Images* 1.25; 2.18; Theodore the Studite *Icons* 2.48–49; Nicephorus *Against Epiphanius* and *Shorter Apology for the Holy Images*. See Ouspensky, *Theology*, 1:131, for the relevant bibliographical references: Ouspensky, Ostrogorsky, Florovsky, Meyendorff, and Schoborn all consider the text by Epiphanius to be dubious, while Holl, Klauser, and Pelikan (*Spirit*, 102) consider it genuine.

68. Irenaeus *Against Heresies* 3.2.1–2 (cited by Pelikan, *Imago*, 62).

important."[69] Examples of such unwritten tradition included the location of Calvary and the tomb, threefold immersion at baptism, praying toward the East, bowing before the cross, and certain aspects of the eucharistic celebration.

Basil had spoken of the authority not only of written texts but of liturgical practice. How, asks Theodore, dare we overthrow "the long-standing ancient customs and traditions? . . . Many teachings which are not written in so many words, but have equal force with the written teachings, have been proclaimed by the holy fathers." In a candid admission Theodore then asks, "So after all, how is it surprising, although it is not written that Christ is the prototype of His image, if the times now require this to be said in opposition to the growing iconoclast heresy?"[70] Employing much the same logic, John concludes, "Just as the written Gospel has been preached to the whole world, so also there has been an unwritten tradition throughout the world to make icons of Christ, the incarnate God."[71] So it was that the final declaration of the Second Ecumenical Council of Nicea (787) was based on "written and unwritten" patristic authority.

4. Whatever roles imperial economics, church-state politics, Old Testament prohibitions, pagan idolatry, patristic authority, and the struggle between sight and sound for epistemological priority may have played in the iconoclastic controversy, the earliest and latest literary evidences (the texts of Eusebius and Epiphanius, Canon 82 of the Council of 692, the Iconoclastic Council of 754, and the final statement of 787) all indicate that the war of words over the role of images was waged on specifically christological grounds. "The question of icons was, from the beginning, linked by the Orthodox to christological teaching."[72] What were the implications of the incarnation for visual images of the invisible God? Christology was not only the most potent weapon in the iconoclastic arsenal, but also the "indispensable key" and "doctrinal heart" of the iconodules' defense of icons.[73]

Eusebius's letter to Constantia, we have seen, attempted to impale the iconodules on the horns of a syllogistic dilemma. Later, Constantine V had charged that "anyone who makes an icon of Christ has failed to penetrate

69. Basil *On the Holy Spirit* 27.66. The text by Basil is quoted in John of Damascus *Divine Images* 1.23 and Nicephorus *Refutation of the Iconoclasts* 3.8.
70. Theodore the Studite *Icons* 1.19; 2.7; cf. Nicephorus's *Refutation* 3.1, which charges the iconoclasts with "taking refuge in tradition" (cited by Pelikan, *Imago*, 54).
71. John of Damascus *Divine Images* 2.16.
72. George Ostrogorsky, "The Combination of the Problem of the Holy Icons with Christological Dogmatics in the Works of the Orthodox Apologists of the Early Period of Iconoclasm," *Seminarium Kondakovianum: Recueil d'études* 1 (Prague, 1927): 36 (cited by Ouspensky, *Theology*, 1:120).
73. Pelikan, *Imago*, 75, 77; see also idem, *Spirit*, 114.

to the depths of the dogma of the inseparable union of the two natures of Christ."[74] And the Iconoclastic Council of 754 convened by Constantine contended that fashioning icons was either impossible or blasphemous:

> What then does the ignorant painter do when he gives a form to that which can only be believed in the heart and confessed with words? The name of Jesus Christ is the name of the God-Man. Therefore, you commit a double blasphemy when you represent Him. First of all, you attempt to represent the unrepresentable divinity. Second, if you try to represent the divine and human natures of Christ on the icon, you risk confusing them, which is monophysitism. You answer that you only represent the visible and tangible flesh of Christ. But this flesh is human and, therefore, you represent only the humanity of Christ, only His human nature. But in this case, you separate it from the divinity which is united with it, and this is Nestorianism. In fact, the flesh of Jesus Christ is the flesh of God the Word; it had been completely assumed and deified by Him. How, then, do these godless persons dare to separate the divinity from the flesh of Christ and represent this flesh alone, as the flesh of an ordinary man? The Church believes in Christ who inseparably and purely united in Himself divinity and humanity. If you represent the humanity of Christ, you separate His two natures, His divinity and humanity, by giving this humanity its own existence, an independent life, seeing in it a separate person, and thus introducing a fourth person into the Holy Trinity.[75]

A material image of Christ, the iconoclasts insisted, necessarily either separated or confused the two natures of Christ: it necessarily either portrayed only Christ's humanity (Nestorianism) or merged both natures (Monophysitism). "Along with describing created flesh, [the iconodule] has either circumscribed the uncircumscribable character of the Godhead, according to what has seemed good to his own worthlessness, or he has confused the unconfused union, falling into the iniquity of confusion."[76]

In response the defenders of images made a series of points by appealing to Chalcedonian Christology and the Council of 451's important distinction between "person" and "nature." First, describing the divine nature is admittedly impossible: "Christ," Theodore admitted, "is describable according to his person, but remains indescribable in his divinity."[77] On this point the defenders of icons could say that they "confessed the same" as the iconoclasts.[78] But second, the iconoclasts were wrong in their under-

---

74. Quoted in Nicephorus *Refutation* 1.41–42 (cited by Pelikan, *Imago*, 73–74).

75. For the text see Ouspensky, *Theology*, 1:124–25.

76. For the text see Pelikan, *Imago*, 78; cf. Theodore the Studite *Icons* 1.3.

77. Theodore the Studite *Refutations of the Iconoclasts* 4.34 (cited by Ouspensky, *Theology*, 1:125).

78. John of Jerusalem *Against Constantine V*, 4 (cited by Pelikan, *Imago*, 79).

standing that the purpose of an icon is to portray the nature of Christ; actually, when an icon portrays Christ, it "is not the nature but the person that is portrayed."[79] Third, because of the incarnation the immaterial God can be represented with a material image; to say otherwise is "to utterly deny that the Word became flesh—which is the height of impiety."[80] But it is not solely his human nature that is portrayed in an icon (separating the human nature from the divine nature would be Nestorianism); rather, "the total divine-human person of Christ" is portrayed.[81]

The Council of Chalcedon had insisted that Christ existed "in two natures," and that the divine and human natures could neither be separated nor confused. The two natures of Christ existed "without confusion, change, division, or separation; the distinction of natures in no way annulled by the union, but rather the characteristics of each nature being preserved." An icon, then, did not attempt to represent either the human or the divine nature alone, but instead the unity and totality of the two natures in a single person. The defenders of icons pointed to the Eucharist,[82] the precrucifixion transfiguration,[83] and even the glorified, post-resurrection Christ[84] as examples demonstrating how the totality of the divine-human person remained at the same time fully divine, fully human, and necessarily localized and therefore circumscribable.

The iconodules thus rejected the Eusebian syllogism that an icon represents either the divinity of Christ (a notion which they agreed was impossible) or the human nature of Christ as distinct from his divinity (a notion which they agreed was heretical). The iconoclasts had failed to recognize a third option, that an icon does not "represent His divinity or His humanity, but His Person, which inconceivably unites in itself these two natures without confusion and without division, as the Chalcedonian dogma defines it."[85]

79. Theodore the Studite Icons 3.34.
80. Ibid., 1.3.
81. Pelikan, Imago, 79.
82. Theodore the Studite Icons 1.10.
83. Theodore the Studite Refutations 3.1.53; Nicephorus Refutation 3.38 (cited by Pelikan, Imago, 95). See also Ouspensky, Theology, 1:159.
84. Theodore the Studite Icons 2.41–47.
85. Ouspensky, Theology, 1:125, 153; see also Meyendorff, Christ, 181–82.

The Witness of the Spirit
Scripture and Tradition

So then, brothers, stand firm and hold to the teachings [traditions] we passed on to you, whether by word of mouth or by letter.

—2 Thessalonians 2:15

Hence it is manifest that they did not deliver all things by epistle, but many things also unwritten, and in like manner both the one and the other worthy of credit. Therefore let us think the Tradition of the Church also worthy of credit. It is a tradition; seek no farther.

—Chrysostom

I praise you for . . . holding to the teachings [traditions], just as I passed them on to you.

—1 Corinthians 11:2

Tradition is the witness of the Spirit.

—George Florovsky

In an unusually graphic way the iconoclastic controversy demonstrated the complexity of Orthodox theological method and its obligatory appeals to the multifaceted criteria of dogmatic authority—Holy Scripture, liturgical custom, patristic consensus, conciliar declaration, and credal statement. In fact, despite the clear statement of the Council of 787 in favor of the iconodules, the conclusions which could be drawn from these theological criteria were neither as simple nor unequivocal as the two sides in the controversy could have hoped. Thus, in this chapter we shall examine in some detail the Orthodox approach to Scripture and tradition as the criteria for theological method.

Any study of Scripture and tradition is admittedly complicated for a number of reasons. Often matters hinge on the definition given to a word or concept, but even this is no simple matter, as Martin Chemnitz demonstrated by showing that there were at least seven distinct meanings of the word *tradition* in the early church.[1] Further, the sheer scope of the literature on the subject has created a theological specialty all its own which requires its own experts. As might be expected, in this body of specialized literature dealing with the historical and theological relationship of Scripture and tradition almost nothing is uncontested. Even ostensibly clear statements are debated down to each word. The Council of Trent (1545–63) is a case in point. Did Trent affirm or deny the "traditional" Catholic view of two equally authoritative sources of revelation (scriptural and extrascriptural) when at its fourth session on April 8, 1546, it changed its original draft from "partly (*partim*) in written books, partly (*partim*) in traditions" to "written books and (*et*) tradition"? That single redaction has been the subject of ongoing debate.[2]

Another factor complicating our study lends some credence to the charge that Western theology lives in its own world and tends to neglect the uniqueness of Eastern theological contributions. Much of the scholarly debate about Scripture and tradition focuses on the differences between Protestants and Catholics on this subject, with little consideration given to the position of Orthodoxy. Of course, the differences between Protestantism and Catholicism on the matter of Scripture and tradition are great, and it would serve no purpose to minimize or ignore those differences. In some ways the Orthodox view of tradition is closer to Catholicism; for example, we can trace a two-source view of revelation back to key figures in both the East (Basil) and the West (Augustine).[3] But it would be a grave error, and miss the whole spirit of Orthodoxy, if we confused the Orthodox view of Scripture and tradition with that found in Catholicism, and contrasted both of these views only with the view of Protestantism.

---

1. David Wells, "Tradition: A Meeting Place for Catholic and Evangelical Theology?" *Christian Scholar's Review* 5 (1975): 55. Thus Robert McAfee Brown, "'Tradition' as a Problem for Protestants," *Union Seminary Quarterly Review* 16.2 (1961): 211–14, urges a philological study of what exactly we mean when we use the word *tradition*.

2. Both George Tavard (*Holy Writ or Holy Church* [New York: Harper, 1959]) and Josef Geiselmann ("Das Konzil von Trient über das Verhältnis der Heiligen Schrift und der nicht geschriebenen Traditionen," in *Die mündliche Überlieferung*, ed. Michael Schmaus [Munich, 1957], 125–206; and "Scripture and Tradition in Catholic Theology," *Theology Digest* 6 [1958]: 73–78) advanced the thesis, now widely accepted by many Catholic theologians, that Trent did not teach the so-called traditional Catholic two-source view. For a dissenting view on this matter see Heiko Oberman, "Quo Vadis? Tradition from Irenaeus to Humani Generis," *Scottish Journal of Theology* 16 (1963): 225–55; Oberman regards the reassessment of Trent by Geiselmann and Tavard as "impossible to accept."

3. Oberman, "Quo Vadis?" 237.

From the perspective of Orthodoxy there is every reason to consider Catholicism and Protestantism not as opposites but as related garments cut from the same piece of cloth. We noted earlier Alexei Khomiakov's point that Eastern tradition is another tapestry altogether.[4] According to Khomiakov, Protestants are crypto-Catholics in the sense that they operate in the same Western framework, the only difference being that Catholics affirm while Protestants deny the same set of theological data. The two operate in the same field but pull in different directions. Orthodoxy plays a different game altogether, insists Khomiakov (see p. 15). This is true in a general way and on a number of specific points, including the role of church art and the doctrine of salvation. It is especially true concerning the matter of Scripture, tradition, and theological method, so much so that John Meyendorff can write that "ultimately, the conflict between East and West resides in two conflicting spiritual perceptions of tradition."[5] More specifically, it is the question of the nature and locus of theological authority, which is another crucial difference between the East and the West.[6]

In Orthodoxy, according to Khomiakov, the church is "the truth—and at the same time the inner life of the Christian"; the church, then, is not an authority, for "authority is something external to us."[7] Even though they draw different conclusions, in the West both Catholics and Protestants operate with identical premises in the sense that they both seek the security of an external authority that would serve as the guarantor of theological truth. In Catholicism this external dogmatic authority came to reside in the teaching magisterium of the church as expressed in the primacy and infallibility of the papacy,[8] whereas in Protestantism there arose,

---

4. Thomas Hopko makes this exact point in his book *Women and the Priesthood* (Crestwood, N.Y:. St. Vladimir's Seminary Press, 1983), 172, as does George Florovsky, who notes that the "universe of discourse" between the East and West has been disrupted and that common understanding will be possible only when this "common universe of discourse" is recovered (*Christianity and Culture* [Belmont, Mass.: Nordland, 1974], 161–62).

5. John Meyendorff, *Catholicity and the Church* (Crestwood, N.Y.: St. Vladimir's Seminary Press, 1983), 97.

6. On the issue of theological authority see Carnegie S. Calian, "The Question of Authority," in *Theology without Boundaries: Encounters of Eastern Orthodoxy and Western Tradition* (Louisville: Westminster/John Knox, 1992), 45–50, and especially the bibliographical references on p. 117, nn. 1, 7. See also James J. Stamoolis, "Scripture and Tradition as Sources of Authority in the Eastern Orthodox Church," M.A. thesis, Trinity Evangelical Divinity School, 1971.

7. Alexei S. Khomiakov, "On the Western Confessions of Faith," in Alexander Schmemann, ed., *Ultimate Questions: An Anthology of Modern Russian Religious Thought* (Crestwood, N.Y.: St. Vladimir's Seminary Press, 1977), 50.

8. Jaroslav Pelikan, *The Emergence of the Catholic Tradition* (Chicago: University of Chicago Press, 1971), 352, 356–57.

in reaction to papal hegemony, the external criterion of *sola scriptura*. By contrast, rather than an external theological authority over and speaking *to* the church, Orthodoxy proposes an idea of internal truth within and living *in* the church—the Spirit of God himself. Orthodoxy offers a view of theological authority that is pneumatic rather than dogmatic. George Florovsky labels "admirable" Khomiakov's explanation that "neither individuals, nor a multitude of individuals within the Church preserve tradition or write the Scriptures, but the Spirit of God which lives in the whole body of the Church."[9] The conclusion of Meyendorff's study of theological authority echoes the same idea: "If Orthodox theology has any contribution to make to the present ecumenical dialogue, it will consist in stressing and showing the *auxiliary* character of authority. It is not authority which makes the Church to be the Church, but the Spirit alone, acting in the Church as Body, realizing the sacramental presence of Christ Himself among men and in men. Authority in the bishops, the councils, Scripture, and Tradition only expresses this presence, but does not replace the goal of human life in Christ."[10] These two different conceptions of theological authority, the one pneumatic and internal, the other dogmatic and external, constitute "the ultimate difference" between Eastern and Western confessions of faith.[11]

Khomiakov overstates his case, of course, and even Meyendorff acknowledges that the sweeping categorical generalizations by Khomiakov are in fact unfair, romantic, and polemical exaggerations. Nevertheless, they serve to remind us that there is a fundamental difference of perspective regarding the matter of Scripture and tradition. For our purposes this is not a difference between the followers of the sixteenth-century Reformers and the Roman pontiff, but between Constantinople and all the West. Khomiakov's overblown rhetoric also offers insight into Orthodoxy's unique view of Scripture, tradition, and the issue of authority in theological method.

9. Alexei S. Khomiakov, "The Church Is One," in W. J. Birkbeck, *Russia and the English Church* (London: S.P.C.K., 1953), 198; George Florovsky, "The Catholicity of the Church," in *Bible, Church, Tradition: An Eastern Orthodox View* (Belmont, Mass.: Nordland, 1972), 46.

10. John Meyendorff, *Living Tradition* (Crestwood, N.Y.: St. Vladimir's Seminary Press, 1978), 44; see also Alexander Schmemann, *Church, World, Mission* (Crestwood, N.Y.: St. Vladimir's Seminary Press, 1979), 186–87.

11. Meyendorff, *Living Tradition*, 27, 77. Meyendorff makes this exact point on pp. 20–21 and cites Irenaeus: "Where the Church is, there is the Spirit of God; and where the Spirit of God is, there is the Church, and every kind of grace; but the Spirit is Truth" (*Against Heresies* 3.24.1). See also John Meyendorff, "Light from the East? Doing Theology in an Eastern Orthodox Perspective," in John D. Woodbridge and Thomas E. McComiskey, eds., *Doing Theology in Today's World* (Grand Rapids: Zondervan, 1991), 346.

In this chapter we will explore the precise differences between, first, Catholicism and Orthodoxy and, second, Protestantism and Orthodoxy on the matter of Scripture and tradition. After that, we shall attempt a positive definition of Orthodoxy's position that Scripture and tradition are the means of the Spirit's witness in the life of the church.

Differences from the Western Positions

Tradition and Papal Primacy

We noted in chapter 2 some of the primary causes of the estrangement between Orthodoxy and Catholicism: liturgical differences, debate over the *filioque* addendum, the Photian Schism of the ninth century, the mutual anathemas in 1054, and the attack on Constantinople in 1204 by Catholic Crusaders. Important as all these were (and are), they pale in comparison with the more fundamental issue of ecclesiastical authority, which "emerges as the central question" that still divides the two bodies of Christians. The pneumatic understanding of an internal authority has made Orthodoxy "stubbornly resist" the papacy as the criterion of truth.[12] Succinctly put, the root of the division was and is a fundamental question: "What comes first, the institution guaranteeing the Truth, or Truth itself?"[13] Whatever similarities there are between Catholics and Orthodox regarding Scripture and tradition, such as the granting of equal respect to both sources as divine revelation and the central role of the church over Scripture as its necessary interpreter, Orthodoxy considers the issue of the papacy so weighty that it sees its relationship with Rome as discontinuous.

In the Catholic West, through a discernible historical development, the bishop of Rome came to be seen as "the final and ultimate criterion of true tradition."[14] Pope Leo the Great (440–61), who at the Council of Chalcedon had claimed a "fullness of power" reserved for popes alone, gave definitive shape to the exegetical argument from Matthew 16:18–19 that Christ conferred on the bishop of Rome a unique, supreme, and universal authority over all Christendom. In a letter written in 446 to Anastasius, bishop of Thessalonica, Leo insisted that while bishops enjoyed a "common dignity," they did not have a "uniform rank"; rather, "the care of the universal Church should converge toward Peter's one chair, and nothing anywhere should be separate from its head." At the First Vatican Council (1869–70), convened by Pope Pius IX, papal primacy and infalli-

12. Meyendorff, *Living Tradition*, 64, 76.
13. John Meyendorff, ed., *The Primacy of Peter in the Orthodox Church* (Crestwood, N.Y.: St. Vladimir's Seminary Press, 1992), 7.
14. Meyendorff, *Living Tradition*, 96.

bility were codified as doctrines of divine revelation. In matters of faith, morals, and jurisdiction, papal pronouncements were "in themselves, and not by virtue of the consensus of the Church, not subject to being changed." It was at this council that Pius made the claim, "I am tradition."[15] Although Vatican II (1962–65) softened the Catholic position somewhat, and gave rise to broader interpretations of the nature of the papacy and infallibility (see, e.g., the works of Hans Küng, Karl Rahner, Avery Dulles, Charles Curran, Edward Schillebeeckx, and Rosemary Ruether), it nevertheless affirmed that "the college of the body of bishops has no authority unless it is understood together with the Roman Pontiff. . . . The pope's power of primacy over all, both pastors and faithful, remains whole and intact."[16]

Orthodoxy has never rejected the primacy of Peter per se. One could even plot a clear historical "pattern of Eastern deference to Rome."[17] We have seen that in the iconoclastic controversy the East appealed to the Roman pontiff for support. In the ninth century Photius of all people affirmed Peter's preeminence, and even after the schism of 1054 major Orthodox writers like Gregory Palamas affirmed the Petrine priority.[18] The reason for this Eastern acceptance of Roman primacy rests in an important distinction. Orthodoxy has always granted Peter a primacy of honor or prestige in a personal sense, but not a primacy of power in any institutional sense. While rejecting the notion that Peter held a "primacy of power" (primatus potestatis), Orthodoxy has always acknowledged him as the "first among equals" (primus inter pares). A strategic turning point in Orthodoxy's attitude toward Peter came after the Latin Crusaders sacked Constantinople in 1204, for at that time Rome began to appoint its own bishops to churches in the East. Most egregious of all from the Orthodox perspective was Pope Innocent III's appointment of an Italian bishop, Thomas Morosini, as patriarch of Constantinople. "All of a sudden the East became more fully aware of an ecclesiological development which had taken place in the West and which it was much too late to stop."[19] Specific polemics against the papacy soon followed.

Acknowledging a personal prestige but not an institutional power for Peter, Orthodoxy vigorously insists upon the "ontological equality" not only of each bishop, but also of every church. The succession of the apos-

15. Robert Strimple, "The Relationship between Scripture and Tradition in Contemporary Roman Catholic Theology," Westminster Theological Journal 40 (Fall 1977): 29.

16. Lumen gentium 3.22 (cited by Meyendorff, Primacy of Peter, 8).

17. Jaroslav Pelikan, The Spirit of Eastern Christendom (600–1700) (Chicago: University of Chicago Press, 1974), 156.

18. Meyendorff, Primacy of Peter, 71–72, 83–90.

19. Ibid., 77.

tolic church passes not unilaterally through the bishop of Rome, but
through every church or the whole church, and through every Christian
who like Peter confesses Christ as the Son of God. Infallibility rests with
the church as a whole, the "pleroma" of all the clergy and people.[20] The
Eastern patriarchs stated this most clearly in an encyclical letter of 1848:
"infallibility resides solely in the ecumenicity of the Church bound
together by mutual love; . . . the unchangeableness of dogma as well as the
purity of rite [is] entrusted to the care not of one hierarchy but of *all the
people of the Church*, who are the body of Christ."[21] This conviction that
the whole people of God is the protector of apostolic tradition does not
imply any sort of congregationalism or ecclesiastical democracy, nor does
it mean that the hierarchy does not assume a special role as the mouth-
piece of the church. Rather, while all the people of God possess the truth,
bishops have the unique duty to teach and proclaim it.[22] The "collective
responsibility of the entire people of God for the preservation of the faith"
finds authoritative expression in a conciliarity and consensus rather than
in the juridical decisions of a single bishop.[23]

Rather than a unilateral or monarchial jurisdiction of a single bishop in
Rome, Orthodox ecclesiology maintains the idea of parallel jurisdiction
among all the churches, with a special honor accorded to the so-called
pentarchy, the five original patriarchal sees of Rome, Constantinople,
Jerusalem, Antioch, and Alexandria. Commenting on Matthew 16:18–
19, Theodore the Studite asks, "Who are the men to whom this order is
given? The apostles and their successors. And who are their successors? He
who occupies the throne of Rome, which is the first; he who occupies the
throne of Constantinople, which is the second; and after them those who
occupy the thrones of Alexandria, Antioch, and Jerusalem. This is the
pentarchic authority in the church; these have jurisdiction over divine
dogmas." Similarly, the sixth ecumenical council (Constantinople, 680–
81) "sent its dogmatic definition 'to the five patriarchal thrones.'"[24]

Orthodoxy rejects claims for papal primacy and infallibility for a number of reasons. Exegetically, the text of Matthew 16 came to be interpreted

20. John Karmiris, *A Synopsis of the Dogmatic Theology of the Orthodox Catholic Church* (Scranton, Pa.: Christian Orthodox Edition, 1973), 88–89, 93, and especially the important historical citations on pp. 98–99 n. 85; Meyendorff, *Living Tradition*, 66, 86; idem, *Pri-
macy of Peter*, 80–82; idem, *Catholicity*, 59; Khomiakov, "Church Is One," 94; Sergius
Bulgakov, "Of the Infallible Exterior Authority of the Church," in *The Orthodox Church*,
rev. ed. (Crestwood, N.Y.: St. Vladimir's Seminary Press, 1988), 54–86.
21. Cited by Khomiakov, "Western Confessions," 55 (emphasis added).
22. Florovsky, *Bible, Church, Tradition*, 53; Timothy Ware, *The Orthodox Church* (Baltimore: Penguin, 1964), 255.
23. Meyendorff, *Catholicity*, 96.
24. Cited by Pelikan, *Spirit*, 164–65.

as referring to Peter's confession rather than to a conferral of a unique ecclesiological status, so that, as Origen observed, every follower of Christ who makes the same good confession becomes a Peter. Historically, it became clear that the many and various appeals to fathers as renowned as Tertullian, Cyprian, Origen, Chrysostom, and the Cappadocians could establish a strong case against any claims for Petrine primacy.[25] Of special import were the canons of the ecumenical councils. Canon 6 of the Council of Nicea indicated that the bishop of Rome was considered equal to the other bishops, and that municipal bishops were to exercise control over their own jurisdictions and so "preserve their privileges." That is, a bishop's primacy was construed in a limited, personal, and geographically regional sense rather than in any universal manner. More important still was Canon 28 of Chalcedon, now considered axiomatic by Orthodox theologians. It clearly enunciated the idea of parallel jurisdiction. Rome had been granted privileges because of its status as the imperial city, and not for any theological reasons. As the New Rome, Constantinople was granted "equal privileges" and "equal rank in ecclesiastical matters" on the same basis.[26]

It is clear, then, that while Protestants might be understandably inclined to link Orthodoxy and Catholicism together on the matter of Scripture and tradition, to do so would be historically and theologically inaccurate. Orthodoxy still considers the schism of 1054 between the East and the West as "the deepest and most fundamental root of later schisms."[27] Moreover, it sees the primary cause of this estrangement as differing conceptions of ecclesiology and theological authority. The subsequent schism between Rome and the Reformers is but a later consequence of this initial division.

Tradition and Sola Scriptura

Though Protestantism's linkage of Orthodoxy and Catholicism on the matter of Scripture and tradition is inaccurate, it is not inaccurate to say that Catholicism and Orthodoxy view the sixteenth-century Reformation and its watchword of *sola scriptura* from a similar negative vantage point. What Heiko Oberman says about Rome's position could be said with equal vigor about the Orthodox position:

25. On Orthodox exegesis of the New Testament and treatment of the early Christian literature on Peter see the two fine essays by Nicholas Koulomzine, "Peter's Place in the Primitive Church," and Veselin Kesich, "Peter's Primacy in the New Testament and the Early Tradition," in Meyendorff, *Primacy of Peter*, 11–34, 35–64.

26. Meyendorff, *Primacy of Peter*, 82; idem, "One Bishop in One City," and "The Council of 381 and the Primacy of Constantinople," in *Catholicity*, 111–42.

27. Meyendorff, *Catholicity*, 79; idem, *Primacy of Peter*, 7.

The sixteenth century witnesses bitter polemics concerning the source and norm of the Church's knowledge of God's revelation. Traditionally this is described as the clash of the *sola scriptura*–principle with the Scripture *and* tradition–principle. Ironically enough, both groups . . . accused each other of undermining the purity and authority of the Word of God. The Reformers pointed to the "ecclesiastical" or "human traditions" as accretions and distortions of the Gospel preserved in Holy Scripture. Spokesmen for the Counter-Reformation accused the Reformers of arbitrary interpretation of Scripture and of a break with the tradition of the Church. In both cases reliance on human authority [was] said to interfere with the rule of obedience to Holy Scripture.[28]

To this general historiography we must add several qualifiers, keeping in mind that the issue between Protestants and Orthodoxy is not a matter of selecting either Scripture or tradition, that is, choosing one and rejecting the other; rather, the issue is two different conceptions of tradition. We can better understand the difference by examining two related aspects of the *sola scriptura* principle.

First, the principle of *sola scriptura* contrasts and differentiates between the normative value of Scripture and tradition, placing the former squarely above and over the latter. It denies that Scripture and tradition are coequal norms for theology. For the Reformers the Bible was the divine, primary, absolute norm of God's revelation, whereas tradition, valuable as it might be, was human, secondary, and relative. From their perspective this truth had been lost, so much so that the gospel had been obscured. Thus Martin Luther complained, "Our opponents skipped faith altogether and taught human traditions and works not commanded by God but invented by them without and against the Word of God; these they have not only put on a par with the Word of God but have raised far above it."[29] Given the historical context, it is easy to understand the Reformers' insistent distinction between Scripture and tradition. Luther would write, "What else do I contend for but to bring everyone to an understanding of the *difference* between the divine Scripture and human teaching or custom, so that a Christian may not take the one for the other and exchange gold for straw, silver for stubble, wood for precious stones?"[30] As an "eloquent symbol and seal" of the Reformers' refusal to subordinate Scripture to tradition, we might recall Luther's burning of the books of canon law at the Elster Gate of Wittenberg on December 10, 1520.[31]

28. Oberman, "Quo Vadis?" 226.

29. Martin Luther, "Lectures on Galatians," in *Luther's Works*, 56 vols. (St. Louis: Concordia, 1958–74), 26:52 (cited by Wells, "Tradition," 50).

30. Martin Luther, "Answer to the Super Christian, Super Spiritual, and Super Learned Book of Goat Emser," in *Works of Martin Luther*, 6 vols. (Philadelphia: Muhlenberg, 1915–32), 3:372 (cited by Alan F. Johnson and Robert E. Webber, *What Christians Believe* [Grand Rapids: Zondervan, 1989], 44 [emphasis added]).

31. Oberman, "Quo Vadis?" 242.

This does not mean that the Reformers categorically rejected tradition, or even disparaged it outright, as is sometimes suggested. It is clear that they even saw themselves as restoring the church to fidelity to the patristic consensus. A reading of John Calvin's *Institutes*, for example, shows his indebtedness to the church fathers. Neither were the Reformers unaware of the dangers of individualistic and private interpretation of Scripture; indeed, they recognized the importance of the church context for the life of faith.[32] What they objected to was the church's elevation of tradition to the status of Scripture, and its arrogation to place itself above Scripture as its mediator. Thus Calvin would write about the "tyranny of human tradition which is haughtily thrust upon us under the title of the Church."[33]

Although it is possible to find Orthodox statements affirming the unique authority of Scripture (see p. 109) as well as occasional acknowledgments of the convergence of the Reformers with the patristic period, it is the Orthodox view that "the Christian faith and experience can in no way be compatible with the notion of *Scriptura sola*" and the explicit rejection of all authority except Scripture.[34] The Bible is not a thing-in-itself that can be isolated or separated from the context of the church and tradition. The mistake of the Reformers, from the Orthodox perspective, is that they divided and separated what is an organic whole, creating an artificial antagonism or what George Tavard calls an "irreconcilable cleavage" between Scripture and tradition.[35] Instead of isolating Scripture as a unique source of revelation and elevating it over and above tradition, Orthodoxy tends to affirm one source for revelation, holy tradition, that comes to us in two forms—written and unwritten: "Scripture and Tradition . . . are equally valid, possess equal dogmatic authority, and are equal in value as sources of dogmatic truth. . . . [This] conception lessens the validity and value of the Holy Scriptures as the primary source of Christian dogma."[36] Thus, while the principle of *sola scriptura* places Scripture above tradition, Orthodoxy tends to see them as two coequal forms of one organic whole.

32. Oberman, "Quo Vadis?" 243, 249; Wells, "Tradition." Calvin, *Institutes*, 4.1.4, quotes the famous words of Cyprian that there is no salvation outside the church. See also Brown, "'Tradition' as a Problem," 207–10.

33. Calvin, *Institutes*, 4.19.18 (cited by Wells, "Tradition," 57).

34. Meyendorff, "Light from the East," 341; idem, *Catholicity*, 49–50, 75, 94.

35. Any number of Orthodox writers make this point: Bulgakov, *Orthodox Church*, 11–12, 24; Thomas Hopko, "The Bible in the Orthodox Church," in *All the Fulness of God: Essays on Orthodoxy, Ecumenism and Modern Society* (Crestwood, N.Y.: St. Vladimir's Seminary Press, 1982), 49; Ware, *Orthodox Church*, 214–15; Meyendorff, *Catholicity*, 94–95; Lazarus Moore, *Sacred Tradition in the Orthodox Church* (Minneapolis: Light and Life, 1984), 5–8; George Tavard in Brown, "'Tradition' as a Problem," 200.

36. Karmiris, *Synopsis*, 5–7.

Secondly, the principle of *sola scriptura* also implies a hermeneutical distinction between Scripture and the church: in the matter of interpreting Scripture, Scripture is over and above the church. The Reformers insisted that God speaks to the reader of the Bible in a direct manner rather than in an indirect manner that is mediated through the church. Ulrich Zwingli makes this exact point when he writes that "all human traditions, authority of Councils, Fathers and papacy, are as nothing before the all-competent self-authenticating authority of the Scriptures. The Bible has no need to be confirmed by the authority of the Church; the Word of God speaks directly from the Scripture to the individual heart and mind."[37] Just as the Reformers placed Scripture over tradition as the primary norm, they likewise placed the Scriptures over the church as the final adjudicator of all theological matters. It was the Word of God that gave birth to the church, Calvin insisted, and not vice versa.

For the Reformers Scripture was both self-authenticating (*autopistos*) and self-interpreting (*Scripturam ex Scriptura explicandam esse*—Scripture is to be explained by Scripture), by which they meant that through the internal testimony of the Holy Spirit, and through what the Westminster Confession calls the "due use of ordinary means," in and of itself Scripture is both trustworthy and understandable. This is why William Tyndale would argue that, given a vernacular translation of the Scriptures, even a ploughboy could have a sufficient if not perfect understanding of God's Word. No external mediator, such as the teaching magisterium of the church or tradition, is needed to certify Scripture. The Reformers believed that "Scripture can and does interpret itself to the faithful from within— Scripture is its own interpreter, *Scriptura sui ipsius interpres*, as Luther puts it—so that not only does it not need Popes or Councils to tell us, as from God, what it means; it can actually challenge Papal and conciliar pronouncements, convince them of being ungodly and untrue, and require the faithful to part company with them. . . . As Scripture was the only *source* from which sinners might gain true knowledge of God and godliness, so Scripture was the only *judge* of what the church had in each age ventured to say in her Lord's name."[38]

It is precisely this view of the self-sufficiency of Scripture, elevated above the church, that Orthodoxy considers to be what Florovsky calls "the sin of the Reformation," the consequences of which are arbitrary, subjective, and individualistic interpretations of the gospel. By con-

37. Ulrich Zwingli, *On the Clarity and Certainty of the Word of God* (1522) (cited by Jordan Bajis, *Common Ground: An Introduction to Eastern Christianity for the American Christian* [Minneapolis: Light and Life, 1991], 38).

38. J. I. Packer, "'Sola Scriptura' in History and Today," in John Warwick Montgomery, ed., *God's Inerrant Word* (Minneapolis: Bethany Fellowship, 1975), 44–45.

trast, Orthodoxy believes that "the Church . . . stands mystically first and is fuller than Scripture."[39] The church in its fullness, as represented by the councils and not by any single hierarch, is the indispensable interpreter of Scripture. In this view Scripture does not stand over the church but within the church, and in that sense its authority is derivative rather than independent and direct. By itself and without the church the Bible would not be understood, or would be liable to great misunderstanding, and thus converts to Orthodoxy pledge that they will "accept and understand Holy Scripture in accordance with the interpretation which was and is held by the Holy Orthodox Catholic Church of the East, our Mother."[40]

Authority in Orthodoxy

The Internal Norm

On the matter of theological authority, Scripture, and tradition, then, Orthodoxy is careful to distinguish itself from both Catholic ideas about papal primacy and Protestant insistence upon the principle of *sola scriptura*. What, then, are the criteria of theological authority in Orthodoxy? The answer is best given in both a negative and positive way.[41]

Negatively, we might say that Orthodoxy does not acknowledge any formal criteria of theological truth that are expressed in an extrinsic, juridical, institutional, or dogmatic form. Gustav Aulen rightly observes that "the Eastern Church will not commit supreme authority to any document, governmental office, councils, or to the Pope, or to any agency through which doctrinal authority would become legally defined."[42] Unlike Catholicism, it has no formal collection of canon law, and even its so-called symbolic books are not formally binding.[43] For Westerners, this "absence of formal criteria or authorities," Meyendorff admits, is "puzzling, . . . nebulous, . . . romantic, . . . unrealistic," apparently "subjectivistic," and even an "embarrassment" of sorts. Nevertheless, "the Orthodox East has never been obsessed with a search for objective, clear, and formally definable criteria of truth, such as either the papal authority

39. Florovsky, *Bible, Church, Tradition*, 48.

40. Ware, *Orthodox Church*, 208–9; see also Bulgakov, *Orthodox Church*, 13–14; Hopko, "Bible in the Orthodox Church," 49–50; and Karmiris, *Synopsis*, 6.

41. Meyendorff, *Catholicity*, 99–101.

42. Gustav Aulen, *Reformation and Catholicity* (Philadelphia: Muhlenberg, 1961), 11–12 (cited by Bajis, *Common Ground*, 113).

43. Bulgakov, *Orthodox Church*, 35; Ware, *Orthodox Church*, 211–12; Karmiris, *Synopsis*, 8–9; Meyendorff, *Living Tradition*, 102; idem, *Byzantine Theology: Historical Trends and Doctrinal Themes* (New York: Fordham University Press, 1974), 79–80.

or the Reformed notion of *sola scriptura*."[44] Meyendorff takes pains to clarify this extremely important point: "This lack in Orthodox ecclesiology of a clearly defined, precise, and permanent criterion of Truth besides God Himself, Christ and the Holy Spirit, is certainly one of the major contrasts between Orthodoxy and all classical Western ecclesiologies. In the West the gradually developed theory of papal infallibility was opposed, after the collapse of the conciliar movement, by the Protestant affirmation of *sola scriptura*. The entire Western ecclesiological problem since the sixteenth century turned around this opposition of two *criteria*, two references of doctrinal *security*, while in Orthodoxy no need for, or necessity of, such a security was ever felt for the simple reason that the living Truth is its own criterion."[45] This, of course, is the exact point made by Khomiakov, that in Orthodoxy the criterion of truth is not external or dogmatic, a speaking *to* the church, but internal and pneumatic, a living Lord *within* the church.

Positively, we might say that the only ultimate theological criterion to which Orthodoxy appeals is the living presence of God himself, who safeguards the church and promises through his Spirit to lead us and guide us into all truth (John 14:25–26; 16:13). This was the pattern established by the original church in council at Jerusalem, which based its decisions on the charismatic criterion: "It seemed good to the Holy Spirit and to us" (Acts 15:28). Thus the Orthodox appeal to Irenaeus: "Where the Church is, there is the Spirit of God; and where the Spirit of God is, there is the Church, and every kind of grace; but the Spirit is Truth."[46]

Ironically, while many people accuse Orthodoxy of a dead, static repetition of ancient tradition and liturgical ritual, a historicism of sorts, it eschews such a notion of tradition in favor of the dynamic, living presence of God who continually vivifies the church. As Florovsky notes, "reference to tradition is not historical inquiry. Tradition is not limited to Church archaeology. . . . Tradition is the witness of the Spirit . . . the constant abiding of the Spirit and not only the memory of words. Tradition is a *charismatic*, not a historical, principle."[47] Tradition is the life of the Spirit in the church, who alone is the ultimate criterion of

44. Meyendorff, *Orthodox Church*, 99–101; see also 102–3; and idem, "Light from the East," 346.

45. Meyendorff, *Living Tradition*, 20.

46. Irenaeus *Against Heresies* 3.24.

47. Florovsky, *Bible, Church, Tradition*, 46–47. Florovsky also states that the teaching authority of the church is not so much "canonical" as it is "charismatic, grounded in the assistance of the Spirit" (pp. 97, 103), and that "ultimately, tradition is a continuity of the abiding presence of the Holy Spirit in the Church, a continuity of Divine Guidance and Illumination" (p. 106).

truth.[48] This, Thomas Hopko insists, is the unanimous position of the Orthodox church, both ancient and modern: "For each of the authors directly studied on this point, and there are about twenty to whom concrete reference could be made here, the Holy Spirit alone remains the ultimate criterion of truth for Christians even though other eternal institutions in the Church, such as [the tradition of the church, including Holy Scripture;] the Councils; and the Church itself are named as the 'highest' and 'supreme' authorities providing formal authorities in the Church. . . . The Church itself taken as a whole cannot and must not remain 'external' to the believer, and indeed not the theologian!"[49] It remains for us to see by what means the witness of the Spirit expresses itself in the life of the church. From this ultimate, internal norm of the Spirit, we now turn to the external, penultimate forms of the Spirit's witness.

The Primacy of Holy Scripture

In general we can say that for Orthodoxy the Spirit speaks to the church through the gospel tradition (*paradosis*), this tradition being defined as a living and authentic continuity with the apostolic past. "The Apostolic Tradition is the gospel, the word and event of salvation, entrusted by Jesus to His disciples who received the authority to proclaim it to the world."[50] Paul transmitted this *paradosis* to the Corinthians (1 Cor. 11:2, 23; 15:3), and referred to it on three occasions as an entrusted deposit which the church must guard (1 Tim. 6:20; 2 Tim. 1:12, 14). Whatever authority or criteria of truth the church possesses resides in its fidelity to this original apostolic *paradosis*. In a comprehensive sense the apostolic tradition finds expression in any number of external forms, all of which are means used by the indwelling Spirit. Timothy Ware, for example, lists seven: Scripture, the seven ecumenical councils, later councils and their dogmatic statements (Orthodoxy's so-called symbolic books), the Fathers, liturgy, canon law, and icons. These external forms constitute an organic whole, and it is only for discussion's sake that we treat them separately. For convenience we can think of them as tradition that is both written (Scripture) and unwritten (extracanonical sources) or, to use a common distinction, written Scripture and oral tradition.

---

48. Vladimir Lossky, *In the Image and Likeness of God* (Crestwood, N.Y.: St. Vladimir's Seminary Press, 1974), 152, 159–60; Emmanuel Clapsis, "Scripture, Tradition, and Authority: Conceptions of Orthodoxy" (Paper given at the Society for the Study of Eastern Orthodoxy and Evangelicalism, Wheaton, Ill., Sept. 26,'1992), 2.

49. Thomas Hopko, "Criteria of Truth in Orthodox Theology," *St. Vladimir's Seminary Quarterly* 15.3 (1971): 123.

50. Clapsis, "Scripture, Tradition, and Authority," 1.

Not all the external forms of the Spirit's witness are of the same nature or value. Tradition is uniquely expressed in our present canon of written Scripture.[51] Although Orthodoxy refuses to consider Scripture apart from the broader context of other forms of tradition, and does not limit authoritative tradition to the biblical canon, it nevertheless accords a unique status to the Bible. Liturgically, this can be seen not merely in Orthodoxy's intense veneration of Holy Scripture (the elevating, incensing, and kissing of the Bible, and its being given the primary place of honor in various processions), but especially in the rich biblical content of the liturgy itself.[52] Doctrinally, and contrary to a common Protestant misunderstanding, Orthodoxy does not endorse a "doctrine of homogenized and unstratified authority," but instead "affirms unequivocally the primary position of Scripture."[53] Scripture is the "supreme expression" of God's revelation.[54] It holds a "place apart" from other forms of tradition, and its inclusion with all other forms of tradition in no way compromises its "originality and its value as the Word of God; the Word of God is above all other sources of faith, especially of all tradition in all its forms." We can even say that Scripture and tradition are "unequal in value" since Scripture alone "has first place."[55] Tradition can never contradict Scripture, and in this sense Scripture is the "main written authority" by which "everything in the church is judged."[56] Scripture is primary; it has no substitute. Nothing can be added to it, and thus even the ancient fathers like Vincent of Lérins and Basil, who recognized an essential role for oral tradition, acknowledged that the Bible was the perfect, self-sufficient, ultimate, and supreme criterion of doctrine.[57] "Complete in itself," Scripture "contains the entirety of the apostolic witness. . . . It is important to note in this connection that whatever value is attributed to Tradition and to the notion of

51. While the Councils of Jassy (1642) and Jerusalem (1672) said that the apocryphal books were "genuine parts of Scripture," Orthodox theologians, though acknowledging their importance more than do Protestants, generally place them on a "lower footing" than the rest of the Old Testament (Ware, *Orthodox Church*, 208–9; see also Bulgakov, *Orthodox Church*, 20; Karmiris, *Synopsis*, 6; Meyendorff, "Light from the East," 341; Bajis, *Common Ground*, 93 n. 9).

52. Meyendorff, *Living Tradition*, 13–14; Clapsis, "Scripture, Tradition, and Authority," 13.

53. Jaroslav Pelikan, *Imago Dei: The Byzantine Apologia for Icons* (Princeton: Princeton University Press, 1990), 45–46; idem, *Spirit*, 16.

54. Ware, *Orthodox Church*, 207.

55. Bulgakov, *Orthodox Church*, 11, 18.

56. Hopko, "Bible in the Orthodox Church," 49–50. John Breck makes this exact point in his book *The Power of the Word* (Crestwood, N.Y.: St. Vladimir's Seminary Press, 1986), 105, as does Gerasimos Papadopoulos, "The Revelatory Character of the New Testament and Holy Tradition in the Orthodox Church," in A. J. Philippou, ed., *The Orthodox Ethos* (Oxford: Holywell, 1964), 109.

57. Florovsky, *Bible, Church, Tradition*, 28, 74–75, 79, 89.

the Church's continuity in the Truth and her infallibility, the Christian Church never added its own doctrinal definitions to Scripture."[58]

The Necessity of Holy Tradition

While the apostolic deposit finds unique articulation in the written tradition of canonical Scripture, it is not confined or limited to the biblical text, but finds fuller expression in extracanonical tradition. Written Scripture is primary but not exclusive; the traditions of the councils and the Fathers are indispensable for a number of reasons.

First, both the church itself and the apostolic kerygma existed for nearly three centuries before the ecumenical councils and the establishment of the scriptural canon. In the Acts of the Apostles the precanonical "word of God" that the apostles preached about Jesus continues to grow and flourish, and even seems to be equated with the church itself (Acts 12:24; 19:20).[59] We also know that Jesus did many things that were never written down (John 20:30–31; 21:25), and that Paul urged the early Christians to accept both the written and unwritten apostolic *paradosis* that he passed on to them (2 Thess. 2:15; 1 Cor. 11:2). The oral message preached to the Thessalonians was rightly received by them as "the word of God" (1 Thess. 2:13; cf. Col. 1:25 and 3:16). Oral tradition is thus a necessary complement or supplement to written Scripture, for the gospel kerygma is not exactly contiguous with the canon of Scripture.

Second, Orthodoxy would insist that nobody operates with a clean slate, a *tabula rasa*, and, accordingly, noncanonical traditions are a practical and hermeneutical inevitability. Although someone might claim to interpret the Scriptures *de novo* in principle, in practice we all read the text not only with theological or denominational presuppositions, but also through the space-time prisms of our individual cultures and experiences. Furthermore, even if a neutral reading were possible, it would hardly be desirable because it would likely lead to arbitrary and errant understandings of the text.[60] Thus it becomes all the more important to locate oneself within the apostolic oral tradition that serves as a hermeneutical context for written Scripture.

Third, liturgical precedent also reveals the importance of noncanonical tradition. We saw in the last chapter that when defending the use of icons, both John of Damascus and Theodore the Studite based their cases squarely on the importance of extrabiblical liturgical tradition. According to Orthodoxy, there are many similar aspects of the life and liturgy of the

58. Meyendorff, *Living Tradition*, 14–16; Calian, *Theology without Boundaries*, 5.
59. Alexander Schmemann, *The Historical Road of Eastern Orthodoxy* (Crestwood, N.Y.: St. Vladimir's Seminary Press, 1977), 42.
60. See Khomiakov, "Western Confessions," 42–43, on this exact point.

church that, while not explicitly contained in or demanded by Scripture, are of undisputed significance to believers.

Pertinent here is a celebrated passage from Basil's *On the Holy Spirit*. In defending the deity of the Holy Spirit, Basil appealed to the fact that widely used doxologies of the church confessed, "Glory to the Father and to the Son *with* the Spirit." While the preposition *with* was not found in Scripture, it had all the weight of liturgical precedent, which for Basil was of enormous significance: "Concerning the teachings of the Church, we have received some from written sources, while others have been given to us secretly, through apostolic tradition. Both sources have equal force in true religion. No one would deny either source—no one, at any rate, who is even slightly familiar with the ordinances of the Church. If we attacked unwritten customs, claiming them to be of little importance, we would fatally mutilate the Gospel, no matter what our intentions—or rather, we would reduce the Gospel teachings to bare words."[61] Basil goes on to list some of the uncontested ancient liturgical customs of the church: making the sign of the cross, praying toward the East, eucharistic invocations, certain baptismal practices, and the renunciation of Satan and his angels. For Basil, not only are certain liturgical traditions of great importance, "they are indispensable for the preservation of right faith."[62]

Tertullian had made the same point, in a similar manner, more than a century earlier. Citing important liturgical practices such as the renunciation of the devil at baptism, threefold immersion, celebration of the Eucharist early in the morning and only by a bishop, prayers for the dead at the Eucharist, celebration of the Eucharist on the anniversary of the deaths of martyrs, abstinence from fasting and from praying in a kneeling position on Sundays, prevention of any part of the bread and wine from falling onto the ground, and other such practices, Tertullian remarks: "If you demand a biblical rule for these observances and others of the same sort, you will find none written. Tradition will be alleged to you as the authority and custom to support them and faith to practice them. You yourself will either see the reason which supports the tradition and the custom and the faith, or you will learn it from someone who will have seen it. Meanwhile you will believe it to be not lacking in authority to which obedience should be owed."[63] In short, in Basil and Tertullian we see a practical example in which the *lex orandi* defines the *lex credendi*. Unless we wish to denude and mutilate the apostolic tradition, according to Basil and Tertullian, we will accept the authority of liturgical precedent, even though it is not contained in Scripture alone.

61. Basil *On the Holy Spirit* 27.66.

62. Florovsky, *Bible, Church, Tradition*, 87.

63. Tertullian *De Corona* 4.1. Origen makes the same point in his *Homilies on Numbers* 5.1.

Fourth, the necessity of the extrabiblical tradition finds broad-based support in the theological methodologies of any number of early fathers, a fact which is of no small significance for Orthodoxy. Tertullian invoked the "rule of faith" and Irenaeus the "canon of truth" against the heretics of their day. Athanasius, the champion of Nicene orthodoxy, had to defend the council against the Arian charge that its conclusions (specifically the term *homoousios*) were innovations. He was convinced that though they were not contained in Scripture, they were nevertheless thoroughly apostolic. In contending against the Arians, who wished to limit the argument to Scripture alone, Athanasius appealed to the larger "scope" (*skopos*) or "rule" (*kanon*) of faith, the tradition and teaching of the catholic church.[64] The stalwart defender of orthodoxy, Epiphanius, noted that some elements of the apostolic faith were "delivered to us through the Scriptures, the others through the Tradition delivered to us by the Holy Apostles." Chrysostom, commenting on 2 Thessalonians 2:15, pointed out that the apostles "did not deliver all things by epistle, but many things also unwritten, and in like manner both the one and the other worthy of credit. Therefore let us think the Tradition of the Church also worthy of credit. It is a tradition; seek no farther."[65] Augustine confessed that "I should not have believed the Gospel, if the authority of the Catholic Church had not moved me."[66] And so, according to Orthodoxy, when we appeal to the apostolic traditions outside of *sola scriptura*, we stand on the firm ground of early patristic consensus and theological method.

Of all the justifications for invoking the extrabiblical apostolic tradition, none is more important for Orthodoxy than the argument that it is a hermeneutical necessity. Hilary of Poitiers noted that "Scripture is not in the reading but in the understanding," a sentiment repeated by Jerome, who rebuked certain heretics because, not having the help of the Holy Spirit, they turned the divine gospel into a human word: "We do not think that [the] Gospel consists of the words of Scripture but in its meaning. . . . In this case Scripture is really useful for the hearers when it is not spoken without Christ, nor is presented without the Fathers, and those who are preaching do not introduce it without the Holy Spirit."[67] The problem of

64. Florovsky, *Bible, Church, Tradition*, 75–83; Clapsis, "Scripture, Tradition, and Authority," 14–21.

65. Epiphanius *Contra Heresies* 61.6; Chrysostom *Homilies on II Thessalonians* 4 (cited by Karmiris, *Synopsis*, 10–11).

66. Augustine *Contra epistolam Manichaei quam vocant Fundamenti* 6 (cited by Oberman, "Quo Vadis?" 235, who compares this text with the text just cited from Basil's *On the Holy Spirit* 27.66). See also Florovsky, *Bible, Church, Tradition*, 73, 91–92.

67. Hilary *Ad Constantium Augustum* 2.9; Jerome *Galatians* 1.1.2 (cited by Florovsky, *Bible, Church, Tradition*, 75, 91).

misunderstanding as a result of private interpreting and twisting of the Scriptures exposes the inadequacy of reading the Bible alone and confirms the hermeneutical necessity of its larger patristic context. This is precisely the problem with heretics, as George Prestige so aptly observed: "Heretics showed that they could be as painstaking in their use of Scripture as the saints. The fact soon became obvious to any intelligent thinker that the principle of 'the Bible and the Bible only' provides no automatically secure basis for a religion that is to be genuinely Christian."[68] Irenaeus and Vincent of Lérins made this point in special ways.

Irenaeus employed two striking analogies. He compared heretics' treatment of Scripture to people who take a beautifully crafted mosaic of a king, rearrange the pieces to depict a dog or a fox, and then have the audacity to claim that their rearrangement is the authentic mosaic because it contains the original materials. Heretics are also like people who arbitrarily rearrange the poetry of Homer so that, while the verses themselves are original, the meaning has been grossly distorted. In other words, it is one thing to have at one's disposal the original material of Scripture, and quite another to use it properly. Only by adhering to the apostolic tradition and the rule of truth will we avoid the hermeneutical distortions of heretics and not mistake foxes for kings or paltry paraphrases for the real Word.[69]

When searching for a means to distinguish the true apostolic faith from heresy, Vincent of Lérins noted that while Scripture is "for all things complete and more than sufficient," even heretics appeal to Scripture. It seems, Vincent observed, that "owing to the depth of Holy Scripture, all do not accept it with one and the same sense, but one understands its words in one way, another in another; so that it seems to be capable of as many interpretations as there are interpreters." To "detect the frauds and avoid the snares of heretics as they rise, and to continue sound and complete in the catholic faith," we need the authority of tradition, specifically, "that which has been believed everywhere, always, by all."[70] This ecumenicity of time and space serves as a hermeneutical prism so that, in the words of Hilary and Jerome, we do not merely read the text but understand it rightly. For Vincent, as Florovsky notes, "Tradition was, in fact, the authentic interpretation of Scripture. And in this sense it was coextensive with Scripture. Tradition was actually 'Scripture rightly understood.' And Scripture for St. Vincent was the only, primary, and ultimate *canon* of Christian truth."[71]

68. George L. Prestige, *Fathers and Heretics* (London: S.P.C.K., 1984), 14–15.

69. Irenaeus *Against Heresies* 1.8.1; 1.9.4.

70. Vincent of Lérins *Commonitorium* 2.

71. Florovsky, *Bible, Church, Tradition*, 75; see also 51, 79; and Bulgakov, *Orthodox Church*, 29.

The Forms of Holy Tradition

Once the necessity of holy tradition as the fuller context of Holy Scripture has been established, a rather obvious problem emerges: not all tradition is good, as both Christ himself and the apostle Paul warned (Matt. 15:3–7; Mark 7:1–13; Col. 2:8). Not all of the many human traditions qualify as the singular holy tradition. Not all traditions have equal value or worth, and some traditions are simply false. Appealing to majority opinion can be problematic, since heresy sometimes flourishes while truth resides in the minority position. Merely appealing to antiquity is not enough since, as Cyprian so well put it, "antiquity without truth is age-old error."[72] Some councils were heretical, like the Robber Council of Ephesus in 449 that exonerated Eutyches. Invoking the Fathers could prove troublesome, as Peter Abelard showed in his Sic et non (c. 1120), a list of 158 topics on which there were variances among the Fathers. The condemnation of Pope Honorius I for the heresy of monothelitism at the Council of Constantinople in 680 demonstrated that even the highest of church authorities might err. All of these points Orthodoxy acknowledges full well, even as they apply not only to the church at large, but also to its own failures to distinguish between the wheat of holy tradition and the chaff of traditions.[73]

We must, in short, be selective, critical, and discriminating when we invoke tradition, testing it to determine if it truly comes from God (1 John 4:1). Recognizing that not all tradition is of equal value or worth, Orthodoxy acknowledges a hierarchy or stratification of the forms of tradition: some are primary and others secondary. Two forms of noncanonical tradition, however, deserve special mention. Having been taught by the Holy Scriptures, we must, according to Maximus the Confessor, also be taught by "the holy teachers and councils," for these possess a status second only to the written Word.[74]

Of all the external forms of tradition, only the first seven ecumenical councils, to which all Orthodox Christians subject themselves, are acknowledged as infallible.[75] Councils, after all, had scriptural precedent (Acts 15). These seven councils, then, serve as unfailing guides in discerning the true and holy tradition, whereas later and local councils may or may not err. So great was the authority of the seven councils that it

72. Cyprian Epistles 74.9 (cited by Florovsky, Bible, Church, Tradition, 99; see also the similar texts by Tertullian and Augustine cited by Florovsky).

73. Ware, Orthodox Church, 205; Lossky, "Tradition and Traditions," in Image and Likeness, 141–68; Meyendorff, Living Tradition, 21–26; Florovsky, Bible, Church, Tradition, 96–100; Karmiris, Synopsis, 7–9; Bajis, Common Ground, 61–62.

74. Maximus the Confessor Relation about the Motion 9 (cited by Pelikan, Spirit, 18).

75. Ware, Orthodox Church, 210; Karmiris, Synopsis, 4–7.

became standard and, shall we say, obligatory theological method to invoke their authority when stating one's theological position. Thus, during the iconoclastic controversy both the Iconoclastic Council of 754 and the iconodule Patriarch Nicephorus of Constantinople, who rejected the council, prefaced their arguments by invoking the "seven holy and ecumenical councils." As Jaroslav Pelikan notes, "so pervasive was this method and so thorough its documentation that if the creeds and doctrinal decrees of the first five councils had been lost, it would be possible to recover their substance from the writings of Sophronius or of Maximus or of their successors."[76]

Secondly, as Jerome warned, we must never approach the Scriptures without the Fathers. Nicodemos of Athos speaks for the entire Orthodox tradition when he writes, "Having read Holy Scripture very carefully, you should also read the holy Fathers who interpret the Scriptures. You will receive no less delight from reading the Fathers than you do from the Scriptures."[77] Yet even the Fathers must be invoked selectively, although Orthodoxy does have a special reverence for the writers of the first four centuries. Most importantly, it was in fact not the opinion of any single father that was to be invoked, but the *consensus patrum*, the opinion of them all.

Maximus challenged his opponents to prove their positions "on the basis of the determinations of the fathers," and if that were impossible, "then let them leave these opinions behind and join us in conforming to what has been reverently determined by the divinely inspired fathers of the catholic church and the five ecumenical councils." Devising "new formulas" or "making up terms according to our own ideas" is presumptuous, deranged, and heretical. "But what has been understood and stated by the saints, that we reverently adduce as our authority."[78]

The Spirit of Truth

Ironically, we have come full circle and, by Orthodoxy's own confession, perhaps even through a vicious circle. Any appeal to tradition, be it Scripture, a council, a father, liturgy, or a Vincentian canon of sorts, is itself insufficient. We would be accepting a theological teaching as true on the basis of an external criterion, but no external criterion can guarantee truth. In fact, Orthodoxy would not even maintain that an ecumenical council guarantees truth, for ecumenical councils are always regarded as

---

76. Pelikan, *Spirit*, 25.
77. Nicodemos of Athos, *Handbook of Spiritual Counsel* (New York: Paulist, 1989), 190. See also pp. 186–88 on the fact that the Scriptures can never err.
78. Maximus the Confessor *Theological and Polemical Opuscula* 9, 19 (cited by Pelikan, *Spirit*, 20).

"charismatic events" rather than as "canonical institutions."[79] It is only and finally the internal witness of the promised Holy Spirit that keeps the church in truth: "Decisive value resides in *inner* catholicity, not in empirical universality. The opinions of the Fathers [or of the councils] are accepted, not as a formal subjection to outward authority, but because of the inner evidence of their catholic truth."[80] While the infallible councils take priority over the fallible Fathers, and the councils reciprocally affirmed that they were merely "following the holy Fathers" in their decisions, in the end the only theological authority for Orthodoxy is a "*charismatic* authority, grounded in the assistance of the Holy Spirit: 'it seemed good to us and to the Holy Spirit.'"[81] Put another way, "faithfulness to Tradition is . . . a participation in Pentecost, and Tradition represents a fulfilment of Pentecost."[82]

79. Florovsky, *Bible, Church, Tradition*, 96–97.
80. Ibid., 52–53.
81. Ibid., 103.
82. George Florovsky, *Creation and Redemption* (Belmont, Mass.: Nordland, 1976), 194.

The Deification of Humanity
Theosis

If the Word is made man, it is that men might become gods.

—Irenaeus

From the Holy Spirit there is the likeness of God, and the highest of all things to be desired, to become God.

—Basil the Great

God became man so that men might become gods.

—Athanasius

[God] has given us his very great and precious promises, so that through them you may participate in the divine nature.

—2 Peter 1:4

For the shepherd David the question came in the middle of the night watch. Alone in the quiet darkness on a Palestinian hillside, he pondered the expansive heavens, the sparkling stars, and the soft moonlight, and, in response, his own feelings of insignificance: "What is man, that Thou dost take thought of him? And the son of man, that Thou dost care for him?" (Ps. 8:4 NASB). Elsewhere the psalmist ponders the sheer transience of life. We live about seventy years, he observes, maybe eighty if we are lucky, and our only pride, the only thing we have to show for it all, is but labor and sorrow. We finish our years with a sigh, our days expire like an exhaled breath or faded flower, and we fly away like windblown dust (Ps. 90:3, 9–10; 103:15–16). King Solomon experimented with all that life had to offer—fame, money, work, pleasure, political power, study—only to acknowledge that often life seemed like a chasing after the wind, a vexing combination of blind chance, futility, and despair, a vanity of vanities that caused him sleepless nights (Ecclesiastes).

Who has not with David, the psalmist, and Solomon pondered similar questions? What is the ultimate reason for my existence that transcends the many penultimate matters that consume my time and energy? Why am I here? Beyond the matter of my job, what is the exact nature of my human vocation, my calling in life? Perhaps this question has come after an especially tiresome day at work, maybe during a solitary winter walk in a snowy forest, or as we linger over a summer sunset beside a favorite lake. Almost all of us have asked the eminently practical question: what is the purpose of my life?

This practical question, voiced by Old Testament saints and contemporary people alike, has exercised the best scholarly minds for millennia. The Sophist philosopher Protagoras (c. 450 B.C.) suggested that man is the center of the universe, the measure of all things (*homo mensura*). In the very first chapter of his *Nicomachean Ethics* Aristotle (384–322 B.C.) raised the question of the purpose of life. He reasoned that our chief end is happiness, but he admitted that there is no agreement upon a definition of happiness—the sick say it is health, the poor say it is riches, the disenfranchised say it is power, and so on. Socrates (469–399 B.C.), in words preserved by Plato's *Apology,* insisted that if we fail to examine our lives and to find a satisfactory reason for existence, then life itself is not worth living. In his epigrammatic *Pensées* Blaise Pascal (1623–62) pondered the paradox of human grandeur and misery: man is only a flimsy reed—but nevertheless a "thinking reed." Perhaps no one put the question more succinctly than did the American pastor-theologian Reinhold Niebuhr (1892–1971). The very first sentences of his book *The Nature and Destiny of Man* pose the following challenge: "Man has always been his own most vexing problem. How shall he think of himself?"

The answer we give to this question of human identity and purpose has profound implications. On the existential plane, our response will guide our lives in the most practical of ways. On the level of a defense of Christianity (apologetics), we observe that in the modern era the most prominent rejections of Christianity have all been what we might call anthropological critiques of religion—that is, they have been based in a particular conception of human nature, be it biological (Charles Darwin), economic (Karl Marx), philosophical (Friedrich Nietzsche), or psychological (Sigmund Freud). On a third level, we observe that many if not most of the major socioethical problems of modern life—abortion, euthanasia, capital punishment, world hunger, women's ordination to ministry, and so on—are rooted in certain conceptions about human identity. The classical questions of politics are also at root based in anthropology—questions, for example, about whether people are inherently good (Jean Jacques Rousseau) or evil (Thomas Hobbes), and whether people are created equal and born with inalienable rights. The frightening failure of politics, exemplified in Somalia's anarchy or the ethnic cleansing in what used to be Yugoslavia, is a painful reminder of our inability to live together in community. Finally, human salvation itself depends upon answering correctly the question of human identity and purpose. John Calvin (1509–64) observed in the very first sentences of his *Institutes of the Christian Religion* (1559) that nearly all of the knowledge that we possess is of two kinds, the knowledge of God and the knowledge of ourselves, and that these two types of knowledge are inextricably connected. My very relationship with God, Calvin insisted, depends in part upon an accurate appraisal of human nature.

In fact, Christianity has spoken definitively about the nature, purpose, and destiny of humanity. The magisterial Westminster Catechism (1647) of Protestant Calvinism, for example, begins with a question about "the chief end of man." Karl Barth (1886–1968), the great Swiss theologian who so vigorously insisted upon the mighty transcendence of God, and who roundly criticized Friedrich Schleiermacher (1768–1834) for reducing theology to anthropology, nevertheless admitted that one could begin a systematic theology of the Christian faith with theological anthropology.

For its part, Orthodox theology in the East likewise places the questions of human destiny, sin, and salvation at the forefront of its entire theological vision, albeit in ways very different from the Western Christian tradition. The long history of Orthodox theology answers the question of the purpose of life with a definitive, unique, and unified response. It is a response that not only is different from Western conceptions of theological anthropology, but also sounds very strange indeed to our ears.

In the *Philokalia*, the collection of fourth- to fifteenth-century Orthodox texts compiled by Nicodemos of Athos (1748–1809), the *Theoretikon* (probably a fourteenth-century text) puts it this way: "Now the purpose of our life is blessedness . . . not only to behold the Trinity, supreme in Kingship, but also to receive an influx of the divine and, as it were, to suffer deification."[1] The contemporary Greek Orthodox theologian Christoforos Stavropoulos summarizes this Orthodox vision in the first pages of his little book *Partakers of Divine Nature*:

1. *Theoretikon*, in *Philokalia*, trans. and ed. G. E. H. Palmer, Philip Sherrard, and Kallistos Ware, 3 vols. (London: Faber and Faber, 1979–90), 2:43.

In the Holy Scriptures, where God Himself speaks, we read of a unique call directed to us. God speaks to us human beings clearly and directly and He says: "I said, 'You are gods, sons of the Most High—all of you'" (Psalm 82:6 and John 10:34). Do we hear that voice? Do we understand the meaning of this calling? Do we accept that we should in fact be on a journey, a road which leads to Theosis? As human beings we each have this one, unique calling, to achieve Theosis. In other words, we are each destined to become a god; to be like God Himself, to be united with Him. The Apostle Peter describes with total clarity the purpose of life: we are to "become partakers of the divine nature" (2 Peter 1:4). This is the purpose of your life; that you be a participant, a sharer in the nature of God and in the life of Christ, a communicant of divine energy—to become just like God, a true God.[2]

"Man," writes Gregory of Nazianzus, "has been ordered to become God."[3]

The purpose of the present chapter is to explore the meaning of these astonishing words. The idea of theosis, divinization, or deification (the words are synonyms) speaks directly to the nature of the Christian's mystical experience of God which we spoke about in chapter 3. With the nocturnal question about feelings of insignificance that David asked on that Palestinian hillside (Ps. 8:4), we must juxtapose the startlingly bold response of his fellow psalmist Asaph that is invoked by Orthodox theology (Ps. 82:6), words that are in fact reiterated by Jesus Christ himself (John 10:34).

Eastern and Western Perspectives on the Work of Christ

As with the emphases explored in the previous chapters, the idea of theosis is a distinctive feature that characterizes Orthodoxy and assumes central importance in its overall theological framework. It is like a continuous golden thread running throughout the centuries of Orthodoxy's ancient theological tapestry. Indeed, most of the major theologians of the East weave this doctrine into the pattern of Eastern Christianity. John Climacus, for whom the idea of theosis is not a major theme, is perhaps the lone exception to this historical rule, although even in Climacus the theme is not entirely absent.

It is not too much to say that the divinization of humanity is the central theme, chief aim, basic purpose, or primary religious ideal of Orthodoxy. Theosis is the ultimate goal towards which all people should

2. Christoforos Stavropoulos, *Partakers of Divine Nature* (Minneapolis: Light and Life, 1976), 17–18.

3. Gregory of Nazianzus *Funeral Oration for St. Basil* (cited by Stavropoulos, *Partakers*, 18).

strive,[4] "the blessed *telos* for which all things were made."[5] In emphasizing this doctrine Orthodox theologians focus on more than what the *Theoretikon* identifies as the purpose of life; for Orthodoxy, deification is "the very essence of Christianity," for it involves the "ineffable descent of God to the ultimate limit of our fallen human condition, even unto death—a descent of God which opens to men a path of ascent, the unlimited vistas of the union of created beings with the Divinity."[6] To paraphrase Athanasius, when God descended, assumed humanity, and was "in-carnated," he opened the way for people to ascend to him, assume divinity, and become "in-godded." In its very definition of the gospel, then, Eastern Christianity presupposes the idea of deification; even when the term is not explicitly mentioned, it is implicitly present "as the content of the salvation proclaimed by the gospel."[7]

Except for the important work by the Catholic scholar J. Gross, and occasional references to the theme,[8] Western theologians in general and Protestants in particular have given only scant attention to the central importance of theosis in Orthodox thought. Nor do they address the doctrine as an important biblical category in its own right. New Testament theologies such as those by George Ladd (1974) and Leon Morris (1986), for example, do not even mention theosis. On the other hand, as early as Gregory Palamas's fourteenth-century work *On Divine and Deifying Participation*, Orthodox thinkers have systematically analyzed the doctrine at length.[9]

4. Georgios I. Mantzaridis, *The Deification of Man* (Crestwood, N.Y.: St. Vladimir's Seminary Press, 1984), 12, 129. See also Timothy Ware, *The Orthodox Church* (Baltimore: Penguin, 1964), 236; John Meyendorff, *Byzantine Theology: Historical Trends and Doctrinal Themes* (New York: Fordham University Press, 1974), 2–3, 225–26.

5. Gregory of Nazianzus *To Thallasios* 60 (cited by Panagiotes Chrestou, *Partakers of God* [Brookline, Mass.: Holy Cross Orthodox, 1984], 36; see also pp. 16–17 and 61 on man's purpose in life).

6. Vladimir Lossky, *In the Image and Likeness of God* (Crestwood, N.Y.: St. Vladimir's Seminary Press, 1974), 97.

7. Jaroslav Pelikan, *The Spirit of Eastern Christendom (600–1700)* (Chicago: University of Chicago Press, 1974), 11; see also p. 46.

8. J. Gross, *La Divinisation du chrétien d'après les Pères grecs: Contribution historique à la doctrine de la grâce* (Paris, 1938) (cited by Mantzaridis, *Deification*, 13). John Karmiris, *A Synopsis of the Dogmatic Theology of the Orthodox Catholic Church* (Scranton, Pa.: Christian Orthodox Edition, 1973), 70 n. 30, cites two German studies by K. Bornhauser (1903) and L. Baur (1916), and a French article by M. G. Congar (1935).

9. In addition to the works by Chrestou, Stavropoulos, Mantzaridis, and Lossky already cited, see Panayiotis Nellas, *Deification in Christ* (Crestwood, N.Y.: St. Vladimir's Seminary Press, 1987); M. Lot-Borodine, "La Doctrine de la déification dans l'Eglise grecque jusqu'au XIe siècle," *Revue de l'histoire des religions* 105 (1932): 5–43; 106 (1932): 525–74; 107 (1933): 8–55; Elias Moutsoulas, *The Incarnation of the Word and the Theosis of Man according to Gregory of Nyssa* (in Greek; Athens, 1965); and Andreas Theodorou, *The Theosis of Man in the Teaching of the Greek Fathers of the Church to John of Damascus* (in Greek; Athens: Theological School of the University of Athens, 1956).

More important still, Eastern treatments of the doctrine of salvation generally construe the dilemma of humanity and the response of God in the work of Christ from a perspective that is different from that of the West. Orthodox theologians contend that in the West the doctrines of sin and salvation have been unduly dominated by legal, juridical, and forensic categories. These categories, they insist, are not only overly negative and alien to the spirit of Eastern Christianity, but, when allowed to dominate, are actual distortions of the biblical message.[10] Ernst Benz suggests that this legal framework predominates in Western thinking (both Catholic and Protestant). He notes how the apostle Paul frames his Epistle to the Romans in terms of divine law and justice, categories that are perhaps taken from Roman civil law, and that his idea of justification by faith answers the question of how guilty people can stand before a just God. Benz suggests that the Catholic church especially, with its doctrines of penance and indulgences, its concepts of the church, the role of the priest, and canon law, developed in this legalistic direction.[11] This accent on legal concepts, in contrast to the idea of mystical union perpetuated in the East, is seen by Orthodoxy as the "real issue that unites the West theologically [that is, both Catholics and Protestants] and divides it from the East."[12]

Tertullian (c. 160–220), who may have been trained as a lawyer and was the first major theologian to write in Latin, is usually credited as the first to interpret the work of Christ in juridical categories, but it is Augustine (354–430) and Anselm of Canterbury (1033–1109) who developed forensic concepts in detail and invested them with full force. John Meyendorff has suggested that the enormous influence of Augustinian legal categories in the West, coupled with Augustine's near total lack of influence in the East (where the work of Christ was understood in terms of theosis), is one of the major theological factors that caused the Eastern and Western churches to drift apart.[13] In his epoch-making work *Cur Deus homo*, a book that influenced almost all subsequent Western treatments of the work of Christ, Anselm argued that the sin of man had offended the majesty and honor of God, and that the justice of God could be served only by making a "satisfaction" or just payment of the penalty. With only

10. Lossky, *Image and Likeness*, chap. 5; Karmiris, *Synopsis*, 38, 55–56.

11. Ernst Benz, *The Eastern Orthodox Church: Its Thought and Life*, trans. Richard and Clara Winston (Garden City, N.Y.: Anchor Books, 1963), 43–47. Here I am following the summary of Benz by James J. Stamoolis, *Eastern Orthodox Mission Theology Today* (Maryknoll, N.Y.: Orbis, 1986), 7–11.

12. Stamoolis, *Orthodox Mission Theology*, 7.

13. Meyendorff, *Byzantine Theology*, 143. See also pp. 32–33, 160–61, 215, 226; Stamoolis, *Orthodox Mission Theology*, 8.

a little work we could adduce further examples of the predominance of juridical categories in Western soteriology. In contemporary evangelical theology, for example, writers like J. I. Packer and John Stott interpret the work of Christ primarily in terms of penal substitution.[14]

One of the best illustrations of this basic difference between the East and the West is the doctrine of justification by faith, so prevalent in the West but almost totally absent from Eastern thought. Martin Luther (1483–1546) argued that Christianity would stand or fall with this doctrine. In his treatise *Two Types of Righteousness* he developed the idea of our external, passive, and alien righteousness in Christ. That God declares sinners righteous on the basis of the perfect righteousness of Christ that is credited to the believer is certainly an idea quite different from notions of mystical union with Christ. In his *Institutes* Calvin described justification by faith as the "hinge on which all true religion turns," and in his precise definition of the doctrine he compares it to an acquittal in the courts of divine justice: "just as a man, deemed innocent by an impartial judge, is said to be justified, so a sinner is said to be justified by God when he asserts his righteousness."[15] In the history of Orthodox theology, on the other hand, it is startling to observe the near total absence of any mention of the idea of justification by faith. Justification by faith has received "short shrift" in Orthodoxy; in fact, the most important text of Orthodox theology, John of Damascus's *Orthodox Faith*, never even mentions the idea.[16]

We have, then, another genuine difference of perspective between the East and the West. But if we left the matter at that, we would be misconstruing the issue. We must add three qualifications to this general theological historiography.

First, Paul himself uses legal categories such as justification by faith, a fact that James Stamoolis, Vladimir Lossky, Benz, and other Orthodox

14. See J. I. Packer, "What Did the Cross Achieve? The Logic of Penal Substitution," *Tyndale Bulletin* 25 (1974): 3–45; John R. W. Stott, *The Cross of Christ* (Downers Grove, Ill.: Inter-Varsity, 1987).

15. John Calvin, *Institutes*, 3.11.2.

16. Benz, *Eastern Orthodox Church*, 50–51; Stamoolis, *Orthodox Mission Theology*, 135. Karmiris's *Synopsis* mentions a number of salvific metaphors but omits justification by faith. See also Meyendorff, *Byzantine Theology*, 160–61, 226; Carnegie S. Calian, *Theology without Boundaries: Encounters of Eastern Orthodoxy and Western Tradition* (Louisville: Westminster/John Knox, 1992), 34, 37; and Nikolai Fyodorov, "The Restoration of Kinship among Mankind," in Alexander Schmemann, ed., *Ultimate Questions: An Anthology of Modern Russian Religious Thought* (Crestwood, N.Y.: St. Vladimir's Seminary Press, 1977), 220. One notable exception to this is the Confession of Faith, Articles 9 and 13, by the controversial "Protestant Patriarch" of Orthodoxy, Cyril Lucaris (1572–1638). For extensive bibliography on Lucaris, see Calian, *Theology without Boundaries*, 115–16, and his entire chap. 3.

theologians acknowledge. This way of interpreting the work of Christ is hardly, then, a distortion or unduly negative. Rather, the idea of justification and legal categories are eminently biblical.

Second, the real issue here seems to be a difference of emphasis—the East emphasizing mystical union through theosis, the West emphasizing juridical categories. No necessity forces us to choose between the two or to see them as mutually exclusive categories that are contradictory. Rather, they, and a host of other New Testament salvation motifs besides (adoption, reconciliation, redemption, ransom, sacrifice, forgiveness, *Christus victor*, propitiation, deliverance), are complementary. We need to affirm them all in order to begin to understand the wonder of God's salvation in Christ.

Third, the historical generalizations are not so neat and clean as some might think. Although the West does not embrace the explicit notion of theosis in any major way, deification is not entirely absent from its tradition. "God received a body and a soul," writes Augustine, "in order that the body and soul of man may be blessed: the soul with his divinity and the body with his humanity."[17] Jaroslav Pelikan has ferreted out references to theosis in several Latin medieval theologians. The canon lawyer and theologian Alger of Liège (died 1131/32) and German exegete Rupert of Deutz (1075–1129) refer to the humanity of Christ as "deified man." Catholic reformer Peter Damian (1007–72) cites 2 Peter 1:4 and notes that Christ "ascended in order to make us participants in his divinity." Bernard of Clairvaux (1090–1153) writes of filling ourselves with God.[18] Further, the West has a well-developed concept of the Pauline idea of union with Christ. In the opening pages of book 3 of his *Institutes* Calvin, for example, before he raises the issue of justification by faith, speaks of believers' being engrafted into or bonded with Christ through the "secret energy of the Holy Spirit."

Conversely, when describing our salvation in Christ, theologians of the East incorporate biblical motifs other than theosis. Athanasius, the preeminent proponent of theosis for Orthodoxy, is a case in point. In his classic *On the Incarnation of the Word*, Athanasius uses a host of biblical motifs to describe the work of Christ, including substitutionary or vicarious atonement, the payment of a debt, the conquest of death and the devil, ransom, and sacrifice. In fact, in the locus classicus of theosis, Athanasius exclaims that the work of Christ is so multifaceted that trying to number his many and various benefits is like trying to count the

17. Augustine *Enchiridion* 26 (cited by Nicodemos of Athos, *Handbook of Spiritual Counsel* [New York: Paulist, 1989], 204).

18. Jaroslav Pelikan, *The Growth of Medieval Theology, 600–1300* (Chicago: University of Chicago Press, 1978), 152; idem, *Imago Dei: The Byzantine Apologia for Icons* (Princeton: Princeton University Press, 1990), 141.

endless waves of the ocean: "Even so, when one wants to take in all the achievements of Christ in the body, one cannot do so, even by reckoning them up, for the things that transcend one's thought are always more than those one thinks that one has grasped."[19] We can say, then, that in addition to theosis Eastern theologians affirm any number of biblical metaphors for salvation, including juridical ones. They acknowledge that the work of Christ cannot be reduced to any single metaphor. Thus, while legal metaphors are truly Pauline and should be affirmed, they should not be allowed to dominate, but should be "relocated" among the host of other biblical images.[20]

In their better moments both Protestant and Orthodox theologians acknowledge that the biblical material presents the work of Christ from a number of different perspectives, and that all of them are necessary for a complete understanding of our salvation in Christ.[21] Nevertheless, the difference in emphasis is real. The West lacks any developed notion of theosis and tends to express the idea of salvation in juridical categories. The Eastern church neglects the concept of justification in favor of deification, a theme which it discovers throughout the Bible and has repeated down through the centuries.

Biblical and Historical Witnesses to Theosis

The Bible speaks extensively about theosis, according to the Orthodox tradition, and thus so must we. The two most direct texts are 2 Peter 1:4 and Psalm 82:6 (= John 10:34–35). If it be objected that these texts are taken out of context, or that finding the doctrine in an array of biblical texts is unconvincing, Orthodox theologians would care little. True exegesis seeks to perceive the hidden meaning of Scripture that lies beyond or beneath the literal words of the text.[22] Sticking to the mere letter of Scripture proves

19. Athanasius *On the Incarnation* 8.54.

20. Vladimir Lossky, *Orthodox Theology: An Introduction* (Crestwood, N.Y.: St. Vladimir's Seminary Press, 1978), 111. See also his similar point in *Image and Likeness*, 100–103. Karmiris, who treats the work of Christ in the rather traditional categories of his roles as prophet, priest, and king, even warns about overemphasizing theosis: "the Greek fathers by no means disregard the other important aspects of the redemptive work of the Saviour" (*Synopsis*, 70 n. 33). So too Dumitru Staniloae, *Theology and the Church* (Crestwood, N.Y.: St. Vladimir's Seminary Press, 1980), 183.

21. Vladimir Lossky, *The Mystical Theology of the Eastern Church* (Crestwood, N.Y.: St. Vladimir's Seminary Press, 1976), 151–55; idem, *Image and Likeness*, 100; Chrestou, *Partakers of God*, 42; Mantzaridis, *Deification*, 27; Stamoolis, *Orthodox Mission Theology*, 9; and Sergius Bulgakov, *The Orthodox Church*, rev. ed. (Crestwood, N.Y.: St. Vladimir's Seminary Press, 1988), 107–9.

22. Mark the Ascetic *On the Spiritual Law: Two Hundred Texts* 26 (in *Philokalia*, 1:112). See also Maximus the Confessor *Two Hundred Texts on Theology* 2.75 (in *Philokalia*, 2:156).

only one's attachment to the senses and the flesh.[23] Although careless allegorization can "kill the Scriptures," the true exegete always seeks a "spiritual interpretation" of God's Word.[24] Further, since the tradition of the church fathers speaks so definitively about the matter, the biblical propriety of the doctrine of theosis is for Orthodoxy beyond debate. In fact, Eastern theologians claim an extensive litany of biblical witnesses to the doctrine of deification. They consider humanity's "organic union" with God to be a constant theme in both Paul and John. Far from being unscriptural, theosis has, according to Orthodoxy, a "solid biblical basis" that goes far beyond the two explicit texts in 2 Peter 1:4 and John 10:34–35.[25]

Moses, who had encountered God in the burning bush, became "like God to Pharaoh" (Exod. 7:1). Later, Moses encountered God in the smoky darkness of Mount Sinai and was transfigured so that his face shone (Exod. 34:30).[26] Peter's being illumined by the bright rays of the transfigured Jesus on Mount Tabor (Matt. 17:1–8) parallels Moses' transfiguration on Sinai as a paradigm for us today whereby we "participate in the divine brightness."[27] Two oft-repeated texts in this connection are 2 Corinthians 8:9 and Hebrews 4:15. Commenting on these texts, Mark the Ascetic (early fifth century) writes that Christ "became what we are, so that we might become what He is. The Logos became man, so that man might become Logos. Being rich, He became poor for our sakes, so that through His poverty we might become rich. In His great love for man He became like us, so that through every virtue we might become like Him."[28] The Johannine corpus is an especially rich witness to theosis (John 3:8; 14:21–23; 15:4–8; 17:21–23; 1 John 3:2; 4:12). Commenting on "John the Theologian" and his many references to our union with God, Peter of Damascus invokes the authority of Christ himself: we become "gods by adoption through grace," and, having become dispassionate, "we have God within ourselves—as Christ Himself has told us."[29] Both Macarius of Egypt

23. Maximus the Confessor *Various Texts on Theology* 4.76 (in *Philokalia*, 2:254). See Neilos the Ascetic *Ascetic Discourse* (in *Philokalia*, 1:210) for an example of a clearly historical narrative interpreted in a spiritual sense.

24. Peter of Damascus *Twenty-four Discourses* 12, 23 (in *Philokalia*, 3:248, 267). Cf. idem, *A Treasury of Divine Knowledge* (in *Philokalia*, 3:144), on the negative impact of allegorizing. On the spiritual interpretation of Scripture, see Bradley Nassif, "Antiochene Theoria in John Chrysostom's Exegesis," Ph.D. diss., Fordham University, 1991.

25. Ware, *Orthodox Church*, 236–37.

26. Hesychios the Priest *On Watchfulness and Holiness* 139 (in *Philokalia*, 1:186).

27. Macarios of Philadelphia (in Nicodemos, *Handbook*, 224).

28. Mark the Ascetic *Letter to Nicolas the Solitary* (in *Philokalia*, 1:155).

29. Peter of Damascus *Treasury* (in *Philokalia*, 3:79); see also Nicodemos, *Handbook*, 186. For patristic references to the other biblical texts see Maximus the Confessor *Various Texts on Theology* 1.42, and Theodoros the Great Ascetic *A Century of Spiritual Texts* 94 (in *Philokalia*, 2:35, 173); *Symeon the New Theologian: The Discourses* (New York: Paulist, 1980), 195, 350.

and Chrysostom interpret the marriage analogy in 1 Corinthians 6:17 as refer-ring to our spiritual marriage in which "the soul is joined to God in an ineffa-ble union."[30] According to Ilias the Presbyter (c. 1100), it is when we attain divine likeness through theosis that we transcend the differences between male and female (Gal. 3:28).[31] We are, writes the apostle Paul, "created to be like God" and "imitators of God" (Eph. 4:24; 5:1).

Maximus the Confessor and Simeon the New Theologian are especially instructive on this point, for they illustrate the depth and breadth of the Orthodox confidence that the idea of theosis is an eminently biblical theme. Maximus discovers the idea of theosis nearly everywhere. In his view, "the purpose of the Lord's Prayer was to point to the mystery of dei-fication. Baptism was 'in the name of the life-giving and deifying Trinity.' When the guests at the wedding in Cana of Galilee . . . said that their host had 'kept the good wine until now,' they were referring to the Word of God, saved for the last, by which men were made divine. When, in the Epistles of the same Apostle John, 'the Theologian,' it was said that 'it does not yet appear what we shall be,' this was a reference to 'the future deification of those who have now been made children of God.' When the Apostle Paul spoke of 'the riches' of the saints, this, too, meant deifica-tion."[32] In addition to the passages already mentioned, Simeon the New Theologian appeals to a broad array of other biblical texts when he expounds the doctrine of theosis (e.g., 1 Cor. 6:15; Col. 3:1; Titus 2:13).[33]

To these biblical texts we can add the historical witness of Orthodoxy's sacra-mental life and theological literature down through the centuries, both of which repeatedly define salvation as divinization. Theosis is "echoed by the fathers and the theologians of every age."[34] In addition to the names already noted, we can briefly mention other important historical witnesses to deification, thus giving us a sense of the near ubiquity of the doctrine in Eastern theology.

The earliest references to theosis occur in Irenaeus (fl. c. 175) and Origen (185–254), both of whom anticipated the Athanasian epigram ("God became man so that men might become gods"). "If the Word is made man," writes Ire-naeus, "it is that men might become gods." According to Origen, when we tran-scend the material realm, the contemplation of God is brought to "its proper ful-fillment," that is, the spirit is "deified by that which it contemplates."[35]

30. Chrysostom *Homilies on Ephesians* 20 (Eph. 5:22–33); Macarius of Egypt *Makarian Homilies* 4.67 and 6.124 (in *Philokalia*, 3:314, 330).

31. Ilias the Presbyter *Gnomic Anthology* 3.25 (in *Philokalia*, 3:50).

32. Pelikan, *Spirit*, 10.

33. *Symeon the New Theologian: The Discourses*, 207, 336, and 361.

34. Lossky, *Mystical Theology*, 134.

35. Irenaeus *Against Heresies* 5, preface; see also 4.2, 5; Origen *On First Principles* 3.6.3 (cited by Vladimir Lossky, *The Vision of God* [Crestwood, N.Y.: St. Vladimir's Seminary Press, 1963], 42, 61–62).

The Cappadocian fathers all continue the theme. In the very first pages of his estimable *On the Holy Spirit* Basil insists that "the goal of our calling is to become like God." He attributes the experience of theosis to the Holy Spirit, who, "being God by nature . . . deifies by grace those who still belong to a nature subject to change."[36] According to Gregory of Nyssa, "God united Himself to our nature in order that our nature might be made divine through union with God."[37] Gregory of Nazianzus echoes the Athanasian epigram: as God became incarnate, man became "endivinized"; to the extent that Christ became a real man, so we become real gods.[38]

Cyril of Alexandria (376–444), one of the most important theologians of the fifth century, commented on 2 Peter 1:4 to note that we are all called to participate in divinity. Although Jesus Christ alone is by nature God, all people are called to become God "by participation." Through such participation we become likenesses of Christ and perfect images of God the Father.[39] In the eighth century John of Damascus insisted that people are created for deification, and that the work of Christ ensures that we might have his image restored in us and so become "partakers of divinity."[40] According to Psellus (died c. 1078), professor at Constantinople, the likeness of the soul to God ultimately means its "ability to make men divine." Like many before him Psellus invoked the standard formula, that God became man that man might become God.[41] Nicholas Motovilov's moving account of the Russian monk Seraphim of Sarov (1759–1833) tells of an Orthodox saint who not only expounded the doctrine of theosis, but who in fact experienced its full effects.[42]

That the liturgical life of Orthodoxy expresses the doctrine of theosis is another testimony to its importance in the Eastern tradition. Not only doctrine and belief (*lex credendi*), but worship and prayer (*lex orandi*), proclaim the ideal of deification. In the canon for the matins of Holy Thursday, the church recites in its worship, "In my kingdom, said Christ, I shall

36. Basil *On the Holy Spirit* 1.2; *Against Eunomius* 3.5.

37. Gregory of Nyssa *Oratio Catechetica* 25; see also Lossky, *Vision*, 80; and Nicholas Arseniev, *Mysticism and the Eastern Church* (Crestwood, N.Y.: St. Vladimir's Seminary Press, 1979), 26.

38. Gregory of Nazianzus *Poem. dogma* 10.5–9 (in Lossky, *Mystical Theology*, 134); *Epistle* 101 (to Cledonius) (in Karmiris, *Synopsis*, 70 n. 31); and "Third Theological Oration" 19 (Oration 29).

39. See Lossky, *Vision*, 98.

40. John of Damascus *Exposition of the Orthodox Faith* 4.4; see also 2.12; 3.18, 20.

41. Psellus *Omnifarious Doctrine* 71; *Oration on the Salutation to Mary* 2 (cited by Pelikan, *Spirit*, 247).

42. For the physical effects of Seraphim's deification see Ware, *Orthodox Church*, 130–32.

be God with you as gods."[43] The ancient Liturgy of Saint James (c. 450), extant in both Greek and Syriac, proclaims: "Thou hast united, O Lord, Thy divinity with our humanity and our humanity with Thy divinity, Thy life with our mortality and our mortality with Thy life; Thou hast received what was ours and hast given unto us what was Thine, for the life and salvation of our souls. Praise be to Thee in eternity."[44]

The hymnology of the fourth-century Christian poet Ephrem the Syrian adds its choruses to the testimony of the liturgy. Since Ephrem wrote in Syriac and was probably ignorant of Greek, his hymns are significant refutations of the common charge that the Orthodox doctrine of theosis is only a pale imitation of Hellenistic philosophy. According to Ephrem, if Adam and Eve had not transgressed the divine command, "they would have acquired divinity in humanity" (*Commentary on Genesis*). In a Nisibene hymn he writes:

> The Most High knew that Adam wanted to become a god,
>> so He sent His Son, who put him on
>> in order to grant him his desire.

In Ephrem's hymn "On Virginity" we read:

> Divinity flew down and descended
>> to raise and draw up humanity.
> The Son has made beautiful the servant's deformity,
>> and he has become a god, just as he desired.

And while Athanasius is typically credited with the definitive epigram of theosis, Ephrem is no less aphoristic. In his hymn "On Faith" he puts the whole matter succinctly:

> He gave us divinity,
> We gave Him humanity.[45]

Defining Theosis

But what exactly does it mean to be "divinized" or to "become god"? In attempting to define theosis, Orthodoxy would have us begin with two cautions. First, remembering the Orthodox predilection for apophatic theology, we must not "seek what is too difficult or investigate what is

43. Ode 4, Troparion 3; see Ware, *Orthodox Church*, 236.
44. Quoted in Arseniev, *Mysticism*, 148.
45. Ephrem the Syrian, in *Hymns on Paradise*, trans. Sebastian Brock (Crestwood, N.Y.: St. Vladimir's Seminary Press, 1990), 72–74.

beyond our power"; instead, we should reflect only "upon what has been assigned to us, for [we] do not need what is hidden" (Ecclesiasticus 3:21–22). Because theosis is ultimately a mystery, we need to use discretion when trying to define it. In some sense theosis defies analysis. Deification, insists Macarius of Egypt (c. 300–390), is "subtle and profound."[46] Gregory Palamas, who devoted an entire treatise to the subject, is nevertheless reluctant to describe the indescribable: "Although we have written at length about stillness . . . we have never dared to write about deification. But now, since there is need to speak, we will speak, reverently, with the Lord's grace, though to describe it is beyond our skill. For even when spoken of, deification remains unutterable: as the Fathers say, it can be identified only by those who have been blessed with it."[47] Union with the divine, asserts Maximus the Confessor, "in the nature of things, cannot be perceived, conceived or expressed."[48]

Second, all of the Eastern theologians, both ancient and modern, uniformly and categorically repudiate any hint of pantheism. Whatever it means to "become god," the essence of human nature is not lost. In this sense human theosis is a relative rather than an absolute transformation. There is a real and genuine union of the believer with God, but it is not a literal fusion or confusion in which the integrity of human nature is compromised. Orthodoxy consistently rejects the idea that humans participate in the essence or nature of God. Rather, we remain distinctly human by nature but participate in God by the divine energies or grace. At no point, even when deified, is our humanity diminished or destroyed.

Thus Maximus writes: "All that God is, *except for an identity in ousia*, one becomes when one is deified by grace." When the Logos became man and deified us, he changed human nature "not in its essential nature but in its quality."[49] In his definition of theosis Anastasius of Sinai (seventh century) insists upon the same distinction: "Theosis is the elevation to what is better, but not the reduction of our nature to something less, nor is it an essential change of our human nature. . . . That which is of God is that which has been lifted up to a greater glory, without its own nature being changed."[50] John of Damascus spoke of "man becoming deified in the way of participating in the divine glory, and not in that of a change into a divine being."[51] Macarius likewise is careful

46. Macarius of Egypt *Makarian Homilies* 4.67 (in *Philokalia*, 3:314).
47. Gregory Palamas *Defense of the Holy Hesychasts* 3.1.32 (in Mantzaridis, *Deification*, 127).
48. Maximus the Confessor *Various Texts on Theology* 4.19 (in *Philokalia*, 2:240).
49. Maximus the Confessor *Book of Ambiguities* 41 (cited by Pelikan, *Spirit*, 267) (emphasis added); *Various Texts on Theology* 2.26 (in *Philokalia*, 2:193).
50. Anastasius of Sinai *Concerning the Word* (in Stavropoulos, *Partakers of Divine Nature*, 19).
51. John of Damascus *Exposition of the Orthodox Faith* 2.12.

to protect the creature-Creator distinction: even when we are deified by grace, "Peter is Peter, Paul is Paul, Philip is Philip. Each one retains his own nature and personal identity, but they are all filled with the Holy Spirit."[52]

Synonyms and Analogies

Keeping these two disclaimers in mind, we can further our definition of theosis by looking at the various synonyms and analogies that Orthodox theologians use to explain the mystery of salvation. Theosis can be described by a number of related words in the vocabulary of the Fathers. It is a transformation, union, participation, partaking, intermingling, elevation, interpenetration, transmutation, commingling, assimilation, reintegration, adoption, or re-creation. Divinization implies our being intertwined with Christ, an influx of the divine, or the attainment of similitude with God.[53]

The most fitting analogy for theosis is the incarnation of God. God and man are "examples of each other," according to Maximus. As God was incarnated, man was "endivinized." But in utilizing this analogy to Christ the Greek fathers are careful to maintain the distinction just emphasized. Our union with God is not a hypostatic one, as with the two natures of Christ, nor a union of essence, as with the three persons of the Trinity. In theosis God "makes man god to the same degree as God Himself became man" except that God "will divinize human nature without changing it into the divine nature."[54] Thus, writes Palamas, "the Logos became flesh, and the flesh became Logos, even though neither abandoned its own proper nature."[55]

Macarius and Chrysostom employ the analogy of marriage to define theosis. Just as two people are joined together in one flesh yet all the while maintain the integrity of their separate identities, just as they share a single existence and hold all things in common, so the believer is joined to God in an "ineffable communion" (see 1 Cor. 6:15–17). Maximus even dares to call this theosis an "erotic union."[56] He also likens theosis to an eighth day of

52. Macarius of Egypt *Makarian Homilies* (in Timothy Ware, *The Orthodox Way* [Crestwood, N.Y.: St. Vladimir's Seminary Press, 1990], 168). On this entire point see Ware, *Orthodox Way*, 237; Mantzaridis, *Deification*, 9, 58; Karmiris, *Synopsis*, 60; Lossky, *Mystical Theology*, 87; Stavropoulos, *Partakers of Divine Nature*, 59; and Meyendorff, *Byzantine Theology*, 38–39, 163–64.

53. I have taken these synonyms from the *Philokalia*. See also C. Kern, "Homotheos et ses synonymes dans la littérature byzantine, in 1054–1954," in *L'Eglise et les Eglises* (Edition de Chevetogne, vol. 2) (cited by Karmiris, *Synopsis*, 70).

54. Maximus the Confessor *Various Texts on Theology* 1.62 (in *Philokalia*, 2:177–78).

55. Quoted in Mantzaridis, *Deification*, 29. See also Lossky, *Mystical Theology*, 87; Ware, *Orthodox Church*, 236; and *Symeon the New Theologian: The Discourses*, 350.

56. Maximus the Confessor *Various Texts on Theology* 3.30 (in *Philokalia*, 2:216); see also Chrysostom *Homilies on Ephesians* 20 (Eph. 5:22–33); Macarius of Egypt *Makarian Homilies* 6.124 (in *Philokalia*, 3:340).

creation—"the transposition and transmutation of those found worthy into a state of deification."[57] Elsewhere Chrysostom compares our union with God to grains of wheat: "Just as the bread is constituted by many grains united together so that the grains cannot be distinguished from one another even though they are there, since their difference is made unapparent in their cohesion, in the same manner we are joined together both to each other and to Christ." Cyril of Alexandria likens our participation in Christ to the joining of wax with wax, to the interpenetration of yeast with a lump of dough, and to red-hot iron penetrated by fire.[58]

From Corruption to Immortality

More specifically, in the Greek tradition theosis signifies the transposition of the believer from a state of corruption and mortality to one of incorruption and immortality. Here again the Eastern tradition has a different emphasis from that in the West. In the Greek fathers the tragedy of Adam's fall is not that all people inherit his guilt, as in the Augustinian tradition. They hold, most certainly, that all people are sinful, and that the fall was an incomparable disaster. But we all sin freely and incur our own guilt. Rather than guilt, in Adam we have inherited death, mortality, and corruption. "The first man brought in universal death," writes Cyril of Jerusalem. Sin originates, Basil the Great insists, in our own free wills: "Do not then go beyond yourself to seek the evil, and imagine that there is an original nature of wickedness. . . . Each of us, let us acknowledge it, is the first author of his own vice."[59]

Panagiotes Chrestou elaborates on this important distinction: "The descendants of Adam inherit him in his entirety, including his nature and his weakness. They did not inherit Adam's guilt, as St. Augustine taught in the West; for, according to the view of the Greek fathers, sin is a personal problem. Adam and Eve on one side, and their descendants on the other, interpenetrate each other in such a way that every man bears by birth that nature which Adam and Eve corrupted . . . . In this way humankind has fallen from the road to life onto the road to death, from incorruption to corruption."[60] According to Anastasius of Sinai, we are heirs of Adam's corruption, but "we are not punished for his disobedience to the

57. Maximus the Confessor Two Hundred Texts on Theology 1.54–55 (in Philokalia, 2:125). On the eighth day of creation see Alexander Schmemann, Introduction to Liturgical Theology (Crestwood, N.Y.: St. Vladimir's Seminary Press, 1986), 77ff.

58. For the analogies of wheat, wax, leaven, and iron see Stavropoulos, Partakers of Divine Nature, 59, 62–63. On the analogy to iron and fire see also Lossky, Vision, 98.

59. Cyril of Jerusalem Catechesis 13.2; Basil That God Is Not Responsible for Evil 8 (cited by Karmiris, Synopsis, 33–34).

60. Chrestou, Partakers of God, 28; see also Pelikan, Spirit, 260; Mantzaridis, Deification, 25, 46; Ware, Orthodox Church, 228–29.

Divine Law. Rather, Adam being mortal, sin entered into his very seed. We receive mortality from him. . . . The general punishment of Adam for his transgression is corruption and death."[61]

The work of God in theosis means the triumph of life over death. Typical are the descriptions given by Simeon the New Theologian and Athanasius. When the Holy Spirit comes upon us, he "regenerates [and] changes [us] from corruptible to incorruptible, from mortal to immortal, from sons of men into sons of God and gods by adoption and grace."[62] In the two passages of *On the Incarnation of the Word* which mention theosis, Athanasius defines it as incorruption. By nature we are mortal, he says, but we are also made in the likeness of God; and if we preserve this likeness, our corruptible nature is deprived of its power and we attain incorruption: "And being incorrupt, [we] would henceforth be as God, as Holy Scripture says, 'I have said, "Ye are gods and sons of the highest, all of you"'" (Ps. 82:6). Through the death of Christ deathlessness has been manifested, and through his shame we inherit immortality.[63]

From Image to Likeness

The Eastern fathers also define theosis as the movement from the divine image to the divine likeness. Many (but not all) Orthodox theologians make this distinction. It was the view of Diadochos of Photiki, Maximus, John of Damascus, Palamas, and others that every person is made in the divine image, but only a few attain the transformation of the distorted image into the divine likeness.[64] That is, we all possess the divine image by nature, but only some acquire the divine likeness through vigilance.

The image of God is the common property of all people, an inherent aspect of every person's human nature by virtue of creation (Gen. 1:26–27). The image refers primarily to our rationality and capacity for free choice. The likeness of God, on the other hand, signifies a potential similitude to God which requires our free cooperation with God's grace. The image might be thought of as potential likeness, and the likeness as realized image.[65] The

61. Anastasius of Sinai *Questions and Answers on Various Chapters* 143 (cited by Karmiris, *Synopsis*, 36).

62. *Symeon the New Theologian: The Discourses*, 337.

63. Athanasius *On the Incarnation* 1.4; 8.54.

64. Diadochos of Photiki *On Spiritual Knowledge* 4, 78, 89; Maximus the Confessor *Four Hundred Texts on Love* 3.24–27; idem, *Two Hundred Texts on Theology* 1.13; John of Damascus *On the Virtues and the Vices*; and Abba Philemon *Discourse* (all in *Philokalia*, 1:253, 280, 288; 2:87, 116, 341, 350, 354).

65. Chrestou, *Partakers of God*, 20–21; Stavropoulos, *Partakers of Divine Nature*, 25; and Mantzaridis, *Deification*, 21. John Hick is one example of a contemporary Protestant who endorses this distinction. See his *Evil and the God of Love*, new ed. of 2d rev. ed. (New York: Macmillan, 1985).

image is static, the likeness dynamic. As we cooperate with God's grace, he renews the distorted image in us so that we attain the likeness and consequently become godlike.

Basil observes that "the image was given to us in our nature, and it is unchangeable; from the beginning until the end it remains. The likeness, on the other hand, we gain and achieve through our cooperation and volition; [it] exists potentially in us, and is energized through the good life and excellent behaviour."[66] Likewise Gregory of Nyssa: we "possess the image of God by being rational; [we] receive the likeness of God by acquiring virtue. In creation I have the image, but I become through the exercise of my free will in the likeness of God."[67]

When by grace and imitation we move from the divine image to the divine likeness, we become an earthly god. We reflect by grace all the many perfections that God alone possesses by nature and essence. In that transfiguration of our nature from image to likeness, we are, according to the words of the psalmist, deified (Ps. 82:6).[68] Salvation, then, "is not possible but by the deification of the saved," writes Pseudo-Dionysius, and "deification is likeness and union with God."[69] Irenaeus sums up the dilemma of man and the remedy of the incarnation of the Word and of the corresponding deification of man through the movement from image to likeness: "The Word of God was made man, assimilating Himself into man, and man into Himself, so that by means of his resemblance to the Son, man might become precious to the Father. For all times long past, it was said that man was created after the image of God, but it was not actually shown; for the Word was as yet invisible, after whose image man was created. Wherefore also he did lose the similitude. When, however, the Word of God became flesh, He confirmed both of these: for He showed forth the image truly, since He became Himself what was His image; and He re-established the similitude after a sure manner, by assimilating man to the invisible Father by means of the visible Word."[70] In this assimilation to God, people move from nature to grace, from the divine image to the divine likeness, from sin to salvation through deification.

The Means of Theosis

We have already anticipated the most practical of questions. Exactly how does one attain theosis? Orthodox theologians are unanimous that

---

66. Basil *On the Creation of Man* (cited by Karmiris, *Synopsis*, 29).
67. Quoted in Nicodemos, *Handbook*, 219.
68. Nicodemos, *Handbook*, 219.
69. Quoted in Nicodemos, *Handbook*, 219.
70. Irenaeus *Against Heresies* 5.16.2 (cited by Karmiris, *Synopsis*, 30).

our final deification will be realized only in the eschaton, with the so-called third birth; nevertheless, a very sure and certain beginning should characterize all Christians in the present age. The *Philokalia* is not only the single most important collection of Orthodox spiritual texts, but an excellent guidebook to the means of theosis. It is, according to its compiler Nicodemos of Athos, the "instrument itself of deification."[71]

Although some compilation apparently began as early as the late fourteenth century, the Greek text of the *Philokalia* (literally, "love of the beautiful") was first published in Venice in 1782, and later in a five-volume edition in Athens (1957–63). The present English version is three volumes, although plans call for a total of five volumes. Compiled by Nicodemos, who discovered the dusty and moth-eaten manuscripts in the monastery at Athos, the *Philokalia* is an anthology of texts written by Orthodox Christians from the fourth to the fifteenth centuries. In addition to contributing an introduction to the anthology, Nicodemos corrected some of the texts through a philological comparison of manuscripts and added short biographies of each author. By some estimates the influence of the *Philokalia* in the Orthodox tradition is second only to the Bible.

Nicodemos's introduction to the *Philokalia* provides a "synoptic expression of all Orthodox spirituality . . . a panoramic view of the history of salvation, creation, fall, and redemption." Deification takes center stage in this worldview, for it is the ultimate purpose of God's creation. The unifying theme throughout the many texts of the *Philokalia*, written over a period of a thousand years and from different cultural perspectives, is precisely how we can fulfill our calling or vocation, which is the summons to theosis or union with God.

Interestingly enough, we can say that for the writers of the *Philokalia*, the gift of theosis comes by grace through faith, and not by works. Especially significant here is Mark the Ascetic's *On Those Who Think That They Are Made Righteous by Works*. On the contrary, we are, insist Maximus and Peter of Damascus, "deified by grace." We "become god through union with God by faith."[72]

To be more exact, the *Philokalia* presents a very clear synergism or cooperation between the grace of God and human effort. Macarius explains the interaction of sovereign grace and human responsibility:

> We receive salvation by grace and as a divine gift of the Spirit. But to attain the full measure of virtue we need also to possess faith and love, and to struggle to exercise our free will with integrity. In this manner we inherit eternal life as a consequence of both grace and justice. We do not reach the final

71. See George S. Bebis, introduction to Nicodemos, *Handbook*, 20–24.
72. Maximus the Confessor, in *Philokalia*, 2:189–90, 243, 246, 263, 267; Peter of Damascus, in *Philokalia*, 3:79.

stage of spiritual maturity through divine power and grace alone, without ourselves making any effort; but neither on the other hand do we attain the final measure of freedom and purity as a result of our own diligence and strength alone, apart from any divine assistance. If the Lord does not build the house, it is said, and protect the city, in vain does the watchman keep awake, and in vain do the labourer and builder work [Ps. 127:1–4].[73]

Thus, faith without works and works without faith are equally rejected (James). In Pauline language, we labor and strive, but only through the empowering grace of God working in us (Phil. 2:12–13; 1 Cor. 15:10–11).

What direction, exactly, does this human effort take? At the risk of oversimplification, we can summarize the *Philokalia* and the human means of theosis in one Greek word, *nepsis*—that is, vigilance, watchfulness, intensity, zeal, alertness, attentiveness, or spiritual wariness. The "neptic" mind-set recognizes the reality of our spiritual warfare, that our Christian life is a strenuous battle, fierce drama, or "open contest" (*Theoretikon*), and responds accordingly.

The vigilance urged by the *Philokalia* will express itself in many ways. Of special concern in the *Philokalia* are our struggle with the passions and vice, which are analyzed at length, and our efforts to attain dispassion and virtue through bodily asceticism (fasting, vigils, prostrations, tears, repentance).[74] Through such dispassion we will attain an inner equilibrium that helps us to "daily wait on God's providence toward us"; whatever form that providence might take, we will be able to receive it "gratefully, gladly, and eagerly."[75] The "science of stillness" (Evagrios of Pontus), contemplation, and the interiorization of prayer through constant invocation of the name of Jesus are also of chief importance. Such prayer, advises Evagrios, must always be with "conscious awareness" and not mere ritual. Related to both dispassion and stillness is our need for detachment from the world, from what Neilos the Ascetic calls our "groveling in the dust of worldliness," empty trivialities, stupid conformity to fashion, and our modern civilized shamelessness. We must be constantly vigilant that we avoid the "false glitter of this life" (Diadochos of Photiki). To all of this we must add the divine gift of discrimination.

To dispassion, stillness, prayer, detachment, and discrimination we can add other means to divinization. We must participate faithfully in the sacraments. Seeking the regular counsel of a guide or spiritual father will save

73. Macarius of Egypt *Makarian Homilies* 1.1 (in *Philokalia*, 3:285). See also Theodoros the Great Ascetic's invocation of Chrysostom to the same effect—*A Century of Spiritual Texts* 68 (in *Philokalia*, 2:28).
74. See Peter of Damascus's list of 228 virtues and 298 vices, *Treasury of Divine Knowledge* (in *Philokalia*, 3:203–6); and John Cassian's analysis, *On the Eight Vices* (in *Philokalia*, 1:73–93).
75. Philotheos of Sinai *Texts on Watchfulness* 20 (in *Philokalia*, 3:24).

us from many sins. Keeping the commandments of God is indispensable: "In the end they make a man god, through the grace of Him who has given the commandments to those who choose to keep them."[76] Above all things we must put on love, for "love makes a man god."[77]

Although the concept of theosis is strange to most Western Christians, the neptic life is nothing exotic or esoteric. It is intended for all Christians and not just those who have taken monastic vows, for as Theognostos observed, the life of the laity "brings us no less close to God than [does] the priesthood."[78] In fact, many priests betray their monastic garb by their style of life. Further, we must never imagine that there is anything mechanical or magical about the many neptic means to godlikeness. Mere ritual or rote practice is the enemy of progress in the Christian life. On this point the *Philokalia* is insistent. Bodily asceticism is useless if it does not lead to moral reformation. Inward intention, whether good or evil, is more important than any outward action. We must turn talk, words, and mere theoretical understanding into practical experience and action.

In the end, according to the Orthodox fathers of the *Philokalia*, even if we were to become "master of the whole world," we still might not escape the "one real disaster" in life—"failure to attain by grace the deification" for which we were created. Conversely, if we avail ourselves of God's grace, and lead a life of spiritual vigilance, we can hope for the "glorious attainment of likeness to God, in so far as this is possible for man."[79]

76. Peter of Damascus *Treasury of Divine Knowledge* (in *Philokalia*, 3:93); see also Nicodemos, *Handbook*, 176, 180, 201.

77. Maximus the Confessor *Various Texts on Theology* 1.27–32 (in *Philokalia*, 2:171).

78. Theognostos *On the Practice of the Virtues* 57 (in *Philokalia*, 3:372).

79. Maximus the Confessor *On the Lord's Prayer*, and *Various Texts on Theology* 2.88 (in *Philokalia*, 2:297, 206).

A Hermeneutic of Love

The Orthodox Church is in her entire structure alien to the Gospel and represents a perversion of the Christian religion, its reduction to the level of pagan antiquity.

—Adolf von Harnack

Orthodox theology is like music made in the conservatory, whereas Protestant theology is like music made in the honky-tonk bars. Protestant Christianity is a cheap, terrible substitute, and an Orthodox believer who knows his own faith will never go there.

—Russian Orthodox priest

With Augustine I affirm a hermeneutics of love in which the fuller understanding of the text remains hidden until Christians learn to live in unity and love with one another.

—Donald Bloesch

In this final chapter we move from description to analysis, from exposition to evaluation. How can we sift for safekeeping the wheat of Orthodoxy discovered by former Protestants like Peter Gillquist from any chaff that would obscure the good news of Jesus Christ? What is a Protestant Christian to make of the Orthodox tradition? Where might we learn from Orthodoxy, and where do we agree to disagree?[1]

1. On the relationship between evangelicals and Orthodoxy see Peter E. Gillquist, *Making America Orthodox: Ten Questions Most Asked of Orthodox Christians* (Brookline, Mass.: Holy Cross Orthodox, 1984); Paul O'Callaghan, *An Eastern Orthodox Response to Evangelical Claims* (Minneapolis: Light and Life, 1984); Jordan Bajis, *Common Ground: An Introduction to Eastern Christianity for the American Christian* (Minneapolis: Light and Life, 1991).

A Context for Critique

In critiquing Orthodoxy, we must keep certain factors in mind. The analysis that follows presupposes an interpretive context guided by two criteria—one moral and one doctrinal.

First, we must beware of the perils of a polemical mind-set. Somewhere between the mutually antagonistic, shrill sounds of Adolf von Harnack's charge of pagan perversion, and the bombastic broadsides launched by my Russian Orthodox priest friend, we begin with the Augustinian dictum of a hermeneutic of love. As we attempt to exegete Orthodoxy, we must remind ourselves that mutual distrust, reciprocal reprisals, and unchecked suspicion will never lead to an accurate reading. Unless we approach one another in love, daring to imagine that each tradition has something of worth to offer to the other, we will, Augustine rightly observed, remain hidden from each other. Surely it is not too much to ask that both Protestant and Orthodox Christians approach one another not merely with the attitude of a spiritual and theological creditor, but as a spiritual debtor of some degree, thanking God for the chance to learn from one another rather than thanking him that we are not like our unfortunate neighbor (Luke 18:9–14). We must, Paul commanded, "accept one another" (Rom. 15:7), even and especially when we disagree with one another.

A hermeneutic of love will look for and discover the best in another, and if we look at contemporary Orthodoxy, we will find some wonderful signs of spiritual life and vigor at which we can only rejoice. It is important that Protestants recognize these positive signs of renewal in the worldwide life of Orthodoxy. The canonization of evangelical mystics such as saints Simeon the New Theologian, Macarius of Egypt, and Seraphim of Sarov are positive signs, as are the clearly evangelical movements within Orthodoxy—"Zoe" in Greece, the "Lord's Army" in Romania, the "Orthodox Brotherhood of Saint Simeon the New Theologian" in America, and the 1987 merger of the Evangelical Orthodox Church with the Antiochian Orthodox Church of North America.[2] The Society for the Study of Eastern Orthodoxy and Evangelicalism, which was organized in 1991, enjoys the support of Orthodox hierarchs and draws upon top scholars from both camps to engage theological issues of mutual concern at its annual meetings.

Russian Orthodoxy is a particular case in point. After seven decades of atheism that did everything in its power to exterminate Christianity, and despite critical shortages of priests (but not of men who want to become priests), of theological education, finances, and worship facilities, the Russian Orthodox Church is showing signs of renewed spiritual life. In a 1993 poll conducted by the All-Russian Center for Studying Public Opinion,

---

2. Bradley Nassif drew my attention to these examples.

45 percent of the 1,650 respondents considered themselves Christians, and 90 percent of those identified themselves as Orthodox. Moreover, 75 percent of the respondents indicated they had been baptized. Among the youth, people with university educations were twice as likely to be believers as were those with only a high school diploma.

The Moscow diocese has grown dramatically. Father Georgii Kochetov, to take one example, led a vibrant congregation of one thousand in preaching God's Word to modern unbelievers and unchurched people. Individuals who wished to be baptized by Father Georgii had to complete an extremely rigorous cathechism class that lasted a year; in a recent year six hundred believers were baptized. A Christian high school, correspondence courses on cassette tapes, an updated and Russified version of the Slavonic liturgy, thirty-two "base communities" that regularly met for prayer and Bible study, Sunday school, and church publications—all these were surely signs of the Spirit's movement in Father Georgii's church.[3] Space permitting, we could also mention many other examples in Russian Orthodoxy, like the All-Church Orthodox Youth Movement, the Children's Center of Orthodox Culture, Saint Dimitri's Orthodox School of Sisters of Mercy, the Orthodox Saint Tikhon Bible Institute, and a Russian Orthodox university.[4] Whatever our differences with Orthodoxy, Protestants must make it known that they not only recognize but fully support such movements of genuine spiritual renewal, that they are eager to see Orthodox churches recover full health, and that our missionary efforts in the former Soviet Union have no desire to convert the converted or steal sheep out of Orthodox parishes.

A hermeneutic of love will also have a sense of perspective. When trying to find our way through the maze of inter-Christian dialogue, it is sobering to think about the global concerns that Christians are called to engage. For example, do not the complexities of interreligious dialogue and world religious pluralism (not to mention religious fundamentalisms of all sorts) overshadow the in-house quarrels of fellow Christians? The same might be said about the many socioethical tragedies of modern life that beg the united, rather than fragmented, efforts of concerned Christians—global hunger, grinding poverty, runaway technology, and so on. Is there not a faint feeling of embarrassment at our internecine conflicts while the world waits for constructive engagement by us on these many critical concerns? I find that thinking about these larger global issues helps me to contextualize my critique of fellow Christians in a rather healthy

3. Unfortunately, because of his progressive measures Father Georgii was removed from his parish to another church—yet another example of the strange trends good and bad under Patriarch Alexei II.

4. Noel Calhoun, "The Russian Orthodox Church 1988-1993" (Unpublished paper, Harvard University, 1993).

way. This does not mean that Christians should ignore or minimize their differences; it means only that we should prioritize them within the broader spectrum of pressing concerns by remembering that we already enjoy agreement upon the primary matters of faith.

Second, there is the doctrinal criterion. A hermeneutic of love is a necessary criterion, but by itself it is not sufficient. Love, without love for truth, can degenerate into softheaded sentimentalism. The worship of God must be done in spirit and in truth (John 4:23–24). Merely accepting one another, as nonnegotiable as that is, is only half of our task. As best as we are able, we must evaluate Orthodoxy as we would any worldview—by the standard of the truth and clarity of the gospel. This doctrinal criterion of truth is as essential as the moral criterion of love.

Paul commanded Timothy to be careful of both: "Watch your life and doctrine closely" (1 Tim. 4:16). Paul himself declared that he would rather perish than preach a different gospel (Gal. 1:6–9). We could cite many similar warnings. Interestingly enough, few theological traditions can claim to have hewn to this requirement of doctrinal fidelity as tenaciously as has Orthodoxy.

At this point four general comments on doctrinal critique are in order. First, as with any confessional critique, we must distinguish between, on the one hand, official church pronouncements and the theology of the hierarchical spokespeople and, on the other, the personalized interpretations of individual thinkers. The official pronouncements and actions of Russian Orthodoxy, for example, have not been favorable toward Protestants in Russia. My priest friend quoted at the beginning of this chapter is a case in point, as were the vigorous efforts by Patriarch Alexei in the summer of 1993 to persuade the Russian Parliament to pass legislation that would have greatly restricted if not eliminated the operations of foreign religious groups in Russia. By most accounts that law would have been enforced if Boris Yeltsin had not dissolved the Russian Parliament that autumn.

On the other hand, a number of individual Orthodox priests exhibit in their own life and thinking a large measure of ecumenicity and empathy toward Protestants, along with strong evangelical inclinations. Father Gleb Yakunin, who opposed the aforementioned legislation on the grounds of free speech and democracy, comes to mind, as does my priest friend Father Evgeny Grushetsky, who invited me to participate as a visiting theologian at the new Humanitarian University of Minsk. Father Georgii Edelstein, who publicly and warmly invites Protestants to work with him in his Kostroma parish north of Moscow, is another example. Father Alexander Borisov, priest at Moscow's Church of Saints Cosmas and Damian, and head of the Russian Bible Society, preached a stirring sermon at the funeral of martyr Alexander Men that would have been the envy of any evangelical pulpiteer. A progressive pastor, Borisov is a leader of the Russian presidential prayer breakfast in Moscow. No doubt there are other such Orthodox priests and leaders.

To use an analogy from Catholicism, there is a difference between official Vatican pronouncements about papal infallibility and the understanding of that doctrine by any number of individual Catholic theologians (e.g., Rosemary Ruether, Hans Küng, Avery Dulles) and lay believers. Likewise, the views of Catholic theologian Paul Knitter on religious pluralism are by his own admission not representative of mainstream Catholic thought. A similar situation applies in Orthodoxy. Whereas the historical documents and official theology of Orthodoxy might make a clear pronouncement about a matter, say, the conclusions that the Second Council of Nicea (787) made about icons, an individual Orthodox theologian might take a more latitudinarian stance. For our purposes, as much as possible we will focus on the official theological positions of Orthodoxy rather than on its specific interpretation by any given individual theologian, for despite its claim to presenting a well-defined, unanimous body of Christian doctrine, in Orthodoxy as in Protestantism and Catholicism one discovers varying degrees of theological leeway.

Second, we must recognize that in the following critique we are making no judgment about any individual's relationship *with* God. Instead, we are studying beliefs *about* God and the gospel—that is, we are analyzing people's theology and not their lives. Too often this distinction is missed, and theological critique slides into spiritual ad hominem suspicion. Ideally these two essentials of Christian identity, doctrine and practice (see 1 Cor. 4:17), should never be separated, but human fallenness dictates otherwise. We all know of unhappy situations where a person with an impoverished theology has a rich relationship with God, as seemed to be the case with Friedrich Schleiermacher, whom Karl Barth fully expected to see in heaven even though his Christology was a "heresy of gigantic proportions." Origen is another case in point. Though he was condemned as a heretic in 553 (three centuries after his martyrdom), his practical piety has been well documented. Despite opening himself up to charges of heresy on any number of counts, Origen insisted he always intended to be "a man of the Church, not the founder of heresy," and that he had no intent whatsoever to "offend against [the church's] canon and Rule of Faith, thus giving scandal."[5]

On the other hand, sometimes Christians with impeccable theology fail to live up to even the basics of the gospel. A chastened evangelicalism has, let us hope, learned from the televangelist fiascos and steady string of fallen and falling pastors both prominent and obscure. Orthodoxy's well-

---

5. Origen *Homilies on Luke* 16; idem, *Homilies on Joshua* 7.6 (cited by Hans Urs von Balthasar, preface to *Origen*, trans. Rowan A. Greer [New York: Paulist, 1979], xi–xii). On Origen's life see Eusebius *Ecclesiastical History* 6.

documented compromise with the Soviet state, whether viewed as a necessity for survival or as a spineless capitulation, is another case in point.

The reciprocity and inseparability of ethical life and theological doctrine constitute a necessary and important study that deserves fuller
inquiry, for Scripture links life and doctrine together in an inextricable
way.[6] In addition to the exhortation to Timothy to watch his "life and doctrine closely" (1 Tim. 4:16) Paul could say to the Corinthians that "my
way of life . . . agrees with what I teach" (1 Cor. 4:17), that obedience in
addition to confession proves our Christian identity (2 Cor. 9:13). James
insists on works of mercy to vindicate words of faith (James 2:14–26). To
correct knowledge of the identity of Jesus ("Who do you say I am?" Matt.
16:15) there must be added an identifiable commitment to Christ in the
person of the poor, the naked, the lonely (Matt. 25:31–46). Doctrinal recognition of Christ is to be fulfilled in ethical encounter with one's neighbor. Fully biblical Christianity never separates the two.

Any denomination or theological tradition has its outstanding saints,
and Orthodoxy is no exception. Protestants eager to dismiss an Orthodox
Christian's claim to have a personal relationship with God through
Christ, or to dismiss Orthodoxy because of its political history, would do
well to recall the many Orthodox saints like Father Alexander Men, Dmitrii Dudko, and countless unknown and unnamed martyrs who suffered
and died for their faith under Soviet atheism. Still, such inquiries, interesting and essential though they are, are not our task here. We simply want
to try to evaluate Orthodox theology and will leave to God, who alone can
judge, any conclusion about the vitality of its spiritual life. In other words,
we are not trying to answer the question of whether a person can be a
Christian, a good Christian, or an evangelical Christian and remain
within the pale of Orthodoxy; I take it for granted that, in principle, being
good Christians is as possible for the Orthodox as it is for Presbyterians,
Baptists, and Catholics. As an acquaintance of mine once observed, it is
no more possible to generalize about whether Baptists (or Presbyterians or
Methodists) are good Christians than whether Orthodox believers are.

Third, because doctrine does have a bearing on one's life (and indeed
on one's eternal destiny), we must at some point tackle the question of
what exactly is the "truth of the gospel" by which a Protestant might evaluate Orthodoxy. We must "test the spirits" to see whether they be of
Christ or false prophets (1 John 4:1). The "eternal life" about which Jesus
spoke presupposes a certain knowledge and truth about God (John 4:23–
24; 17:3); presumably, wrong knowledge could misdirect or subvert the

6. Daniel B. Clendenin, "Barth on Schleiermacher: Yesterday and Today," in Robert
Streetman and James Duke, eds., *Barth and Schleiermacher: Beyond the Impasse?* (Philadelphia: Fortress, 1988), 173–75.

quest for eternal life. To recognize Jesus merely as one of the prophets is simply wrong. Renewal movements of all sorts—the sixteenth-century Reformation, the Anabaptists who followed it, nineteenth-century Wesleyan holiness movements, modern-day charismatics, Catholic lay renewals, mainline reform, and even monastic reforms within Orthodoxy such as were championed by Simeon the New Theologian in the tenth and eleventh centuries—all of these remind us of the sad fact that at times true life in Christ and the knowledge of God, in all its kingdom fullness, can be obscured, concealed, and even subverted by, among other things, dead ritualism, political compromise, theological interpretations that absolutize the relative, major on the minors, make peripheral matters central, or subvert theological nonessentials into essentials. At some point we must determine if, how, and to what extent Orthodoxy has done this (the same critique, of course, must be applied to all Christian confessions).

Our rule of faith, then, must be the essentials of the gospel rather than any of its nonessentials. Even this is no small matter to define with precision, as becomes apparent by efforts throughout the history of the church to define the sine qua non or final essence of Christianity—Johann Arndt's *True Christianity*, Søren Kierkegaard's later works, Harnack's *What Is Christianity?* Stephen Sykes's *Identity of Christianity*, and liberation theology's attempts to define true faith as socioeconomic preference for and liberation of the poor. Still, we must not overestimate the difficulty. The recent efforts by Donald Bloesch, Thomas Oden, and Robert Webber all point us to the methodological standard of an identifiable core, a "consensual tradition" (Oden) or "catholic evangelicalism" (Bloesch) of Christian beliefs that, as Vincent of Lérins of the fifth century put it, have been believed "everywhere, always, and by all."

On any given theological matter we will try to be as insistent as the gospel. Where a matter is left ambiguous, say, baptism for the dead (1 Cor. 15:29) or the descent of Christ into Hades (1 Peter 3:18–22), we will approach it with some latitude. Where the history of church exegesis is clear, say, on the deity of Christ, we will remain more narrow and insistent.

Finally, as will already be obvious, the present book makes no pretense of considering Orthodox theology in a comprehensive sense. Important matters such as ecclesiology, the sacraments, liturgy, the role of Mary and the saints, and the unique history and theology of church-state relationships are not considered. Any final Protestant engagement of Orthodoxy would have to address these and other important areas.

Lessons from Orthodox Life and History

It is a truism to observe that Christians have often taken it upon themselves to ostracize one another from the kingdom of God. Reformed people overlook Wesleyans, dispensationalists stigmatize charismatics, the High Church spurns the Low (and, of course, the reverse of these relationships also holds). The truism applies to Orthodoxy as well, which in chapter 2 we referred to as "the forgotten family." Western Christians typically do not know about Orthodoxy, ignore it, or confuse it with Catholicism. Though we have noted some identifiable reasons for this anonymity of Orthodoxy, we need to rediscover the full-orbed work of the Spirit across confessional lines rather than succumb to partisan appeals that divide the body of Christ ("I follow Paul," etc., 1 Cor. 1:10–17). Theologically, we need to experience anew the catholicity of the church, the fullness of each individual church, and the unity of all the church across space and time, "for we were all baptized by one Spirit into one body" (1 Cor. 12:13).[7] Thus we must be "diligent to preserve the unity of the Spirit in the bond of peace" (Eph. 4:3 NASB). This catholicity, although not without problems of definition, is mentioned in both the Nicene and Apostolic creeds, and has always been considered one of the four essential marks of the true church. It signals not uniformity but unity, diversity but not division.

Of the many lessons evangelicals might learn about the work of the Spirit in the life and history of the Eastern Orthodox Church, I will mention just three. The first grows out of the fact that for much of its history Eastern Orthodox Christianity has lived under political, cultural, and religious conditions that were, by any outward measure, extremely adverse. The four patriarchates of the eastern Mediterranean—Constantinople, Alexandria, Antioch, and Jerusalem—have existed as a Christian minority under the Muslim hegemony that began to take shape in the eighth century. The Orthodox churches of Eastern Europe and the former Soviet empire (Russia, Serbia, Romania, Bulgaria, Georgia, Poland, Albania, and what used to be Czechoslovakia), which constitute some 85 percent of worldwide Orthodoxy, have lived through the nightmare of violent persecutions at the hands of atheistic communism.[8] Having kept the faith in these two historico-

7. Cf. Ignatius *To the Smyrnaeans* 8.2: "Wherever Jesus Christ is, there is the catholic church."

8. Timothy Ware, *The Orthodox Church* (Baltimore: Penguin, 1964), 126. On Orthodoxy under Islam see Steven Runciman, *The Great Church in Captivity: A Study of the Patriarchate of Constantinople from the Eve of the Turkish Conquest to the Greek War of Independence* (New York: Cambridge University Press, 1968); Theodore Papadopoullos, *Studies and Documents Relating to the History of the Greek Church and People under Turkish Domination* (New York: AMS, 1973); Timothy Ware, *Eustratios Argenti: A Study of the Greek Church under Turkish Rule* (New York: Oxford University Press, 1964). On Orthodoxy under atheistic communism see Dmitry V. Pospielovsky, *A History of Marxist-Leninist Atheism and Soviet Antireligious Policies*, 3 vols. (New York: St. Martin's, 1987–88); idem, *The Russian Church under the Soviet Regime, 1917–1982*, 2 vols. (Crestwood, N.Y.: St. Vladimir's Seminary Press, 1984).

cultural contexts as a persecuted minority, Orthodoxy has experienced biblical truths that Christians in the West ought to learn. Orthodoxy can help
refocus our attention on a central theme of New Testament Christian identity—that the people of God is often a people that suffers.

Western Christians, most of whom have experienced little if any serious
persecution, need to rediscover the significance of Christian suffering found
throughout the pages of the New Testament, in the early church, and across
the world today. Jesus warned his followers about persecution on his account
(Matt. 5:10–11; 10:18, 22; 13:21; 24:9). Luke records the fulfilment of that
warning (Acts 5:41). Every epistle of Paul except Titus mentions Christian
suffering, either of Paul or of his readers. The books of Hebrews, James, especially Peter, Jude, and Revelation all witness to the reality of suffering in the
life of the early church. Early Christian literature like the *Martyrdom of Poly-
carp*, the *Passion of Saints Perpetua and Felicitas*, and Origen's *Exhortation to
Martyrdom* continues this theme that characterized much early Christian life
until the Edict of Toleration issued by Emperor Galerius on April 30, 311.[9]
Reflecting on these historical texts might be a good place for Western Christians to begin to contemplate this mark of Christian identity.

Western Christians have been quick to seek and find God through his
mighty acts of power, victory, prosperity, and miracle (a *theologia gloriae*),
but far too slow to recall that God's ultimate act of self-revelation was
through suffering on a cross, and that those who would follow the Suffering Servant must pattern their lives after his (a *theologia crucis*). Somehow
we must rid ourselves of the self-serving and facile "isn't God good?!" attitude. Paul taught that God is to be discovered not so much through his
startling displays of power and miraculous interventions, but through
times of great suffering, testing, and human weakness (2 Cor. 12:7–10).
Orthodox believers have experienced this sobering truth. May we in the
West have the grace and wisdom to learn from their experience, rejecting
our triumphalistic attitudes in favor of the more biblical idea of knowing
God through the way of the cross.

The second area in which we have much to learn from Orthodoxy is its
self-conscious adherence to apostolic tradition (*paradosis*), its well-
developed historical consciousness that the gospel is an inheritance from
those who have gone before us, its determination to pattern its entire Christian identity after the life of the early church, its creeds and councils. By
contrast, evangelicals sometimes in their reading of the Bible and experiencing of Christianity act as if they were the first to discover those truths.
We too easily ignore and sometimes even eschew the function of tradition
as the rich repository of the church's beliefs, confessions, and worship

9. Eusebius *Ecclesiastical History* 8.17.6–10.

throughout all times and places. Orthodoxy can help us move beyond our
tendencies toward theological amnesia and ahistorical attitudes to recapture
a sense of historical continuity with the church down through the centuries.
Because of its minority status in Muslim and atheistic environments, Orthodoxy has long exhibited a strong tendency to conserve the historical deposit
of faith. Accordingly, evangelicals will find Orthodoxy to be a close ally in
the defense of the faith against erosions by modernity.

Developing a sense of Christian historical consciousness will have at
least two benefits. First, it will help us to differentiate between what the
church has always considered the essential, nonnegotiable core of Christian identity and the nonessential, negotiable particularities of any given
confession, time, or place. We will find the principle behind this differen-
tiation spelled out by the early church fathers, as in Vincent of Lérin's dictum, Irenaeus's "canon of truth," the notion of a *regula fidei*, and Athanasius's "scope of faith."[10] Likewise in the Reformation Era John Calvin,
Martin Luther, and Philipp Melanchthon, and later John Wesley, invoked
the concept of *adiaphora* ("things indifferent") to discriminate between
the essentials of Christianity and, on the other hand, matters which Scripture neither commands nor forbids, neutral issues to be decided by each
local church as long as they do not impede or obscure the gospel (1 Cor.
8:1–9:23; Gal. 2:3–5; 5:13–15; and Col. 2:16–23).[11] With this historical
background in view, we can approach our theologizing with a renewed
sense of priorities or hierarchy in doctrine (cf. Paul's reference to matters
"of first importance" in 1 Cor. 15:3), confidence about what really matters
and what does not, and, having this solid anchor, freedom to think cre-
atively about less clear theological issues.

The second benefit of a renewed historical consciousness will be a sense
of theological modesty, the awareness that all of our best theologizing is limited by our finitude, sinfulness, and historicocultural experience. We will
also feel genuine gratitude for all the saints of God that have gone before us.
To help us develop this sense of historical consciousness, we might well
examine the recent works of Drew University theologian Thomas Oden,
which present a thoroughgoing theology of historical consensus.[12]

A third conspicuous characteristic of Orthodox life and history is its
near total integration of theology and worship. This blending of theology

---

10. George Florovsky, *Bible, Church, Tradition: An Eastern Orthodox View* (Belmont,
Mass.: Nordland, 1972), chap. 5.

11. John Calvin, *Institutes*, 4.2.1. On Wesley see Donald A. Thorsen, *The Wesleyan
Quadrilateral* (Grand Rapids: Zondervan, 1990), 159–62.

12. Thomas Oden, *Systematic Theology*, 3 vols. (San Francisco: Harper and Row, 1987–
92); see also Daniel B. Clendenin, "Thomas Oden," in Walter Elwell, ed., *Handbook of
Evangelical Theologians* (Grand Rapids: Baker, 1993), 401–11.

and worship gives Orthodoxy its thoroughly liturgical character. From the perspective of Eastern Christianity, Western Christianity typically exhibits a breach or rupture between theological study and liturgical experience. Orthodoxy has not been immune from this pattern, but to the extent that it has followed the West in this respect, it has cut itself off from its natural historical roots.[13] For by most accounts the integration of theology and worship in the liturgy is the very heart or essence of Orthodoxy. Whereas in the West theology and worship tend to be discrete and even dissimilar activities, in Orthodoxy they are a single, inseparable act. This explains Orthodoxy's repeated appeal to the Evagrian aphorism, "If you are a theologian, you will pray truly. And if you pray truly, you are a theologian."[14] Likewise, many see the sum and substance of Orthodoxy as encapsulated in the dictum that "the rule of prayer and worship is the rule of faith and doctrine" (lex orandi est lex credendi).

Orthodoxy does not neglect scholarly study, nor should evangelicals. We do so to our own peril. But Western believers might learn from Orthodoxy that the ultimate context of academic study must be the Christian community at worship. Without the liturgical context of worship, theology becomes "scholastic" in the worst sense of the word, rather than a guide to worshiping God in spirit and in truth.

General Problems

Orthodox Christianity is not without its own set of problems and weaknesses, and for the most part its scholars and priests are well aware of this. Its unrelenting insistence that it alone is the one true church of Christ on earth must be questioned, especially as it impinges upon the necessity of Christian unity. This matter is somewhat ironic given Orthodoxy's problems of intense nationalism and ethnocentricity vis-à-vis not only non-Orthodox Christians, but also the various branches within Orthodoxy. Although officially condemned by the Synod of Constantinople in 1872, phyletism, which is the identification of the interests of the secular state with the Christian church, and even racism remain stubborn and prevalent weaknesses of modern Orthodoxy.[15]

13. Alexander Schmemann, Introduction to Liturgical Theology (Crestwood, N.Y.: St. Vladimir's Seminary Press, 1986), 10; George Florovsky, The Ways of Russian Theology, 2 vols. (Belmont, Mass.: Nordland, 1979, 1987), 1:134 (see also Florovsky's chapter on the "contamination" of Orthodoxy by Western "school theology," 114–48).

14. Evagrios On Prayer 61.

15. John Meyendorff, Living Tradition (Crestwood, N.Y.: St. Vladimir's Seminary Press, 1978), 86–91, 105–6, 112, 120–21, 200; Ware, Orthodox Church, 77, 89, 174–75; Alexander Schmemann, "The Idea of Primacy in Orthodox Ecclesiology," in John Meyendorff, ed., The Primacy of Peter in the Orthodox Church (Crestwood, N.Y.: St. Vladimir's Seminary Press, 1992), 167–71; and Nicolas Zernov, Eastern Christendom: A Study of the Origin and Development of the Eastern Orthodox Church (New York: Putnam, 1961), 173–74.

Further, resolute historical consciousness can easily turn to historicism, a fossilization of the past. The criticism that Orthodoxy is backward-looking and plagued by a medieval mind-set is not without some warrant, for at times it exhibits both a romantic and uncritical attitude toward the church fathers. This petrification of the past can distort or supplant the living biblical witness. Another problem is that the patristic inheritance is neither as monolithic nor as uniform as Orthodoxy sometimes suggests (here Peter Abelard had a point). Further, the dogmatic incorporation of the past into the life of the church tends to sacrifice contextual interaction with contemporary cultural issues. Incorporating the patristic past is necessary, but merely repeating it is dangerous.

A related danger is that love for liturgy can turn into rote ritualism. Russian Orthodoxy's insistence, for example, on maintaining its liturgy in ninth-century Slavonic, which few modern Russians fully understand, is a case in point. There is little doubt that some of the successes of Western missionaries in the former Soviet Union can be partially attributed to new and more contemporary forms of worship and discipleship.

Critique of the Distinctive Emphases of Orthodoxy

God's Majesty and Mystery: Apophaticism

In chapter 3 we focused on the apophatic character of Orthodox theology as fundamental to its entire theological mind-set, this "negative way" of "denial" being defined as a radical prostration of the intellect before the living God. In his essence or nature, as he is in himself, God is absolutely incomprehensible and inaccessible. As John of Damascus put it, all that is comprehensible of God in his essence is his incomprehensibility.[16] But this by no means implies that we cannot know or experience God. In his energies, in his condescending grace, we know and experience God in a valid but limited way. Against any notion of ontological ineffability or theological agnosticism Simeon the New Theologian and Gregory Palamas both defended the legitimacy and even necessity of a direct experience of God.

In Orthodoxy the impenetrable mystery of God is not a puzzle to decipher or a defect to expunge; it is something to contemplate and adore. Theological mystery moves toward mystical union. Thus in the East theology (*theologia*) tends not so much toward rational deductions from abstract propositions, although such work is not entirely absent in Orthodoxy, but toward contemplation (*theoria*) and vision. In the *Philokalia*, for example, "theology" is understood less as a level of erudition and more as a level of spiritual experience.

16. John of Damascus *Exposition of the Orthodox Faith* 1.4.

The biblical witness to the nature of God lends strong support to apophaticism. No one has seen or can see God (John 1:18). He lives in unapproachable light (1 Tim. 6:16). His ways are unsearchable and unfathomable (Job 11:7–8; Rom. 11:33–36). Even the angels, who enjoy a more certain knowledge of God, shield their vision of him (Isa. 6:2). Between the divine and human wisdom there is a qualitative difference (Isa. 55:8–9; 1 Cor. 1:18–31; 3:18–23). As the psalmist put it, "Our God is in heaven; he does whatever pleases him" (Ps. 115:3; cf. 135:6).

Apophaticism is demanded not only by the divine nature, but also by our human condition. As John Calvin observed in his *Institutes*, "the fault of dullness is within us." We are finite. Our intellectual capacities and historicocultural experiences are varied and relative. The fall and our inherent sinfulness compromise not only our wills and our capacity to do the good, but also our minds and their capacity to know the Good. Suppression of truth, futile thinking, and darkened, depraved minds limit our theological knowledge (Rom. 1:18, 28; Eph. 4:17–18). We will never know God now as we will in the eschaton (1 Cor. 13:12; 1 John 3:2–3).

The way of denial is a necessary component of any truly biblical theological method. It is a constant warning against the rationalistic impulses in some evangelical theological methods, tendencies that would domesticate the transcendent God. Apophaticism is a constantly needed reminder of the virtue not of skepticism or agnosticism, but of theological modesty. A truly biblical theological method adores the mystery rather than eliminates it. Here the priority of faith seeks understanding.[17]

Orthodox apophaticism not only helps in the method of theology. It helps in our consideration of the nature of theology by reminding us that truly biblical theology is experiential as well as intellectual. God is not merely a transcendent object of detached intellectual scrutiny. He is also an immanent Subject who, as Gregory Palamas and Simeon the New Theologian insisted, must be experienced directly. Cyril of Jerusalem was correct when he observed that God as the object of intellectual study and God as the Subject of a personal relationship cannot be separated: "The method of godliness consists of these two things: pious dogmas and the practice of virtue. God does not accept dogmas apart from good works. Nor does He accept works that are not based on pious dogmas."[18] For Orthodoxy, true theology involves not only intellectual erudition but a spiritual experience with the living God; this conception can correct Western models of theology which tend to be academic reflection on propositions.

17. Anselm *Proslogion* 1.
18. Cyril of Jerusalem *Catechesis* 4.2.

The insights of Orthodoxy about both the method and nature of theology can be found in the Protestant tradition. It was the genius of John Wesley (1703–91) to insist upon the experiential or experimental nature of true theology, warning us of mere formality or outside religion that would be the undoing of true heart-religion. According to Donald Thorsen, Wesley sees a positive and necessary role for experience in correcting theological methods that are rigidly scholastic or only conceptualist.[19] In the Reformed tradition, Calvin insisted on a knowledge of God that did not merely "flit about in the brain" but instead was a transforming piety. Likewise Philipp Spener (1635–1705), who in his *Pia desideria* (1675) insisted that spiritual renewal is equally important as theological dogmatics. More recently, Neoorthodox theologians like Emil Brunner (1889–1966) have argued that God's revelation is not only propositional but especially personal. God reveals not simply information, but his very self. For Brunner, the biblical concept of truth, as opposed to the Western philosophic, is encounter. Biblical truth is not simply I-It but I-Thou, an encounter with the living God.[20]

Nor is the Western tradition bereft of mystery in theology. One thinks of Søren Kierkegaard and Karl Barth, who insisted on the radical otherness of God. Likewise Protestant scholasticism made helpful distinctions between the infinite knowledge of God that is known only to himself (*theologia archetypa*) and the finite and imperfect knowledge of God that is available to creatures (*theologia ectypa*)—whether to angels, the blessed saints in heaven, or pilgrim wayfarers on earth (*theologia viatorum*).

Thus Orthodox apophaticism reminds us that in our rational theological method we must always incorporate the mysterious, and that in addition to the necessary work of the intellect theology must always include personal, life-transforming encounter. Further, the transcendence of God means that our knowledge of him, though it can be valid, is limited. His immanence signals that God in his self-revelation is not just an objective proposition for the intellect, but a loving Subject to be adored in worship.

Images of Christ: Icons

When one compares the internal architecture of Protestant and Orthodox churches, the former with whitewashed walls and the latter with hardly a square foot not covered with some art form, one senses just how

19. Thorsen, "The Authority of Experience," in *Wesleyan Quadrilateral*, 201–25. Randy Maddox, "John Wesley and Eastern Orthodoxy: Influences, Convergences, and Differences," *Asbury Theological Journal* 45.2 (Fall 1990): 29–53, notes explicit convergences on this and other points.

20. See Emil Brunner, *Wahrheit als Begegnung* (Zurich: Zwingli, 1938); *Truth as Encounter*, rev. ed. (London: SCM, 1964).

different the worlds of Protestantism and Orthodoxy are. The Orthodox icon is perhaps the most obvious and, for the Protestant, controversial example of these differences.

Historically, iconoclasm has almost been part and parcel of Protestantism. We have tended toward either a benign neglect of the role of aesthetics in theology and worship or at times even a rather calculated iconoclasm. The Protestant Reformers would whitewash the walls of churches that had images. To take a contemporary example, in his widely influential book *Knowing God* J. I. Packer categorically insists that Christians must never make use of *any* visual or pictorial representations of God in their worship: "There is no room for doubting that the [second] commandment obliges us to dissociate our worship, both in public and in private, from all pictures and statues of Christ, no less than from pictures and statues of His Father."[21] Jacques Ellul's *Humiliation of the Word* is another example of a Reformed iconoclasm that emphasizes the priority of the Word and the danger of images within the Christian community.

While there are some good reasons to question the use of icons, do Protestants need to go so far as to consider Christians who use icons as "rejected and cursed out of the Christian Church," to use the words of the Iconoclastic Council of 754? Might we not pause to consider how and why, despite the complex theological and political history of icons, an ecumenical council finally ratified their use? Might not Orthodox theology and its appeal to the strategy employed by Basil the Great help us to reconsider the role of liturgical tradition (what the church has practiced and confessed, often before its theological justification) as a source for theology?

Conversely, related questions can be asked of Orthodoxy. Cannot Orthodoxy acknowledge that the complex political, historical, and theological factors surrounding the final endorsement of icons make their use something less than mandatory? It is obvious that icon use enjoyed something far less than a unified support in the history of the early church, not to mention a large number of negative statements by Christian apologists. George Florovsky is quite helpful here, acknowledging as he does that the support of the church was one of the strongest weapons in the iconoclastic arsenal. Furthermore, does it really serve any useful purpose, given this murky theological history of the icon, to continue to insist with the Council of 787 that Christians who reject icons are evil, pernicious, and subversive heretics? Does it help the cause of Christ today to commemorate the Council of 843 every year with the

---

21. J. I. Packer, *Knowing God* (Downers Grove, Ill.: Inter-Varsity, 1973), 39–40; see also Packer's entire chapter and similar comments by Donald Bloesch, *A Theology of Word and Spirit* (Downers Grove, Ill.: Inter-Varsity, 1992), 94–102.

public anathematization of iconoclastic believers? I think not. Instead, icons just might be an issue that both Protestant and Orthodox believers can relegate to the category of *adiaphora*.

Orthodox icons raise for Protestant Christians a generally neglected but important theological question—the nature and function of a wide-ranging and truly Christian aesthetic. Perhaps Protestants have been too reluctant to explore, as does Canon 82 of the Council of 692, what the doctrines of creation and incarnation imply regarding the goodness of the material world. What explains this neglect of or hostility toward aesthetics in theology? It seems that we must constantly fight against Docetic or Gnostic inclinations that treat the material world as evil. The statements by John of Damascus and Theodore the Studite about the sanctification of our senses and the glorification of matter might be helpful here, as might consideration of what would be entailed in a full-fledged Christian metaphysics of matter.

But having acknowledged the legitimacy of a Christian aesthetic or materialism, Protestants rightly question the propriety of assigning icons the same status and function as the gospel, as did the Council of 787. Does Orthodoxy really want to affirm that what the gospel text renders in words is adequately conveyed simply in color (Council of 869)? Is there not something inherently unhealthy in Orthodoxy's insistence that theology is best crystalized in images rather than in words, and that for uneducated people images are a sufficient substitute for the Word explained? In short, icons are by no means sufficient to teach us "all we need to know"—which was the response of one Orthodox priest when asked why his church did not offer more doctrinal teaching.[22] Images must never replace or subvert the Word. But rightly understood they can be a joyous supplement in the manner, if not content, of worship.

Orthodoxy makes an explicit distinction between the absolute worship that is due to God alone and the relative respect or veneration that can be paid to an icon, to a saint, or even to one another. Further, when offering relative veneration to an icon, Orthodoxy insists that the worship is directed to God alone, the prototype, and not to the material image. Protestants should acknowledge the helpfulness of this distinction and recognize with Theodore the Studite that although the "outward form" of veneration can look the same as absolute worship, the "inward intention" is very different.

But precisely at this point Protestants again raise an important question. Is there often not an apparent discrepancy between the Orthodox doctrine and the actual practice of icons? How many lay Orthodox believ-

22. Harvey Cox, *Many Mansions* (Boston: Beacon, 1988), 132.

ers understand and follow the complex theological distinctions regarding the nature of worship? Cannot the use of icons degenerate very easily into something quite counterproductive to encountering God? Of course, this is a question that is difficult to answer because the key issue is a person's inward intention. And who can determine that?

Perhaps an analogy from the Protestant tradition will be helpful. Because of widespread practical abuses that vitiate theological justifications, some Lutheran and Reformed theologians have discouraged the continuation of infant baptism (Kierkegaard, Barth, Jürgen Moltmann). Likewise, were not the theological polemics of Luther and Calvin against images driven by their frustration with practical abuses? If liturgical practice can support a theological position, as the Orthodox insist, then liturgical abuses must be accounted for and factored in as well. Even *adiaphora* can impede or obscure the gospel. Within Orthodox Christianity some theologians have begun to note this problem.[23] Furthermore, the *Philokalia* itself gives extensive warnings about our susceptibility to being deceived by sense perception.

The Spirit's Witness: Scripture and Tradition

In chapter 5 we saw how Orthodoxy attempts to distinguish itself from both the Protestant insistence on *sola scriptura* and Catholic doctrines of papal primacy. Instead of an external authority of book or pope, Orthodoxy proposes the pneumatic and internal authority of the Holy Spirit.

In fact, as we saw, Orthodoxy is not at all consistent about the relationship between Scripture and tradition. Although there are Orthodox statements about the absolute primacy of Scripture over tradition, for the most part Orthodoxy clearly states that other forms of tradition—icons, councils, ecumenical creeds—are coequal and even infallible sources of theological authority. Protestants rightly respond that the mere fact of the formation of the scriptural canon demonstrates that the early church considered all other sources of theological authority as secondary. The church's reception of the canon demonstrated its acknowledgment of an "unambiguous authority amidst the confusing claims of pseudepigraphic literature and oral traditions."[24]

On the other hand, Protestants need to recognize the historical context of Orthodoxy's emphasis on tradition. In the early centuries of Christianity, the church struggled with attempts by Gnostic and Arian heretics to use the Scripture to their own ends. Vincent of Lérins, for example, com-

23. E.g., Alexander Yelchaninov, in George P. Fedotov, A *Treasury of Russian Spirituality*, 2 vols. (Belmont, Mass.: Nordland, 1975), 2:451, 463–64.

24. Heiko Oberman, "Quo Vadis? Tradition from Irenaeus to Humani Generis," *Scottish Journal of Theology* 16 (1963): 250.

plains in his *Commonitorium* that all the heretics claim scriptural support for their positions. In response, the early church developed notions of tradition, the rule or canon of Christian truth, in order to distinguish the true from false exegesis of the Word. From the historical perspective, then, the emphasis on tradition is quite understandable, as is the Reformation emphasis on Scripture over tradition in its own historical circumstances.

We should also observe that Orthodoxy in general is not sufficiently critical in its invocation of the Fathers, creeds, and councils. These extra-canonical sources, often viewed somewhat romantically by Orthodoxy, are not as unified and monolithic as sometimes implied. Orthodoxy needs to recover the Reformation insight that tradition can subvert as well as support the witness of the Spirit in Scripture.

But if Orthodoxy is not sufficiently critical of these patristic sources, for its part Protestantism is not sufficiently attentive to the historical and ecclesiastical context of Scripture. Entering the world of Orthodoxy can ameliorate Protestant tendencies to an ahistorical reading of Scripture. Protestants must understand that tradition has a role in the life, worship, and reflection of the Christian community. To reach that understanding, they need to be more precise as to exactly what they mean by *sola scriptura*. Within the historical context of the Reformation (and early-twentieth-century fundamentalism), where many saw institutional tradition and traditions as obscuring or even falsifying the gospel, the appeal to Scripture alone was understandable, and perhaps even necessary. But, as Harold Brown observes, from another perspective it is "misleading to think that Scripture produced the Church." With Orthodoxy (and Catholicism) Protestants must acknowledge that the church preceded and gave birth to written Scripture. Further, it is "misleading to think that Scripture alone can create a full structure of Christian life and Christian worship." The various forms of tradition amplify, positively or negatively, the text of Scripture. Brown concludes: "We evangelical Protestants of today, even as we insist on the normative principle of *sola scriptura*, can no longer maintain the fiction that the early congregations were products of the Scripture principle, or at least not of the Scripture principle alone."[25]

Protestants, then, should insist that Scripture is the primary but not exclusive source for Christian life and theology. While Scripture is in a class by itself (*sui generis*), tradition is both a practical inevitability (no one can avoid it) and a hermeneutical necessity. Exploring the mind of the church in its interpretation of Scripture down through the centuries will help us to avoid the real dangers of private, subjectivistic interpretations.

25. Harold O. J. Brown, "Orthodoxy: An Evangelical Perspective" (Paper given at the Society for the Study of Eastern Orthodoxy and Evangelicalism, Wheaton, Ill., September 26, 1992), 5.

Protestants will also feel kinship with the Orthodox insistence that the succession of apostolic truth is the responsibility of the entire church and not of a single hierarch or group of hierarchs. With Orthodoxy, Protestants might agree that the bishop of Rome enjoys a primacy of honor as the first among equals, but not any primacy of power. The ontological equality of every priest and bishop, of every church, and of all the people of God as the protector of the truth of the gospel, is a healthy corrective to Roman tendencies. Whether the Orthodox hierarchy has in practice been able to avoid similar tendencies to ecclesiastical hegemony is another question.

Finally, with its ultimately pneumatic understanding that ecclesiastical authority rests in the work and witness of the Holy Spirit, Orthodoxy reminds Protestants of a truth they often neglect. While recognizing the legitimacy and even necessity of external norms of theological authority, at the same time we must acknowledge that these norms are penultimate in nature. The final triumph of the gospel over the gates of hell (Matt. 16:18) depends ultimately on the work of God himself. Recovering the role of the Spirit in the doctrine of scriptural authority is a healthy challenge for Protestants.

The Divinization of Humanity: Theosis

The centrality of theosis to Orthodoxy is, like the centrality of icons, quite foreign to Protestant theology. In chapter 6 we saw that theosis or divinization has at least three interrelated meanings. It is the mystical union with God whereby believers are transformed; the movement from death, mortality, and corruption to life, immortality, and incorruption; and the ascent from the image of God (possessed by all people) to his very likeness (given to those who cooperate with divine transforming grace).

Theosis is an area that, while enjoying only modest biblical support, has a long and certain patristic heritage. Theosis has been little explored by Protestant evangelicals who, while tipping their hat to the panoply of biblical metaphors for the work of Christ, nevertheless tend to focus primarily on justification by faith and substitutionary atonement. A study of church history, however, makes us aware of support for the well-defined, Eastern exegetical tradition that places Christian anthropology at the center of its vision. As the major rejections of Christianity in the last two centuries have been based in anthropological critiques (Darwin, Marx, Freud), and as many of the critical cultural issues of our day (abortion, euthanasia, hunger, illiteracy) beg for a robust theological anthropology, Protestants might want to reconsider the priority they give to the Christian view of what it means to be a human being created in the image of God and for union with him.

Protestants should be reassured by the fact that Orthodoxy is careful to explicitly reject any hints of pantheism in its doctrine of theosis. The general idea, that believers are transformed through mystical union into the divine nature, finds support in the Pauline teaching that the image of God, distorted but not lost in the fall, is being progressively renewed in us (Col. 3:10), so that we are increasingly conformed to the likeness of Christ (Rom. 8:29). In Paul's words, we become more like Christ and God. In Peter's vocabulary, we come to share the divine nature.

Orthodoxy's emphasis on the necessity of human cooperation with the grace of God, which is understood in the *Philokalia* as a "neptic" struggle, should find a welcome reception among Protestants. Paul's own self-understanding was that God's grace in his life was not without effect or in vain, for he himself "worked hard" (1 Cor. 15:10–11; 2 Cor. 6:1). As God works in us, we work out our salvation, not by self-effort or by any inherent ability (Pelagius), but by the transforming grace of God that works in us to will and do his will (Phil. 2:12–13). James, too, insists that true faith is vindicated or justified by the response of human work (James 2:14–26). The Orthodox emphasis on the importance of the human response toward the grace of God, which at the same time clearly rejects salvation by works, is a healthy synergistic antidote to any antinomian tendencies that might result from (distorted) juridical understandings of salvation.

Protestantism can offer a threefold critique of the theology of theosis. First, Orthodoxy might reconsider whether the slender biblical support for theosis, found explicitly only in two texts, and even then questionably so (2 Peter 1:4 and John 10:34–35), warrants the disproportionate emphasis given to it in the overall theological schema. Reconsideration is especially necessary if the emphasis on theosis neglects more-central biblical motifs that depict the work of Christ or, worse, suggests that other biblical motifs like justification by faith are unduly negative Augustinian distortions rather than Pauline categories. Some Orthodox thinkers do a better job at recognizing the full biblical witness to the work of Christ. Vladimir Lossky, for example, explicitly endorses substitutionary atonement.[26]

Second, some of the evidence for theosis, like the distinction between image and likeness, finds little support in contemporary biblical scholarship (a point acknowledged by some Orthodox thinkers).

Third, it is important in biblical theology to distinguish between the doctrines of salvation and sanctification.[27] While one can justifiably argue that any believer who experiences salvation can and should undergo sanctification, this is not to equate the two experiences or doctrines. A case

26. Vladimir Lossky, *Orthodox Theology: An Introduction* (Crestwood, N.Y.: St. Vladimir's Seminary Press, 1978), 110.
27. Bajis, *Common Ground*, 253 n. 45.

could be made that theosis is better understood as the experience of sanctification rather than salvation, and that Orthodoxy confuses the two at
this point.

Theosis and other biblical metaphors for the work of Christ need not
be understood as contradicting one another. There is no reason that they
cannot be seen as complementary. The East emphasizes the crucial idea of
mystical union and divine transformation, while the West tends to stress
the believer's juridical standing before a holy God. Both conceptions, and
others beside, find biblical support and deserve full theological expression.

The witness of the gospel is intrinsically dependent upon the unity of
the church. Only when fellow believers are brought to "complete unity"
(John 17:23), only when we convincingly love one another, will the world
understand that God in Christ loves them. No doubt, as Calvin observed
in his *Institutes*, the church "swarms with many faults," but even then we
should never be guilty of what he called "an immoderate severity." Wesley,
too, provides us with a useful model. Although he had his differences with
Catholics, and did not hesitate to state those differences forcefully when
he thought that the essentials of the gospel were compromised, he was also
quite insistent that a demonstrable conciliatory posture is mandatory for
believers.[28]

The witness of the gospel is also intrinsically dependent upon a rightly
formulated and clearly proclaimed word of truth. Both the theological
content and type of expression are critical. The content of the gospel must
be clearly formulated and then find expression in ecclesiastical wineskins
that effectively proclaim the good news. The evangelistic means must suit
the end of a clear and distinct message.

By convincingly practicing a hermeneutic of love, and insisting upon
the essentials rather than the nonessentials of Christian teaching, Protestant and Orthodox Christians will begin to incarnate the marks of the true
body of Christ—the one, holy, catholic, and apostolic church—and obey
the clear command of our Lord.

28. Thorsen, *Wesleyan Quadrilateral*, 159–62.

Epilogue
Orthodox-Evangelical Dialogue: Past, Present, and Future

A Muscovite Past

Every book is in part a product of its own social location and the author's personal biography, and this book is no exception. In September 1991 my family moved to Moscow State University, where for the next four years I served as a visiting professor in the faculty of philosophy's department of scientific atheism. When I left in June of 1995, this department had been renamed the department of philosophy of religion and religious studies in order to reflect some curricular changes. I will always be grateful for the kindness and gracious reception with which the people in this department welcomed me, especially given the extraordinarily difficult circumstances under which they lived and worked in those years. As a visiting professor, I was paid a full professor's salary by the university for the first two years, which in those days was $20 a month.

Just three months after moving to Moscow, on December 24, 1991, we celebrated Christmas Eve in the American embassy with friends, and Mikhail Gorbachev appeared on television and shocked the world with his resignation speech.[1] The next weekend we stood in Red Square as the Russian flag displaced the newly defunct Soviet flag atop the Kremlin buildings. In the park outside of our apartment on Lenin Avenue, people formed a gauntlet of two long lines and began their fledgling experiment with capitalism by selling anything and everything—a dried, stiff fish; a pack of cigarettes; plumbing fixtures; homemade VCR tapes; odd pieces of clothing; and so forth. By all accounts, the fulcrum of history was shifting.

These tectonic shifts in politics, economics, and culture were matched by similar shifts in the religious world. At midnight on Saturday April 25, 1992, for the first time since the 1917 Bolshevik Revolution, Easter bells rang out from the Kremlin's Ivan the Great bell tower. Russian Orthodoxy,

---

1. For the text of Gorbachev's speech see Daniel B. Clendenin, *From the Coup to the Commonwealth* (Grand Rapids: Baker, 1992), 155–59.

which celebrated one thousand years of Christianity in 1988 and had
endured seventy years of virulent atheism, was poised for resurgence and
revival. But having suffered what might have been the greatest martyrdom
in the history of Christianity, Russian Orthodoxy emerged greatly weak-
ened.[2] It also had made its share of concessions and compromises with the
Soviet regime. The tidal wave of Western missionaries eager to evangelize
further complicated matters; by 1992 at least eight hundred organizations
had descended upon the former Soviet Union.[3] No wonder that even the
likes of Billy Graham received a lukewarm reception from the patriarch
during his Moscow crusade. Recovering from near obliteration, grappling
with the consequences of accommodation, and adjusting to religious pluralism remain challenges for today's Russian Orthodox Church. For both
good and ill, the church emerged as the one cultural institution, next to
the military, that still commanded significant social influence; despite
Marxist predictions, the church had decidedly not withered away.

During my second year at Moscow State University, I researched the
first edition of this book, presenting the manuscript material to students
and professors in university seminars and lectures. These university students offered a unique perspective and valuable critique. On the one
hand, they were the offspring of parents whose generation, as far as I could
tell from my limited experiences, had been thoroughly assimilated to
Soviet atheism. For the most part, my students and their parents were cyn-
ical and critical about religion. In numerous conversations people would
tell me with all candor something to the effect, "I have never felt a need
for God or ever believed in God." People were intellectually curious about
religion but not existentially hungry for religion. On the other hand, other
students recounted how they had been secretly baptized by their grandpar-
ents, or how they enjoyed making what was then a political statement by
attending an Orthodox worship service. A few of them had chosen to be
baptized as teenagers. One extremely conservative Orthodox priest,
Andrei Kuraev, lectured to huge, overflow crowds at Moscow State University, urging students to embrace the faith. Whether they loved or hated
Kuraev, the students clearly found his subject engaging. Overall, then,
whether critical or supportive, my students were eager to discuss Orthodoxy and how it compared with Western Protestantism.

So too were my professor colleagues, but almost to a person they dis-
tanced themselves from Russian Orthodoxy, which they considered a
hopelessly "medieval mind-set," as one friend put it. For them, Orthodoxy,
with its black robes, long beards, and ninth-century Slavonic chants, was

2. See pp. 44–45 for the statistics that reveal the magnitude of this martyrdom.
3. Clendenin, *Coup*, 166–67.

reactionary, authoritarian, and badly compromised by political accommo-
dations during the Soviet period. The Russian church might have won the
hearts of the ordinary faithful among the peasants in the villages, but for
the most part it had lost the university, intellectual crowd. In this sense it
has always appeared to me that the Soviet program of atheism was very
successful.

I have recounted elsewhere how my four years at Moscow State University resulted in an ambivalent posture toward Russian Orthodoxy.[4] There
I was, a Protestant theologian teaching in a department of atheism in a
country that boasted a millennium of Orthodox faith. As a believer, I was
filled with respect, admiration, and even awe for Russian Orthodoxy. But
I also concurred with many of the misgivings articulated by my atheist
friends. In addition, I had my own uniquely Protestant disagreements.
Consequently, I have a deep respect for Orthodoxy but none of the
romanticism that so many American converts exude about having discovered "the one true church of Christ on earth." Other scholars who have
lived and worked in Orthodox countries have expressed similar ambivalence.[5] In their more honest moments, even evangelical Protestant converts to Orthodoxy have admitted how unwelcome they felt in "the least
Americanized form of Christianity in the United States."[6] Frank Schaeffer
complains openly about the vast differences separating the true, undefiled
Orthodox church and the ethnocentric, exclusivistic, and overall mori-
bund faith that he thinks characterizes many cradle Orthodox.[7]

Eventually, I dealt with my decided ambivalence by making two important distinctions. First, just as with Protestantism and Catholicism, it is

4. Daniel B. Clendenin, "Why I'm Not Orthodox," *Christianity Today* 41.1 (Jan. 6,
1997).

5. I am thinking of Bradley Nassif, "New Dimensions in Eastern Orthodox Theology,"
in David Dockery, ed., *New Dimensions in Evangelical Thought* (Downers Grove, Ill.: Inter-
Varsity, 1998), 92–117; Bradley Nassif, "The Evangelical Theology of the Eastern Orthodox Church," in James Stamoolis, ed., *Three Views on Eastern Orthodoxy and Evangelicalism*
(Grand Rapids: Zondervan, forthcoming); Donald Fairbairn, *Eastern Orthodoxy through
Western Eyes* (Louisville: Westminster John Knox, 2002), and Gerald Bray as recounted in
Bradley Nassif, "Eastern Orthodoxy and Evangelicalism: The Status of an Emerging Dia-
logue," *Scottish Bulletin of Evangelical Theology* 18.1 (Spring 2000): 33. For an appreciative
treatment of how Protestants can enrich their faith by learning about Orthodoxy, see
Donald Fairbairn, "Not Just 'How' but 'Who': What Evangelicals Can Learn from the
Orthodox," *Evangel* (Spring 1999): 10–13.

6. Timothy Weber, "Looking for Home: Evangelical Orthodoxy and the Search for the
Original Church," in Bradley Nassif, ed., *New Perspectives on Historical Theology: Essays in
Memory of John Meyendorff* (Grand Rapids: Eerdmans, 1996), 96.

7. Weber, "Looking for Home," 119, cites passages in Schaeffer's book *Dancing Alone:
The Quest for Orthodox Faith in the Age of False Religions* (Brookline, Mass.: Holy Cross
Orthodox Press, 1994).

important not to make sweeping generalizations. I came to differentiate at least seven "faces" of Orthodoxy: (1) the official positions and pronouncements made by the patriarch; (2) the actions and attitudes of any given local priest, which can vary greatly; (3) the text traditions of the church fathers and ecumenical councils, which Western converts have rediscovered; (4) the reform movements in the national churches (even charismatic Orthodox Christians, for example); (5) the ordinary faithful as distinguished from the writing scholars; (6) the national churches, which are intensely ethnocentric (Romanian, Greek, Russian, etc.); and (7) the mainly American and British converts to Orthodoxy. The cradle Orthodox in these national churches abroad typically exist as a religious majority and often persecute other Christian groups as "sects"; whereas here in America the tables are turned, and the convert Orthodox exist within a minority subculture that is overshadowed by the mainstream Protestants and Catholics.

Second, although there are some significant theological differences between Orthodoxy and evangelicalism, for the most part these are differences of emphasis rather than absolute contradictions, and thus there is no reason why they cannot gratefully learn from one another.[8] What unites the two remains more important than what separates them.

The American Present

At about this same time (the late 1980s and early 1990s) in America, observers began to take note of a small but significant trend among Protestant evangelicals. People were converting to Eastern Orthodoxy. Conversions to the Roman Catholic and Episcopalian churches and Catholic-evangelical dialogue had become almost commonplace,[9] but conversions to Orthodoxy were something new. Today, ten to fifteen years later, this American evangelical attraction to and engagement with Orthodoxy continues.

Many Protestant clergy have converted to Orthodoxy to escape the liberalism of their mainline churches or to embrace a sense of Christian history and liturgy that they found sadly wanting in their churches.[10] Among laypeople, Frederica Mathewes-Green, a syndicated columnist for Religion News Services and commentator for National Public Radio, does a

8. This point is one of the many strengths of Fairbairn's book and also of Nassif's work.

9. See Scott Hahn, *Rome Sweet Rome: Our Journey to Catholicism* (Ignatius Press, 1994); and Patrick Madrid, ed., *Surprised by Truth: 11 Converts Give the Biblical and Historical Reasons for Becoming Catholic* (Basilica Press, 1994). Most notable might be Charles Colson and Richard John Neuhaus, eds., *Your Word Is Truth: A Project of Evangelicals and Catholics Together* (Grand Rapids: Eerdmans, 2002).

10. Peter Gillquist, ed., *Coming Home: Why Protestant Clergy Are Becoming Orthodox* (Ben Lomond, Calif.: Conciliar Press, 1992).

winsome job of exemplifying the enthusiasm and zeal of lay converts.[11] In the intellectual world, prominent scholars such as Jaroslav Pelikan, a historian at Yale, and Richard Swinburne, a philosopher at Oriel College, Oxford, have converted to Orthodoxy.

Why do Protestants continue to convert to Orthodoxy? On an experiential level, I believe that Mathewes-Green speaks to the numerous reasons when she suggests that some are looking for the "true, apostolic church," others long for liturgy, others seek theological stability that is less enamored by the zeitgeist, others appreciate the call to spiritual disciplines whose goal is mystical union with God, while others find Orthodoxy a welcoming home for their deep spiritual hunger.[12] Another explanation is that these conversions form part of a larger social and cultural trend as documented by Colleen Carroll in her book *The New Faithful: Why Young Adults Are Embracing Christian Orthodoxy*.[13] Carroll focuses on the baby buster generation born between 1965 and 1983, and mainly upon Catholics, but her overall thesis dovetails with what is happening with Protestant conversions to Orthodoxy. Timothy Weber offers a third perspective, arguing that for evangelicals these conversions reflect in part a crisis of identity dating back two decades and surrounding the issues of biblical inerrancy, social ethics, the charismatic movement, and a growing feeling of being detached from the historic, catholic traditions of the faith.[14]

Church growth statistics also tell a story. According to Mathewes-Green, about half of the students in Orthodoxy's two largest seminaries are converts, as are about half of the bishops in the Orthodox Church of America. In the Antiochian Archdiocese, the number of churches in America has tripled in the last few decades, due almost entirely to conversions, and the number of its priests who are converts is 78 percent.[15] Similarly, Peter Gillquist suggests that today about 80 percent of converts to Orthodoxy come from evangelical and charismatic backgrounds.[16] If these

11. Frederica Mathewes-Green, *Facing East: A Pilgrim's Journey into the Mysteries of Orthodoxy* (San Francisco: Harper, 1997); and *At the Corner of East and Now: A Modern Life in Ancient Christian Orthodoxy* (New York: Putnam, 2000). For similar conversions to Orthodoxy in England, see Michael Harper and Peter Gillquist, eds., *A Faith Fulfilled: Why Are Christians across Great Britain Embracing Orthodoxy?* (Ben Lomond, Calif.: Conciliar Press, 1999).

12. Mathewes-Green, *At the Corner of East and Now*, 119.

13. Colleen Carroll, *The New Faithful: Why Young Adults Are Embracing Christian Orthodoxy* (Chicago: Loyola Press, 2002). For her references to Eastern Orthodoxy, see 35, 57–60, and 64. By "Orthodoxy" Carroll means a belief in the Apostles' Creed and, more broadly, a return to conventional morality.

14. Weber, "Looking for Home," 98–102.

15. Mathewes-Green, *At the Corner of East and Now*, 120; *Facing East*, 126. Her husband is one such convert priest.

16. Nassif, "Eastern Orthodoxy and Evangelicalism," 23.

trends continue, these demographic changes could have a seismic impact on the Orthodox church here in America.

Here we must make two significant caveats. First, Orthodoxy in America is small and might be getting smaller. Overall, Orthodoxy is but a minor part of America's religious landscape. Statistics for religious bodies are notoriously difficult to verify and politically controversial, but some rough, comparative estimates are helpful. Mathewes-Green cites a figure of 3.5 million Orthodox in America, or about 1.3 percent of the country's population.[17] This would compare with David Barrett's figures for Jews (5.6 million), Muslims (4.1 million), Buddhists (2.4 million), and Hindus (1 million) in America.[18] Evangelicals of all sorts number about 40 million, Mormons 3 to 5 million, and the Church of God in Christ, America's largest black denomination, about 5 million. Catholics (62 million), all Baptists (34 million), Lutherans (10 million), and Methodists/Wesleyans (14 million) put the size of Orthodoxy in America in even greater perspective.[19]

Second, as Carroll points out, in the largest survey of American churches ever done, a 2001 study by the Hartford Institute for Religious Research, new church development has overall *declined* among Orthodox and Catholic bodies and surged among Mormons and evangelical Protestants.[20] The second and third generations of Orthodox immigrants, writes Nassif, "have hemorrhaged out the doors of the church in large numbers due to the church's apparent irrelevance to their lives and their inability to pray the liturgy in the English language."[21] As an ethno-religious subculture peripheral to mainstream American culture, these declines are not surprising. As I will discuss below, Orthodoxy's declining fortunes appear to be faring even worse on a global scale.

For all those who have converted to Orthodoxy, there might be exponentially more who have left Orthodox churches, some who have no doubt joined Protestant churches and parachurch movements. That is a study that remains to be done. It is important to remember then that overall Orthodoxy in America is a small group, it is likely declining, and because of its ethnocentric roots as an immigrant church, it remains tangential to mainstream American culture.

Another important observation: Despite all of these fascinating developments, most of the dialogue among Orthodox and Protestants has been

17. Mathewes-Green, *At the Corner of East and Now*, 120.

18. David Barrett, *World Christian Encyclopedia* (Oxford: Oxford University Press, 2001). Figures for Muslims range from about 1 million to the 8 million claimed by the Islamic Society of North America.

19. See www.adherents.com/rel_USA.html for these figures.

20. Carroll, *The New Faithful*, 69.

21. Nassif, "Eastern Orthodoxy and Evangelicalism," 22.

generated by Protestants who are interested in Orthodoxy. There is nothing close to a reciprocal, broad-based interest in Protestantism on the part
of Orthodox scholars, priests, and laypeople.[22] Mathewes-Green admits,
for example, how surprised some Orthodox churches and leaders have
been when Protestants wanted to join their fold, and in his study of the
1987 conversion of 2,000 evangelicals under the leadership of Peter
Gillquist, Weber shows how hard it was for them to "come home" to a
church that did not exactly open the door to welcome them.[23]

In sum, Orthodox converts form an important minority in a small part
of American religious life. The "dialogue" between the two groups tends
to be generated and sustained by the interest of Protestants. From my perspective this is a wonderfully positive development that has generated an
exponential amount of good in proportion to its small size. What does the
future hold? Where will the conversation proceed from here?

The Spirit Today in History and Liturgy

As we think about the future of Orthodox-evangelical dialogue, I
would like to begin with a twofold appeal to love and gratitude. The commandment to love one another is the second greatest commandment
according to Jesus, without which it is impossible to claim that we have
fulfilled the first and greatest commandment to love God (1 John 4:20–
21). Let us listen again, then, to some of the best voices of both the East
and the West by circling back to the preface and conclusion of this book,
where both traditions urge this twofold love of God and neighbor as the
ultimate criterion for engagement.

In commending his *Four Hundred Texts on Love*, Maximus the Confessor
(580–662), one of Orthodoxy's greatest theologians, urged his readers to
employ a criterion of charity so that reading led to conversion of the soul
rather than conquest of the author. Furthering our love of God and neighbor, he says, should always be the ultimate test and goal of reading rightly.

> If anything in these chapters should prove useful to the soul, it will be re-
> vealed to the reader by the grace of God, provided that he reads, not out of
> curiosity, but in the fear and love of God. If a man reads this or any other
> work not to gain spiritual benefit, but to track down matter with which to
> abuse the author, so that in his conceit he can show himself to be the more
> learned, nothing profitable will ever be revealed to him in anything.

22. So too Nassif, "Eastern Orthodoxy and Evangelicalism," 31, 39, 50. See his article
for the notable exceptions.
23. The converts were rebuffed by the Orthodox jurisdictions of Constantinople,
Greece, and Rome before being enthusiastically welcomed by the Antiochian church.

168 Eastern Orthodox Christianity

168 Eastern Orthodox Christianity

168   Eastern Orthodox Christianity

Our reading of a text, and by extension our "reading" of each other, should contribute to the growth of our souls and the love of God rather than to intellectual curiosity, hubris, polemics, or mutual abuse. The scientific wisdom we seek should never be an end in itself (knowledge) but rather a means to a far greater end (love), for as Paul warned, knowledge "puffs up" whereas love "builds up" (1 Cor. 8:1–2).

Saint Augustine (354–430), perhaps the greatest theologian of the West, similarly invokes the love of God and neighbor as the primary hermeneutical principle for interpreting the Bible. In *On Christian Doctrine* (1.36) he writes:

> Whoever, therefore, thinks that he understands the divine Scriptures or any part of them so that it does not build the double love of God and our neighbor does not understand it at all. Whoever finds a lesson there useful to the building of charity, even though he has not said what the author may be shown to have intended in that place, has not been deceived.

Even an errant understanding of Scripture that misconstrues the author's intention but still generates love, says Augustine, is preferable to any ostensibly correct interpretation that neglects the "double love" for which we must work and pray. With Donald Bloesch, I believe that without the prior goal and criterion of this twofold love, Orthodox and Protestant believers will always remain "hidden from each other,"[24] and with Maximus, I affirm that without love nothing significant or useful will result. Here I think the Orthodox East has a helpful reminder for evangelical Protestants who are so given to propositional truth, and that is its insistence that true theology is a style of life, a form of worship and prayer. The Spirit does not place a premium on ignorance, and theology requires an intellectual disposition that we ignore to our peril, but Evagrios said it best when he defined theology incarnationally: "If you are a theologian, you will pray truly. And if you pray truly, you are a theologian."[25]

I can speak only as a Protestant, so I will leave it to our Orthodox partners to articulate their own reasons for gratitude, but if I am correct, there seems to be a broad consensus that the Orthodox contribution coming our way clusters around what I would call a recovery of history and a return to liturgy. In the remainder of this epilogue, I would like to explore these two issues.

24. See p. 139.

25. Evagrios, *On Prayer*, 61. On this subject see Alan Jacobs, *A Theology of Reading: The Hermeneutics of Love* (Boulder: Westview Press, 2001), the purpose of which, says Jacobs, is to make "an academic case for governing interpretation by the law of love." A brief review of Jacobs's book can be found in Mark Walhout, "Reading, Writing and Charity," *Books and Culture* (July–August 2002): 35.

Recovery of History

For some time now Protestants, particularly evangelicals, have had a growing awareness of and discomfort with their recognition that in many ways they have been cut off, or have cut themselves off, from more catholic and historic expressions of Christian faith. In essence, evangelicals have promulgated a decidedly ahistorical faith. Sometimes this expresses itself in sheer ignorance of or disinterest in history, at other times by a superficial understanding of the nature and function of the doctrine of *sola scriptura,* and at other times in hubris in thinking that as "Bible believers" they have kept the faith undefiled from social, political, cultural, and historical forces. But about twenty-five years ago this began to change, when Robert Webber, Donald Bloesch, and Thomas Howard gathered a number of evangelicals together for a conference of like-minded "orthodox evangelicals."[26] The conference resulted in the document entitled "The Chicago Call: An Appeal to Evangelicals" (1978). Among other concerns, the call specifically lamented the evangelical neglect of history and its sectarian spirit, urging a return to a faith more deliberately connected to the early fathers, councils, creeds, and "the catholicity of historic Christianity." What, exactly, that meant remained unclear for many but not for Orthodox believers.

I believe that evangelicals and all Protestants owe a debt of gratitude to Orthodoxy for answering this question with its bold claim to be the one, holy, catholic, and apostolic church, the only true church of Christ on earth, and that there is an absolute identity and historical continuity of this Orthodox Church from the time of the apostles to the present day. Orthodoxy has thus helped to rescue us from what E. P. Thompson once called "the enormous condescension of posterity" and what C. S. Lewis referred to as our modern propensity to "chronological snobbery." They remind us, in Chesterton's words, that we must always give "votes to the most obscure of all classes, our ancestors."[27] For this we should remain eternally grateful. This particular view, though, comes at a high price, for it insists that to recover a sense of history demands a uniquely ecclesiastical choice, requiring the believer to return to the Orthodox Church.

But in upping the historical ante, Orthodoxy also invites several related questions. Must one join the Orthodox Church in order to embrace catholic and historic Christianity or to experience salvation? Is their claim of

26. Weber, "Looking for Home," 96–98. Cf. Robert Webber and Donald Bloesch, eds., *The Orthodox Evangelicals: Who They Are and What They Are Saying* (Nashville: Thomas Nelson, 1978), as cited by Weber.

27. The quote from Thompson is cited by Grant Wacker, *Heaven Below: Early Pentecostals and American Culture* (Cambridge, Mass.: Harvard University Press, 2001), 266. Mathewes-Green cites the Chesterton quote in *At the Corner of East and Now,* 42.

unbroken historical continuity with the apostles a credible one? Is it the "purest and fullest" expression of the faith? We should pause here to remember that Orthodoxy is hardly the only Christian group to make these types of claims. There is a long, sad tradition of Christians excommunicating each other, both literally and figuratively, of demonizing each other as an Other. Orthodoxy might distinguish itself only by making this historical claim most clearly and unapologetically.

As a Protestant I believe that Orthodoxy is wrong to make this claim. Florovsky once observed that the Christian tradition is a pneumatic or spiritual matter rather than just an appeal to history. Tradition, said Florovsky, is the witness of the Spirit. If we ask where the Spirit is working and witnessing today, where the Christian *paradosis* is taking root and producing fruit, I would wager that he moves forward to the future in time and place, and not just backwards to recover the historical past of a limited geography. Let me suggest four reasons for this.

Theological Perspective

From a mere human perspective, and that is the only perspective that anyone has, I think that we can describe the Spirit's work in history today in a theological sense. By this I mean that it appears that much of the vigorous tradition and witness of the Spirit around the world today is taking place in the charismatic movement. From its obscure beginnings with Charles Parham, founder of Bethel Bible School in Topeka, Kansas, and William Seymour, a black pastor with one eye who founded the Apostolic Faith Gospel Mission at 312 Azusa Street in Los Angeles, in a little less than one hundred years what we broadly describe as the "pentecostal movement" has exploded to number about 500 million Christians. According to current projections, in fifty years their number will double to one billion. They constitute the largest distinct group of Christians except for Roman Catholics (who number about one billion) and exist in every country and in every denomination, Orthodoxy included.[28]

Size is not everything, of course, and one can easily find the excessive and the bizarre at the margins of some charismatic movements. Nor should we miss the irony that classic Pentecostalism, which insists that it is normative for every believer to experience the "baptism in the Spirit" and to speak in tongues as evidence of this baptism fullness, relegates all noncharismatic believers to a second-class status much as the Orthodox do with their ecclesial claim. But it beggars the Christian imagination to make the Orthodox claim, either in its "hard" version, that it is the only

28. For the best treatment of Pentecostalism in America, see Wacker's book already cited. For global Pentecostalism, see Murray Dempster, Byron Klaus, and Douglas Peterson, eds., *The Globalization of Pentecostalism* (Oxford: Regnum, 1999).

true church, or even in its "soft" version, that it is the "fullest" expression of the gospel, when most of the rest of the global communion of saints sees the Spirit clearly moving in history far beyond the confines of Orthodoxy.

Sociological Perspective

To this theological perspective we can add a sociological perspective that in many ways overlaps with these observations, but it is a perspective the magnitude and implications of which many people in the West, believers and unbelievers alike, have failed to see.[29] If we ask where the Spirit is moving in history, a social scientific perspective would tell us that global Christianity has experienced a massive shift in its center of gravity, from the wealthy and primarily white regions of the northern hemisphere to the poor and nonwhite regions of the southern hemisphere. These changes roughly follow the trends of population growth, where we observe declines in the north and explosive growth in the south.

Here and in the West among northern, liberal-minded believers, there is enormous pressure for a new reformation of sorts to address a church crisis that clusters around a handful of issues—declining attendance, clergy celibacy, sexual scandals, homosexuality, the ordination of women, and so forth. But seen globally, this is a minor trend, for as Philip Jenkins documents, at the same time what he calls an "epochal" counter-reformation has already occurred in the south that is oriented toward traditional theology, a literal belief in the supernatural (seen in healing and exorcism), and an overall conservative stance on social and political issues. With the failure of governments in many of these nations to provide basic goods, services, health care, education, and so forth, the leaders in these ascendant Christian movements enjoy increased social and political power. This southern counter-reformation, says Jenkins, far overshadows and runs "utterly contrary to the dominant cultural movements in the rest of the world."[30]

But the "rest of the Christian world" now matters far less than it used to matter, for the exponential growth of the church is taking place in Africa, Latin America, and Asia. Africa had about 10 million Christians in 1900 out of a population of about 107 million people (9 percent); today it has 360 million Christians out of 784 million (46 percent). In fifty years, half of the world's Christian population will be in Africa and Latin Amer-

29. Missiologists have long been making the following observations, beginning with the 1982 publication of David Barrett's *World Christian Encyclopedia*. I am following Philip Jenkins, "The Next Christianity," *The Atlantic Monthly* (October 2002): 53–68. For his book-length version of the same, see Philip Jenkins, *The Next Christendom: The Coming of Global Christianity* (Oxford: Oxford University Press, 2002).

30. Jenkins, "The Next Christianity," 55.

ica, and only about 20 percent of believers will be non-Latino whites. The implications of this could be staggering. In the Catholic Church, "the next time a papal election takes place, fifty-seven of the 135 cardinals eligible to vote, or more than 40 percent, will be from southern nations. Early this century they will constitute a majority."[31] By then, three-quarters of Catholic members will come from Africa, Asia, and Latin America. Pentecostals, notes Jenkins, stand in the "vanguard" of this sea change. The Anglican communion has already experienced this power shift. At its 1998 Lambeth Conference, only 316 of the registered bishops were from the United States, Europe, and Canada, while Africa and Asia accounted for 319, allowing southern bishops to vote as a bloc and defeat northern proposals for gay rights.[32]

From this sociological perspective, the projected demographic future appears especially grim for Orthodoxy in particular. Because most of Eastern Orthodoxy is concentrated in an increasingly de-Christianized Europe, where populations are shrinking, Jenkins projects that it will "suffer acutely" in the coming decades. True, the largest Orthodox church (Russia) might be experiencing resurgence and revival, but overall "the long term future of the church must be in doubt. . . . In the worst-case scenario, the total number of Orthodox believers in the world by 2050 might actually be less than the Christian population of a single nation like Mexico or Brazil."[33] Is Orthodoxy where we sense the Spirit moving in history? From an empirical, sociological perspective, not especially, at least when compared with the rest of the global church.

Biblical Perspective

Third, from a biblical perspective, Orthodoxy comes uncomfortably close to equating the kingdom of God with its own church or insisting that the kingdom comes only or primarily through its church. As with Catholicism, which has more recently acknowledged the legitimacy and integrity of Christian identity outside of its church, one can find qualifications and nuances in Orthodoxy, but in general it is an open question whether a person can be saved outside of its church.[34] For Orthodoxy, the gospel tradition finds its fullest expression in the Eucharist, and it is through the Eucharist, closed to people outside of its membership, that the kingdom of God is not only represented but also actualized.[35]

31. Ibid., 62.
32. Jenkins, *The Next Christendom*, 202–3.
33. Ibid., 96.
34. For a significant exception see, for example, Timothy Ware, *The Orthodox Church* (New York: Penguin, 1997), 247–48, 308.
35. See Fairbairn, *Eastern Orthodoxy through Western Eyes*, 27.

How should we understand the relationship of the kingdom of God to any particular church? Is the Spirit's kingdom work in human history identical to one church, which is what traditional Catholic and Orthodox theology teaches, or is it reasonable to believe that we must distinguish (but never separate) the realities of church and kingdom?

George Ladd makes five biblical observations about this relationship that I find compelling.[36] First, the church is not the kingdom; the two are intricately related but different. Second, the kingdom creates the church, rather than vice versa. By entering the kingdom one participates in the church, but by entering the church one does not necessarily participate in the kingdom. Third, the mission of the church is to witness to the kingdom rather than to build the kingdom, for the kingdom always comes as a gift of grace. Fourth, the church can be the instrument of the kingdom, with human experience telling us that this variously occurs to a greater or lesser degree. Finally, since it possesses the keys of the kingdom (Matt. 16:19), the church is the custodian of the kingdom. In sum, we cannot separate the visible church and the invisible kingdom, but neither should we identify them as closely as the Orthodox church teaches: "They remain two distinguishable concepts: the rule of God and the fellowship of men."[37]

Taken together, I believe that these three observations—theological, sociological, and biblical—cast significant doubt on the Orthodox claim about its church in history. Instead, I believe that it is reasonable, even compelling, to affirm that we see the Spirit working all across the world to inaugurate God's kingdom, far outside the narrow confines of Orthodoxy. But so much for the historical present and the projected future. What about Orthodoxy's more limited claim about the historical past, that Orthodoxy alone has kept the gospel tradition in unbroken continuity from the time of the apostles and the original, New Testament church? This brings me to my fourth point.

Historical Perspective

Orthodoxy is not the only church to claim such continuity. As Weber and fellow historians have noted, so-called "restorationism" and "primitivism" are common strains in American Christianity. The basic scheme suggests that after a pristine period, the early church fell into error and departed from its original, pure past. For example, the time of Constantine is often cited as a turning point when it is thought that the church capitulated to the state. Or again, restoration meant returning the church to its unpolluted condition, as many Protestants understand the meaning of the

36. George Ladd, A *Theology of the New Testament* (Grand Rapids: Eerdmans, 1974), 111–19.
37. Ibid., 119.

Reformation. The unique twist of Orthodoxy is not that it claims to restore a fallen past but that it claims never to have departed from apostolic continuity in the first place, thus its claim to "unbroken succession." It comes as no surprise that when Gillquist and his followers, who openly admit that what they sought was the "original, New Testament Church," found the Orthodox Church that made this uncompromising successionist claim, they were a match made in heaven. The best Orthodox scholars nuance their successionist arguments, and popular versions among converts do not represent its best thinking, but this nevertheless remains the Orthodox claim.

At best this successionist claim can only be a relative as opposed to an absolute claim. The early days of the apostles were not as pure as are claimed (cf. Corinth, Colossae, or Galatia) nor was the postapostolic period as polluted as imagined. Oden, for example, in seeking to promote a catholic orthodoxy based upon a broad patristic consensus of the first five centuries, admits that we can only approach a proximate consensus, not an ideal or absolute consensus. The historical evidence is far too mixed to say otherwise. If taken as an absolute ideal, the Vincentian Canon—that one should only accept that which has been believed "everywhere, always, by all"—applies almost nowhere, at any time, among anyone. Take but one example dear to Orthodoxy, the iconoclastic controversy. If the original apostolic tradition remained clear and unbroken, why did it take almost eight hundred years to arrive at its position? It is because the scriptural warrant, creeds, history, liturgy, written evidence, unwritten traditions, archaeological evidence, artistic practices, and the like of the early, and not so early, church remain ambiguous, debated, and equivocal. Both iconoclasts and iconodules could make reasonable claims from history. As Weber notes, "Successionists must be highly selective and ignore all evidence to the contrary. They must also maintain an idealized and naïve view of the past. In the end, successionism is based on one's theology or ideology not on any critical historical analysis."[38] I believe that Orthodoxy's historical claim to unbroken apostolic succession is just that; it is a theological claim that is, ironically, uncritically unhistorical.

Return to Liturgy

Let me conclude with some reflections on the matter of renewed interest, again especially among evangelicals, in liturgy. The Chicago Call previously mentioned also lamented evangelicals' weaknesses in this area and urged a greater appreciation for sacramental traditions. Similarly, in his contribution to the Rose Hill Conference, Harold Brown observes that

38. Weber, "Looking for Home," 109.

evangelicals tend to have a deficient sense of the importance of the church, worship, and liturgy.[39] Worship must be more than self-expression, more than a few good songs followed by a lecture, and more than feeling good at the end of some upbeat songs and a time of "sharing" (in which case, as Mathewes-Green notes, there can only be "performance anxiety" for the celebrants and the audience).[40] Orthodoxy (along with Catholicism and some liturgical Protestant traditions) has much to teach evangelicals here.

It goes without saying that one need not become Orthodox (or Catholic) to enter a deeper and more substantial liturgical life. Protestants have their own "high church" traditions. Orthodoxy is only one of many good choices believers who want more liturgy might make.

When you read the New Testament with an eye toward liturgy and worship, you immediately notice that it is long on description of the life of the early church, and short on prescription. It tells us a little bit of what was happening back then in those first house churches—much less than we would like and even less about what we *must* do today. As Brown observes, once we have believed the gospel and try to fill out a life of discipleship in a worshiping community, we are left to follow human traditions rather than specifically mandated, divine instructions. These many and varied "liturgies," if I may call them that, are inevitable and necessary. But as Brown warns, they are also potentially dangerous. Why? Protestants are "minimalists" who intend to keep things pure and simple (or so we think) and thus tend to ignore liturgical tradition as if they could live without it, as if they did not have their own "liturgy" (literally, "public work"), or as if liturgical tradition necessarily obscures or encumbers pure Christian faith and practice. Orthodoxy or more liturgical traditions tend to be "maximalist," their danger being a failure to remember that these liturgical traditions are a human invention that may or may not prove edifying to believers. In a word, the problem is that these inevitable and necessary liturgical traditions create conflict and divisions. So, with Brown, I suggest that "we may observe these traditions and honor them as suitable, acceptable, and even necessary, but we must avoid claiming that they are mandatory, determinative, or obligatory."[41] Such advice is consonant with the New Testament, which describes these inevitable "traditions of men" as sometimes positive (2 Thess. 2:15; 3:6) and at other times negative (Mark 7:3; Col. 2:8).

39. Harold O. J. Brown, "Proclamation and Preservation: The Necessity and Temptations of Church Tradition," in James Cutsinger, ed., *Reclaiming the Great Tradition: Evangelicals, Catholics, and Orthodox in Dialogue* (Downer's Grove, Ill.: Inter-Varsity, 1997), 81.

40. Mathewes-Green, *At the Corner of East and Now*, 171.

41. Brown, "Proclamation and Preservation," 85, 87.

Liturgy is an area of *adiaphora*, something neither good nor bad in itself. We should encourage believers to make their liturgical choices wisely, acknowledging that latitude and freedom are necessary and even good. I close with a story of two liturgical choices, one made by Ed Rommen, an evangelical Protestant missionary-scholar turned Orthodox, and James Stamoolis, a cradle Orthodox turned evangelical Protestant. In their friendly exchange, each admits that the liturgical inheritance that they received from their respective communities proved, in the end, to be personally unsatisfying.

For Rommen, the typical evangelical worship with which he had grown up and even fostered as a missionary, scholar, and church planter had grown increasingly problematic. The services seemed to have devolved to taped music, stage performances, casual pep rallies, glib and even impious commentary, an infrequently celebrated Lord's Supper, poorly prepared sermons littered with even poorer attempts at humor and self-disclosure, and so on. After visiting and investigating at least eight other church traditions, he attended an Orthodox service: "I was so overwhelmed by the worship service that I came away with the feeling that this was what I had been looking for." Less than a year later, Rommen converted to Orthodoxy.

Stamoolis grew up in an Orthodox home, describes himself as devoted, and even served as an altar boy. He is empathetic to Rommen's story, but he made the opposite liturgical journey. Why? The same problem of liturgical dissatisfaction: "There were forms, but they were devoid of meaning, there were homilies in our Orthodox parish, but they did not speak of the mysteries of faith but of the necessity to support the activities of the parish, [and] my fellow parishioners were more interested in social conversation than divine communion." It was only with an evangelical presentation of the gospel, says Stamoolis, that worship came alive and spoke to him, and thus he converted to Protestantism.[42]

Conclusion

To what degree are Orthodoxy and Protestantism compatible? This, of course, depends upon who you read, but I think Nassif makes an astute observation. He suggests that if viewed from the viewpoint of the way evangelicals describe themselves, that is, from the viewpoint of their essential characteristics (Christology, Scripture, conversion, and evangelism), then there is significant compatibility. But if viewed from the opposite direction, that is, from the way that Orthodox believers define them-

42. For the Stamoolis and Rommen exchange, see www.missiology.org/EMS/bulletins/bulletins.htm.

selves, then the two are rightly seen as significantly less compatible.[43] This likely helps to explain what we noted above, that evangelicals tend to be much more interested in Orthodoxy than the reverse.

For this dialogue to continue, and it would be a tragedy if it did not, two things need to happen. First, it would be wonderful if far more Orthodox believers were more intentional about engaging evangelicals. For example, Nassif has noted that far more evangelical seminaries offer courses on Orthodoxy than Orthodox seminaries offer on evangelicalism. This is all the more curious when you consider that in America evangelicalism is approximately ten times the size of Orthodoxy.

Finally, we must not allow the shrill voices of the margins, the more dogmatic and polemical voices among us, to control the conversation. We need to listen to the Timothy (Kallistos) Wares and Thomas Odens of the world rather than the Frank Schaeffers. The former clearly intend to engage, learn, and respect; whereas the latter seem intent upon correcting and converting. The latter path leads only to a monologue with very few listeners; the former path invites the possibility of dialogue and mutual enrichment.

43. Nassif, "The Evangelical Theology of the Eastern Orthodox Church."

Bibliography

Alexeev, Wassilij, and Theofanis G. Stavrou. *The Great Revival: The Russian Church under German Occupation*. Minneapolis: Burgess, 1976.

Anglican-Orthodox Dialogue: The Dublin Agreed Statement of 1984. Crestwood, N.Y.: St. Vladimir's Seminary Press, 1985.

Anglican-Orthodox Dialogue: The Moscow Agreed Statement of 1976. London: S.P.C.K., 1977.

Arseniev, Nicholas. *Mysticism and the Eastern Church*. Crestwood, N.Y.: St. Vladimir's Seminary Press, 1979.

Atiya, Aziz S. *A History of Eastern Christianity*. Notre Dame: University of Notre Dame Press, 1968.

Bajis, Jordan. *Common Ground: An Introduction to Eastern Christianity for the American Christian*. Minneapolis: Light and Life, 1991.

Baker, Derek. *The Orthodox Churches and the West*. Oxford: Basil Blackwell, 1976.

Beeson, Trevor. *Discretion and Valour: Religious Conditions in Russia and Eastern Europe*. Rev. ed. Philadelphia: Fortress, 1982.

Benz, Ernst. *The Eastern Orthodox Church: Its Thought and Life*. Translated by Richard and Clara Winston. Garden City, N.Y.: Anchor Books, 1963.

Billington, James H. *The Icon and the Axe: An Interpretive History of Russian Culture*. New York: Random House, 1966.

———. *Russia Transformed: Breakthrough to Hope*. New York: Free, 1992.

Blackmore, R. W., et al. *The Doctrine of the Russian Church*. Willits, Calif.: Eastern Orthodox Books, 1973.

Bociurkiw, Bohdan R., and John W. Strong, eds. *Religion and Atheism in the U.S.S.R. and Eastern Europe*. Toronto: University of Toronto Press, 1975.

Bourdeaux, Michael. *Gorbachev, Glasnost and the Gospel*. London: Hodder and Stoughton, 1990.

———. *Patriarch and Prophets: Persecution of the Russian Orthodox Church Today*. New York: Praeger, 1970.

———. *Religious Ferment in Russia: Protestant Opposition to Soviet Religious Policy*. New York: St. Martin's, 1968.

———. *Risen Indeed: Lessons in Faith from the USSR*. Crestwood, N.Y.: St. Vladimir's Seminary Press, 1983.

———, and Lorna Bourdeaux. *Ten Growing Soviet Churches*. Bromley, Kent: MARC Europe, 1987.

Bratsiotis, Panagiotes. "Fundamental Principles and Main Characteristics of the Orthodox Church." In *The Orthodox Ethos*, edited by A. J. Philippou, 23–31. Oxford: Holywell, 1964.

———. *The Greek Orthodox Church*. Notre Dame: University of Notre Dame Press, 1968.

Bulgakov, Sergius. *The Orthodox Church*. Rev. ed. Crestwood, N.Y.: St. Vladimir's Seminary Press, 1988.

———. *The Wisdom of God: A Brief Summary of Sophiology*. New York: Paisley, 1937.

Buss, Gerald. *The Bear's Hug; Christian Belief and the Soviet State, 1917–86*. Grand Rapids: Eerdmans, 1987.

Calian, Carnegie S. *Icon and Pulpit: The Protestant-Orthodox Encounter*. Philadelphia: Westminster, 1968.

———. *Theology without Boundaries: Encounters of Eastern Orthodoxy and Western Tradition*. Louisville: Westminster/John Knox, 1992.

Carroll, Colleen. *The New Faithful: Why Young Adults Are Embracing Christian Orthodoxy*. Chicago: Loyola Press, 2002.

Cavarnos, Constantine. *The Icon: Its Spiritual Basis and Purpose*. Belmont, Mass.: Institute for Byzantine and Modern Greek Studies, 1973.

Chmykhalov, Timothy, and Danny Smith. *The Last Christian: The Release of the Siberian Seven*. Grand Rapids: Zondervan, 1986.

Chrestou, Panagiotes. *Partakers of God*. Brookline, Mass.: Holy Cross Orthodox, 1984.

Chrysostomos, Archimandrite. *Contemporary Eastern Orthodox Thought: The Traditionalist Voice*. Belmont, Mass.: Nordland, 1982.

Clendenin, Daniel. "Why I'm Not Orthodox." *Christianity Today* 41.1 (Jan. 6, 1997).

Coniaris, Anthony M. *Introducing the Orthodox Church: Its Faith and Life*. Minneapolis: Light and Life, 1982.

Conquest, Robert. *The Great Terror: Stalin's Purge of the 1930s*. New York: Oxford University Press, 1990.

———. *The Harvest of Sorrows: Soviet Collectivization and the Terror-Famine*. New York: Oxford University Press, 1986.

———. *Religion in the U.S.S.R.* New York: Praeger, 1968.

———, ed. *The Last Empire: Nationality and the Soviet Future*. Stanford, Calif.: Hoover Institution Press, 1986.

Constantelos, Demetrios J. *The Greek Orthodox Church: Faith, History, and Practice*. New York: Seabury, 1967.

Copleston, Frederick C. *Philosophy in Russia*. Notre Dame: University of Notre Dame Press, 1986.

———. *Russian Religious Philosophy*. Notre Dame: University of Notre Dame Press, 1988.

Curtiss, John S. *Church and State in Russia: The Last Years of the Empire, 1900–1917*. New York: Octagon, 1940.

———. *The Russian Church and the Soviet State, 1917–1950*. Boston: Little, Brown, 1953.

Cutsinger, James, ed. *Reclaiming the Great Tradition: Evangelicals, Catholics and Orthodox in Dialogue*. Downers Grove, Ill.: Inter-Varsity, 1997.

Demetrakopoulos, George H. *Dictionary of Orthodox Theology: A Summary of the Beliefs, Practices, and History of the Eastern Orthodox Church*. New York: Philosophical Library, 1964.

Doulis, Thomas, ed. *Journeys to Orthodoxy: A Collection of Essays by Converts to Orthodox Christianity*. Minneapolis: Light and Life, 1986.

Dudko, Dmitrii. *Our Hope*. Crestwood, N.Y.: Saint Vladimir's Seminary Press, 1977.

Durasoff, Steve. *Pentecost behind the Iron Curtain*. Plainfield, N.J.: Logos International, 1972.

———. *The Russian Protestants: Evangelicals in the Soviet Union, 1944–1964*. Rutherford, N.J.: Fairleigh Dickinson University Press, 1969.

Dvornik, Francis. *Byzantium and the Roman Primacy*. New York: Fordham University Press, 1966.

Ellis, Jane. *The Russian Orthodox Church: A Contemporary History*. Bloomington: Indiana University Press, 1986.

Evdokimov, Paul. *The Art of the Icon: A Theology of Beauty*. Torrance, Calif.: Oakwood, 1990.

———. *L'Orthodoxie*. Paris: Delachaux and Niestlé, 1959.

Fairbairn, Donald. *Eastern Orthodoxy through Western Eyes*. Louisville: Westminster John Knox, 2002.

Fedotov, George P. *The Russian Religious Mind*. New York: Harper and Row, 1965. (2 vols. Cambridge, Mass.: Harvard University Press, 1946, 1966. Vol. 1, *Kievan Christianity: The Tenth to the Thirteenth Centuries*; Vol. 2, *The Middle Ages: The Thirteenth to the Fifteenth Centuries*.)

———. *A Treasury of Russian Spirituality*. 2 vols. Belmont, Mass.: Nordland, 1975.

Feuter, Paul. "Confessing Christ through the Liturgy: An Orthodox Challenge to Protestants." *International Review of Missions* 65 (1976): 123–28.

Fletcher, William C. *Religion and Soviet Foreign Policy, 1945–1970*. New York: Oxford University Press, 1973.

———. *The Russian Orthodox Church Underground, 1917–1970*. New York: Oxford University Press, 1971.

———. *Soviet Believers: The Religious Sector of the Population*. Lawrence, Kans.: Regents Press of Kansas, 1981.

———. *Soviet Charismatics*. New York: Peter Lang, 1985.

———. *A Study in Survival: The Church in Russia, 1927–1943*. New York: Macmillan, 1965.

Florensky, Pavel. *The Pillar and Ground of the Truth* (in Russian). Godstone, Eng.: Gregg, 1971.

Florovsky, George. *Collected Works*. 14 vols. Belmont, Mass.: Nordland, 1972–79 (vols. 1–5); Vaduz, Liech.: Büchervertriebsanstalt, 1987–89 (vols. 6–14). Vol. 1, *Bible, Church, Tradition* (1972); Vol. 2, *Christianity and Culture* (1974); Vol. 3, *Creation and Redemption* (1976); Vol. 4, *Aspects of Church History* (1975); Vols. 5–6, *The Ways of Russian Theology* (1979, 1987); Vol. 7, *Eastern Fathers of the Fourth Century* (1987); Vol. 8, *Byzantine Fathers of the Fifth Century* (1987); Vol. 9, *Byzantine Fathers of the Sixth to Eighth Centuries* (1987); Vol. 10, *Byzantine Ascetic and Spiritual Fathers* (1987); Vol. 11, *Theology and Literature* (1989); Vol. 12, *Philosophy* (1989); Vols. 13–14, *Ecumenism* (1989).

Fouyas, Methodios. *Orthodoxy, Roman Catholicism, and Anglicanism*. New York: Oxford University Press, 1972.

French, Reginald M. *The Eastern Orthodox Church*. New York: Hutchinson's University Library, 1951.

Gill, Joseph, and Edmund Flood. *The Orthodox: Their Relations with Rome*. London: Darton, Longman, and Todd, 1964.

Gillquist, Peter E. *Becoming Orthodox: A Journey to the Ancient Christian Faith*. Brentwood, Tenn.: Wolgemuth and Hyatt, 1989.

———. *Making America Orthodox: Ten Questions Most Asked of Orthodox Christians*. Brookline, Mass.: Holy Cross Orthodox, 1984.

———, ed. *Coming Home: Why Protestant Clergy Are Becoming Orthodox*. Ben Lomond, Calif.: Conciliar Press, 1992.

Goricheva, Tatiana. *Talking about God Is Dangerous: The Diary of a Russian Dissident*. New York: Crossroad, 1987.

Greek Orthodox Theological Review 22.1 (1977): 357–463; 27.1 (1982): 2–82 (Orthodox–Southern Baptist dialogues).

Hadjiantoniou, George A. *Protestant Patriarch: The Life of Cyril Lucaris*. Richmond: John Knox, 1961.

Harper, Michael and Peter Gillquist, eds. *A Faith Fulfilled: Why Are Christians across Great Britain Embracing Orthodoxy?* Ben Lomond, Calif.: Conciliar Press, 1999.

Hebly, J. A. (Hans). *Protestants in Russia*. Grand Rapids: Eerdmans, 1976.

Hill, Kent R. *The Soviet Union on the Brink: An Inside Look at Christianity and Glasnost*. Portland: Multnomah, 1991.

———. *Turbulent Times for the Soviet Church*. Portland: Multnomah, 1991.

Hopko, Thomas. *All the Fulness of God: Essays on Orthodoxy, Ecumenism and Modern Society*. Crestwood, N.Y.: St. Vladimir's Seminary Press, 1982.

———. "Criteria of Truth in Orthodox Theology." *St. Vladimir's Theological Quarterly* 15.3 (1971): 121–29.

———. *Lenten Spring: Readings for Great Lent*. Crestwood, N.Y.: St. Vladimir's Seminary Press, 1983.

———. *The Orthodox Faith*. 4 vols. Crestwood, N.Y.: St. Vladimir's Seminary Press, 1984.

———. *Winter Pascha: Readings for the Christmas-Epiphany Season*. Crestwood, N.Y.: St. Vladimir's Seminary Press, 1984.

———. *Women and the Priesthood*. Crestwood, N.Y.: St. Vladimir's Seminary Press, 1983.

House, Francis. *Millennium of Faith: Christianity in Russia, 988–1988*. Crestwood, N.Y.: St. Vladimir's Seminary Press, 1988.

Hussey, Joan M. *The Orthodox Church in the Byzantine Empire*. New York: Oxford University Press, 1986.

Karmiris, John. *A Synopsis of the Dogmatic Theology of the Orthodox Catholic Church*. Scranton, Pa.: Christian Orthodox Edition, 1973.

Kline, George L. *Religious and Anti-Religious Thought in Russia*. Chicago: University of Chicago Press, 1968.

Landmarks: A Collection of Essays on the Russian Intelligentsia, trans. Marian Schwartz (New York: Karz Howard, 1977).

Lane, Christel. *Christian Religion in the Soviet Union: A Sociological Study*. Winchester, Mass.: Allen and Unwin, 1978.

Lapeyrouse, Stephen L. *Towards the Spiritual Convergence of America and Russia*. Santa Cruz, Calif.: Stephen L. Lapeyrouse, 1990.

Lossky, Vladimir. *In the Image and Likeness of God*. Crestwood, N.Y.: St. Vladimir's Seminary Press, 1974.

———. *The Mystical Theology of the Eastern Church*. Crestwood, N.Y.: St. Vladimir's Seminary Press, 1976.

———. *Orthodox Theology: An Introduction*. Crestwood, N.Y.: St. Vladimir's Seminary Press, 1978.

———. *The Vision of God*. Crestwood, N.Y.: St. Vladimir's Seminary Press, 1963.

Makrakis, Apostolos. *An Orthodox-Protestant Dialogue*. Chicago: Orthodox Christian Educational Society, 1966.

Maloney, George A. *A History of Orthodox Theology since 1453*. Belmont, Mass.: Nordland, 1976.

Mantzaridis, Georgios I. *The Deification of Man*. Crestwood, N.Y.: St. Vladimir's Seminary Press, 1984.

Marshall, Richard H., Jr., ed. *Aspects of Religion in the Soviet Union, 1917–1967*. Chicago: University of Chicago Press, 1971.

Mathewes-Green, Frederica. *At the Corner of East and Now: A Modern Life in Ancient Christian Orthodoxy*. New York: Putnam, 2000.

———. *Facing East: A Pilgrim's Journey into the Mysteries of Orthodoxy*. San Francisco: Harper, 1997.

Medvedev, Roy A. *Let History Judge: The Origins and Consequences of Stalinism*. Rev. ed. New York: Columbia University Press, 1989.

———. *On Stalin and Stalinism*. New York: Oxford University Press, 1979.

Meyendorff, John. *The Byzantine Legacy in the Orthodox Church*. Crestwood, N.Y.: St. Vladimir's Seminary Press, 1982.

———. *Byzantine Theology: Historical Trends and Doctrinal Themes*. New York: Fordham University Press, 1974.

———. *Byzantium and the Rise of Russia*. Crestwood, N.Y.: St. Vladimir's Seminary Press, 1989.

———. *Catholicity and the Church*. Crestwood, N.Y.: St. Vladimir's Seminary Press, 1983.

———. *Christ in Eastern Christian Thought*. Crestwood, N.Y.: St. Vladimir's Seminary Press, 1975.

———. *Imperial Unity and Christian Divisions*. Crestwood, N.Y.: St. Vladimir's Seminary Press, 1989.

———. *Living Tradition*. Crestwood, N.Y.: St. Vladimir's Seminary Press, 1978.

———. *The Orthodox Church*. Crestwood, N.Y.: St. Vladimir's Seminary Press, 1981.

———. *Orthodoxy and Catholicity*. New York: Sheed and Ward, 1966.

———. *St. Gregory Palamas and Orthodox Spirituality*. Crestwood, N.Y.: St. Vladimir's Seminary Press, 1974.

———. *The Vision of Unity*. Crestwood, N.Y.: St. Vladimir's Seminary Press, 1987.

———, ed. *The Primacy of Peter in the Orthodox Church*. Crestwood, N.Y.: St. Vladimir's Seminary Press, 1992.

———, and Joseph McLelland, eds. *The New Man: An Orthodox and Reformed Dialogue*. New Brunswick, N.J.: Agora Books, 1973.

———, and Robert Tobias. *Salvation in Christ: A Lutheran-Orthodox Dialogue*. Minneapolis: Augsburg, 1992.

Nassif, Bradley. "Eastern Orthodoxy and Evangelicalism: The Status of an Emerging Dialogue." *Scottish Bulletin of Evangelical Theology* 18.1 (Spring 2000): 21–55.

———, ed. *New Perspectives on Historical Theology: Essays in Memory of John Meyendorff*. Grand Rapids: Eerdmans, 1996.

Nesdoly, Samuel J. *Among the Soviet Evangelicals*. Carlisle, Pa.: Banner of Truth, 1986.

New Valamo Consultation: The Ecumenical Nature of Orthodox Witness. Geneva: World Council of Churches, 1978.

Nichols, Robert L., and Theofanis G. Stavrou. *Russian Orthodoxy under the Old Regime*. Minneapolis: University of Minnesota Press, 1978.

Niesel, Wilhelm. *Reformed Symbolics: A Comparison of Catholicism, Orthodoxy, and Protestantism*. London: Oliver and Boyd, 1962.

Nissiotis, Nikos. "The Unity of Scripture and Tradition." *Greek Orthodox Theological Review* 11.2 (Winter 1965–66): 183–208.

O'Callaghan, Paul. *An Eastern Orthodox Response to Evangelical Claims*. Minneapolis: Light and Life, 1984.

Oden, Thomas. *The Rebirth of Orthodoxy*. San Francisco: Harper, 2002.

———. *Two Worlds: Notes on the Death of Modernity in America and Russia*. Downers Grove, Ill.: InterVarsity, 1992.

The Orthodox Church and the Churches of the Reformation: A Survey of Orthodox-Protestant Dialogue. Faith and Order paper 76. Geneva: World Council of Churches, 1975.

The Orthodox Church in the Ecumenical Movement: Documents and Statements, 1902–1975. Edited by Constantin G. Patelos. Geneva: World Council of Churches, 1978.

Orthodox Study Bible. Nashville: Thomas Nelson, n.d.

Ouspensky, Leonid. *Theology of the Icon*. Crestwood, N.Y.: Saint Vladimir's Seminary Press, 1978. (2 vols. Crestwood, N.Y.: St. Vladimir's Seminary Press, 1991.)

———, and Vladimir Lossky. *The Meaning of Icons*. Rev. ed. Crestwood, N.Y.: St. Vladimir's Seminary Press, 1982.

Pain, James, and Nicolas Zernov, eds. *A Bulgakov Anthology*. Philadelphia: Westminster, 1976.

Paraskevas, John E., and Frederick Reinstein. *The Eastern Orthodox Church: A Brief History*. Washington, D.C.: El Greco, 1969.

Parsons, Howard L. *Christianity Today in the U.S.S.R.* New York: International Publishers, 1987.

Paul of Finland, Archbishop. *The Faith We Hold*. Crestwood, N.Y.: St. Vladimir's Seminary Press, 1980.

Pelikan, Jaroslav. "Fundamentalism and/or Orthodoxy." In *The Fundamentalist Phenomenon*, edited by Norman J. Cohen, 3–21. Grand Rapids: Eerdmans, 1990.

———. *Imago Dei: The Byzantine Apologia for Icons*. Princeton: Princeton University Press, 1990.

———. *The Spirit of Eastern Christendom (600 1700)*. Chicago: University of Chicago Press, 1974.

Petro, Nicolai N., ed. *Christianity and Russian Culture in Soviet Society*. Boulder, Colo.: Westview, 1990.

Philokalia. Translated and edited by G. E. H. Palmer, Philip Sherrard, and Kallistos Ware. 3 vols. London: Faber and Faber, 1979–90.

Pollock, John C. *The Faith of Russian Evangelicals*. New York: McGraw-Hill, 1964.

———. *The Siberian Seven*. Waco: Word, 1979.

Pomazansky, Michael. *Orthodox Dogmatic Theology: A Concise Exposition*. Platina, Calif.: St. Herman of Alaska Brotherhood, 1983.

Pospielovsky, Dimitry V. *A History of Marxist-Leninist Atheism and Soviet Antireligious Policies*. 3 vols. New York: St. Martin's, 1987–88.

———. *The Russian Church under the Soviet Regime, 1917–1982*. 2 vols. Crestwood, N.Y.: St. Vladimir's Seminary Press, 1984.

Powell, David E. *Antireligious Propaganda in the Soviet Union*. Cambridge, Mass.: MIT Press, 1975.

Pushkarev, Sergei, and Gleb Yakunin. *Christianity and Government in Russia and the Soviet Union: Reflections on the Millennium*. Boulder, Colo.: Westview, 1989.

Quenot, Michel. *The Icon: Window on the Kingdom*. Crestwood, N.Y.: St. Vladimir's Seminary Press, 1991.

Ramet, Pedro. *Cross and Commissar: The Politics of Religion in Eastern Europe and the U.S.S.R.* Bloomington: Indiana University Press, 1987.

Sahas, Daniel J. *Icon and Logos: Sources in Eighth-Century Iconoclasm*. Toronto: University of Toronto Press, 1986.

Sawatsky, Walter. *Soviet Evangelicals since World War II*. Scottdale, Pa.: Herald, 1981.

Schaeffer, Frank. *Dancing Alone: The Quest for Orthodox Faith in the Age of False Religions*. Brookline, Mass.: Holy Cross Orthodox Press, 1994.

Scheffbuch, Winrich. *Christians under the Hammer and Sickle*. Grand Rapids: Zondervan, 1974.

Schmemann, Alexander. *Church, World, Mission: Reflections on Orthodoxy in the West*. Crestwood, N.Y.: St. Vladimir's Seminary Press, 1979.

———. *The Eucharist: The Sacrament of the Kingdom*. Crestwood, N.Y.: St. Vladimir's Seminary Press, 1988.

———. *For the Life of the World: Sacraments and Orthodoxy*. Crestwood, N.Y.: St. Vladimir's Seminary Press, 1973.

———. *The Historical Road of Eastern Orthodoxy*. Crestwood, N.Y.: St. Vladimir's Seminary Press, 1977.

———. *Introduction to Liturgical Theology*. Crestwood, N.Y.: St. Vladimir's Seminary Press, 1986.

———. *Of Water and the Spirit: A Liturgical Study of Baptism*. Crestwood, N.Y.: St. Vladimir's Seminary Press, 1974.

———. "Russian Theology: 1922–1972." *St. Vladimir's Theological Quarterly* 16.4 (1972): 172–94.

———. "Towards a Theology of Councils." *St. Vladimir's Theological Quarterly* 6.4 (1962): 170–84.

———, ed. *Ultimate Questions: An Anthology of Modern Russian Religious Thought*. Crestwood, N.Y.: St. Vladimir's Seminary Press, 1977.

Schneirla, William. "Orthodoxy and Ecumenism." *St. Vladimir's Theological Quarterly* 12.2 (1968): 86–88.

Sherrard, Philip. *The Greek East and the Latin West*. New York: Oxford University Press, 1959.

Solovyev, Vladimir. *Lectures on Godmanhood*. New York: Hillary, 1948.

———. *Russia and the Universal Church*. London: N.p., 1948.

———. *A Solovyev Anthology*. Edited by S. L. Frank. Westport, Conn.: Greenwood, 1974.

Solzhenitsyn, Alexander, ed. *From under the Rubble*. Chicago: Regnery Gateway, 1981.

Spinka, Matthew. *The Church and the Russian Revolution*. New York: Macmillan, 1927.

———. *The Church in Soviet Russia*. Westport, Conn.: Greenwood, 1980.

Stamoolis, James J. *Eastern Orthodox Mission Theology Today*. Maryknoll, N.Y.: Orbis, 1986.

———, ed. *Three Views on Eastern Orthodoxy and Evangelicalism*. Grand Rapids: Zondervan, forthcoming.

Staniloae, Dumitru. *Theology and the Church*. Crestwood, N.Y.: St. Vladimir's Seminary Press, 1980.

Stavropoulos, Christoforos. *Partakers of Divine Nature*. Minneapolis: Light and Life, 1976.

Stroyen, William B. *Communist Russia and the Russian Orthodox Church, 1943–1962*. Washington, D.C.: Catholic University of America Press, 1967.

Struve, Nikita. *Christians in Contemporary Russia*. New York: Scribner, 1967.

Szczesniak, Boleslaw, ed. *The Russian Revolution and Religion: A Collection of Documents concerning the Suppression of Religion by the Communists, 1917–1925*. Notre Dame: University of Notre Dame Press, 1959.

Tarasar, Constance, ed. *Orthodox America, 1794–1976: Development of the Orthodox Church in America*. Syosset, N.Y.: Orthodox Church in America, 1975.

Theological Dialogue between Orthodox and Reformed Churches. Edited by Thomas F. Torrance. Edinburgh: Scottish Academic Press, 1985.

Thrower, James. *Marxist-Leninist "Scientific Atheism" and the Study of Religion and Atheism in the U.S.S.R.* Hawthorne, N.Y.: Mouton, 1983.

Ugolnik, Anthony. *The Illuminating Icon*. Grand Rapids: Eerdmans, 1989.

———. "The Orthodox Church and Contemporary Politics in the USSR." Unpublished paper, 1991.

Ware, Timothy. *The Orthodox Church*. Baltimore: Penguin, 1964.

———. *The Orthodox Way*. Crestwood, N.Y.: St. Vladimir's Seminary Press, 1990.

Yancey, Phil. *Praying with the KGB: A Startling Report from a Shattered Empire*. Portland: Multnomah, 1992.

Zernov, Nicolas. *Eastern Christendom: A Study of the Origin and Development of the Eastern Orthodox Church*. New York: Putnam, 1961.

———. *Moscow, the Third Rome*. New York: Macmillan, 1937.

———. *The Russian Religious Renaissance of the Twentieth Century*. New York: Harper, 1963.

———. *The Russians and Their Church*. Crestwood, N.Y.: St. Vladimir's Seminary Press, 1978.

Scripture Index

Subject Index

185